GRAMMAR & STLYE

AT YOUR FINGERTIPS

Lara M. Robbins

ALPHA
A member of Penguin Group (USA) Inc.

ALPHA BOOKS

Published by the Penguin Group

Penguin Group (USA) Inc., 375 Hudson Street, New York, New York 10014, USA

Penguin Group (Canada), 90 Eglinton Avenue East, Suite 700, Toronto, Ontario M4P 2Y3, Canada (a division of Pearson Penguin Canada Inc.)

Penguin Books Ltd, 80 Strand, London WC2R 0RL, England

Penguin Ireland, 25 St. Stephen's Green, Dublin 2, Ireland (a division of Penguin Books Ltd.)

Penguin Group (Australia), 250 Camberwell Road, Camberwell, Victoria 3124, Australia (a division of Pearson Australia Group Pty. Ltd.)

Penguin Books India Pvt. Ltd., 11 Community Centre, Panchsheel Park, New Delhi—110 017, India

Penguin Group (NZ), 67 Apollo Drive, Rosedale, North Shore, Auckland 1311, New Zealand (a division of Pearson New Zealand Ltd.)

Penguin Books (South Africa) (Pty.) Ltd, 24 Sturdee Avenue, Rosebank, Johannesburg 2196, South Africa

Penguin Books Ltd., Registered Offices: 80 Strand, London WC2R 0RL, England

International Standard Book Number: 978-1-59257-657-9
Library of Congress Catalog Card Number: 2006920583

09 08 07 8 7 6 5 4 3 2 1

Interpretation of the printing code: The rightmost number of the first series of numbers is the year of the book's printing; the rightmost number of the second series of numbers is the number of the book's printing. For example, a printing code of 07-1 shows that the first printing occurred in 2007.

Printed in the United States of America

Note: This publication contains the opinions and ideas of its author. It is intended to provide helpful and informative material on the subject matter covered. It is sold with the understanding that the author and publisher are not engaged in rendering professional services in the book. If the reader requires personal assistance or advice, a competent professional should be consulted.

The author and publisher specifically disclaim any responsibility for any liability, loss, or risk, personal or otherwise, which is incurred as a consequence, directly or indirectly, of the use and application of any of the contents of this book.

Most Alpha books are available at special quantity discounts for bulk purchases for sales promotions, premiums, fund-raising, or educational use. Special books, or book excerpts, can also be created to fit specific needs.

For details, write: Special Markets, Alpha Books, 375 Hudson Street, New York, NY 10014.

Publisher: **Marie Butler-Knight**
Editorial Director: **Mike Sanders**
Managing Editor: **Billy Fields**
Executive Editor: **Randy Ladenheim-Gil**
Senior Development Editor: **Christy Wagner**
Production Editor: **Megan Douglass**
Copy Editor: **Krista Hansing**
Cover/Book Designer: **Kurt Owens**
Indexer: **Johnna Vanhoose Dinse**
Layout: **Chad Dressler**
Proofreader: **Aaron Black**

Dedicated to the ones I love …

Merry and Jerry Bush, for their constant love and support, and a place to call Home in Missouri.

Gail and Phil Rector, for always counting me as family.

Christie and Dan Brinkman, for our enduring friendship as we continue to grow up together, and for a loving place to escape to in Hawaii. Mahalo.

Renee and David Harney, for two of the world's three greatest nieces: Madeline and Annabelle.

And Chelsea Peterson, for being the first of the world's greatest nieces!

CONTENTS

Chapter 1	**Nouns and Pronouns**	**1**
1.1	Nouns	2
1.2	Compounds	8
1.3	Pronouns	11
1.4	Noun and Pronoun Properties	17
Chapter 2	**Verbs**	**21**
2.1	Verbs	22
2.2	Verb Forms	31
2.3	Verb Properties	34
2.4	Subject and Verb Agreement	42
Chapter 3	**Modifiers**	**45**
3.1	Adjectives	46
3.2	Adverbs	50
3.3	Modifiers: Regular, Dangling, and Misplaced	52
Chapter 4	**Prepositions and Conjunctions**	**55**
4.1	Prepositions	56
4.2	Prepositional Phrases	59
4.3	Conjunctions	61
Chapter 5	**Sentence Structure**	**67**
5.1	Basic Sentence Structure	68
5.2	Types of Sentences	71
5.3	Parallelism	80
5.4	Figures of Speech	82
5.5	Stylistic Devices	88
Chapter 6	**Punctuation**	**93**
6.1	Use of Punctuation	94
6.2	Periods	95
6.3	Commas	98
6.4	Question and Exclamation Marks	105
6.5	Ellipses	106
6.6	Colons and Semicolons	107
6.7	Quotation Marks	109
6.8	Apostrophes	111

6.9 Hyphens, Dashes, and Slashes 113
6.10 Parentheses and Brackets 117

Chapter 7 Plurals and Possessives.....119
7.1 Plurals 120
7.2 Possessives 126

Chapter 8 Capitalization.....133
8.1 Personal Names and Titles 134
8.2 Proper Nouns 141

Chapter 9 Special Type Treatment 147
9.1 Italics 148
9.2 Boldface 159
9.3 Small Capitals 160
9.4 Serif versus Sans Serif 162
9.5 Underlining 164

Chapter 10 Spelling and Abbreviations 165
10.1 Spelling 166
10.2 Word Choices 181
10.3 Abbreviations 186

Chapter 11 Numbers, Signs, and Symbols.....199
11.1 Numbers 200
11.2 Signs and Symbols 207

Chapter 12 Trademarks, Copyrights, Permissions, and Fair Use 211
12.1 Trademarks 212
12.2 Copyright Information 216
12.3 Permissions 221

Chapter 13 Citation 227
13.1 Source Citation 228

Chapter 14 Documentation and Reference 237
14.1 Footnotes 238
14.2 Endnotes 242
14.3 Glossaries 245
14.4 Bibliographies 246
14.5 Indexes 252

Appendix A Words to Go Glossary 261
Appendix B Reference and Resource Bibliography 275
Index 281

INTRODUCTION

> The difference between the *almost*-right word & the *right* word is really a large matter—it's the difference between the lightning bug and the lightning.
>
> —Mark Twain

Words are the foundation of everything. All societies (civilized and otherwise), relationships, and actions begin with words—whether thought, spoken, or written. Words and their considered and selective use are the keys to conveying and comprehending all manner of ideas, plans, hopes, and desires.

Words are my business and a personal passion. As senior managing editor for the Berkley Publishing Group, it is important for me to know how to use words and punctuation both correctly and to greatest effect. These are not always one and the same. When I am working with the words of *The New York Times* bestselling authors such as Nora Roberts, Tom Clancy, or Patricia Cornwell, it is imperative that I get it right. The same is true when I review the copy that will be used on a book's cover. Hundreds of thousands of people purchase the novels and self-help, inspirational, and historical titles I work on each year. I must get it right.

Here's the rub: Although I'm a good speller, I'm not a great speller. In my seventh-grade spelling bee, I only made it to third place. I was done in by the word *illustration*. Many would say it is important to know one's strengths—I say it is more important to know the weaknesses and to use them as opportunities for growth. I learned from early spelling mistakes and now make quick use of all manner of reference books—I keep online, CD, and hardback copies of *Merriam-Webster's Collegiate Dictionary*, 11th edition, close at hand both at work and at home. I use them every day.

If you're like me, the correct application of grammar and punctuation rules might come rather naturally. Perhaps for you, as for me, the flipside of such a lucky coin has been that it hasn't always been easy to explain the "how" of it to others. I liken my abilities with word usage and style to my driving skills: I always get where I am going, but I rarely know the street names. This proves to be less than helpful when providing driving directions to others.

Still, it is not necessary to be the most talented student of word usage. What you might lack in natural ability, you can obtain by disciplined study. This is possible for everyone. When I began in publishing fourteen years ago as a temping receptionist, I knew I had to learn the rules. So I studied and I practiced and then I practiced some more.

Now, in my capacity as the senior managing editor for a major publishing house, I am called upon daily to provide grammar and punctuation directives that are both correct and easily understood. With driving directions, I can grab a map and simply highlight the way for someone. Providing guidance with grammar and punctuation is a bit more challenging. It has been and continues to be crucial that I understand the rules governing language usage and style.

Many style and reference guides were consulted for confirmation of the rules I've presented in this book. *The Chicago Manual of Style* is one of the style guides that was consulted; however, the most-recent edition (fifteenth) asserts some changes to traditional rules that I do not support. Although there are many schools of thought regarding writing styles, it is my assertion that the governing grammar and punctuation rules are universal. *Grammar and Style at Your Fingertips* provides the tools you need to navigate your writing or reading journey.

How This Book Is Organized

The purpose of this book is to assist writers and readers in pursuit of both expression and understanding through the use of words and punctuation. The rules in the following pages provide easy access for a greater understanding of the traditional bricks-and-mortar grammar and punctuation rules. These are the foundation of written communication. Each step builds upon the step before.

First up are chapters identifying the parts of speech: nouns, pronouns, verbs, adjectives, adverbs, prepositions, and conjunctions. Next is a chapter concerning spelling issues. A sentence structure chapter brings together the parts of speech.

Punctuation chapters follow, presenting usage rules and examples for periods, commas, colons, semicolons, etc. The next chapters progress through the governing plural, capitalization, italicization, and other special-treatment rules. A vast listing of correct newspaper, magazine, and online titles, and the proper treatment of each, is also provided. A chapter follows with rules regarding the treatment of numbers, signs/symbols, and trademarks. A complete listing of proofreader's marks is included in that chapter. I've also included chapters on permissions issues and documentation matters. Wrapping it all up is a glossary and a resources appendix.

Throughout this book, you'll notice ***SEE ALSO***s. These are included to provide cross-references to other areas in the book that relate directly to what's discussed in the text or provide more information on a related topic.

WORDS TO GO . . . WORDS TO GO . . . WORDS TO GO

Words to Go are quick definitions of grammar and punctuation terms discussed within the chapter. These definitions are provided to enhance your understanding of the material covered.

Acknowledgments

The creation of this book required the help of many. First, I would like to thank my agent and dear friend, Jacky Sach, for suggesting I take on this project in the first place. It was my first foray into life on this side of the page, and a truly scary journey, but I'm ever so glad to have had the opportunity.

I must also thank my editor, Randy Ladenheim-Gil, for her kind patience. After so many years chasing down late manuscripts in my role as managing editor, it was a less-than-comfy position to find myself looking at the wrong side of a due date. I'm so happy we made it! And much appreciation goes to Christy Wagner, who has been such a kind editorial guide through the development stage of the book.

I most definitely want to acknowledge Jennifer Eck, who provided me with invaluable research, aid, and assistance toward the completion of this book. I cannot guarantee my sanity would have held together without Jennifer's calm and capable approach to each task set before her. This will come as no surprise to those who have worked with Jennifer for lo these many years. She is a pro through and through and a true expert in this field.

There are many others who have contributed in positive ways to the person and writer I am today—and many continue to affect the person and writer I hope to be in the future. I must mention a few: Merry and Jerry Bush, who gave me a true home and sense of self when I was on my own at fifteen. Mrs. (Blanche) Kelly, who was my favorite English/drama teacher and helped me find my voice onstage and basically forced me to write my first story. Mr. (Douglas) MacRae, who was my favorite guitar-playin' history teacher/basketball coach and taught me to love to learn. Leonard Walls, wherever you are, who taught me to take chances. There are many others, so … to the rest of you-who-know-who-you-are: Thank you!

Special Thanks to the Technical Editor

Grammar and Style at Your Fingertips was reviewed by an expert who double-checked the accuracy of what you'll learn here, to help us ensure that this book gives you everything you need to know about grammar and style. Special thanks are extended to David A. Salomon, Ph.D.

David A. Salomon is associate professor of English and chair of the Department of English and Modern Languages at The Sage Colleges in Troy and Albany, New York. He has published scholarly work in medieval and Renaissance English literature and religion, and has been teaching writing and literature at the college level for twenty years.

Trademarks

All terms mentioned in this book that are known to be or are suspected of being trademarks or service marks have been appropriately capitalized. Alpha Books and Penguin Group (USA) Inc. cannot attest to the accuracy of this information. Use of a term in this book should not be regarded as affecting the validity of any trademark or service mark.

1

NOUNS AND PRONOUNS

1.1 Nouns

1.2 Compounds

1.3 Pronouns

1.4 Noun and Pronoun Properties

1.1 NOUNS

Common Nouns

Proper Nouns

Common Versus Proper Nouns

Count Nouns

Mass Nouns

Nouns are the building blocks of sentences. A noun is a word used to represent general classes of people, places, and things or something a bit more intangible, such as ideas. Nouns can appear in either common or proper form and will fall into one of two categories: count or mass. As you might have already guessed, nouns are generally the stars of our sentences; therefore, there is much to be done by, for, and to nouns.

WORDS TO GO . . .WORDS TO GO . . .WORDS TO GO

A **noun** is a word that identifies a person, place, thing, or idea.

Common Nouns

Common nouns, or simple nouns, are exactly that: common, everyday, run-of-the mill words used to identify a person, place, thing, or idea. Common nouns do not provide specificity or point to one certain thing or idea. They also do not require any special capitalization treatment. Except when used as the first word in a sentence, these words are generally presented in their **lowercase** form.

WORDS TO GO . . .WORDS TO GO . . .WORDS TO GO

Lowercase means to write a word without using capital letters.

Here are some examples of common nouns:

People: sister, teacher, doctor, gardener
Places: town, school, hospital, yard
Things: shoe, pizza, radio, house
Ideas: faith, beauty, truth, goodness

Proper Nouns

A proper noun, often referred to as a proper name, is still a noun, but it identifies a *specific* person, place, or thing. Unlike with the common noun, the first letter of a proper noun is always going to be capitalized, regardless of the placement within a sentence or title. Let's look at an example:

You should visit Elsberry; that town is enchanting.

Here, *town* is a common noun and is set lowercase. The name of the town, *Elsberry*, is a proper noun and as such it is capitalized.

Common Versus Proper Nouns

It's easy enough to identify a proper name and to understand that the first letter of a proper noun will be and should be capitalized. However, it's not unusual to find yourself stumped when trying to figure out whether words should be lowercased and left as common nouns or capitalized as proper nouns. The following table lists some examples of common and proper nouns.

	Common Nouns	Proper Nouns
People	woman	Queen Elizabeth
	girl	Madeline
	actor	George Clooney
	judge	Judge Judy
Places	city	New York City
	farm	Double D Ranch
	store	Wal-Mart
	park	Yosemite National Park
	cathedral	St. Patrick's Cathedral
Things	team	Boston Celtics
	car	Ford Mustang
	language	Spanish
	soda	Pepsi
	marker	Sharpie
	hurricane	Hurricane Katrina

SEE ALSO 12.1, "Trademarks"

It is often particularly challenging to determine whether to capitalize or leave a word lowercase when a common noun switches gears and is used as a proper noun or within a proper name. For instance, is it the *President* (capped) or the *president* (lowercase)? Which treatment is correct?

In many cases, the determining factors are the placement and the use of the word in the context of a phrase or sentence. Civil, military, or other professional titles are usually lowercased when used to indirectly reference a person without using the person's name or when the person's titles follow their name. Such titles are generally capitalized only when used alone in a direct-address context or when positioned to directly precede a personal name. In that latter position, the title actually becomes an extended part of the person's name.

SEE ALSO 8.1, "Capitals"

Back to the *President* versus *president* debate:

> Speaking with the president would be a memorable experience.
>
> John Adams was the second president of the United States.
>
> I awoke from a dream in which President Al Gore was dancing with Tipper at the Inaugural Ball, following his landslide 2008 election.

Let's look at some more examples:

> This was Assistant District Attorney Rienzi's first big win.

In this example, *Assistant District Attorney* is a proper noun. It's a title preceding a personal name.

> "I want to talk with you, Detective."

In this example, *Detective* is a proper noun used as a direct-address title in place of a personal name.

> When the smoke cleared, only the detective remained standing.

The detective is used here as a common noun in an indirect reference.

Sometimes official titles are lowercased even when they precede a personal name. These are **appositives**. The title comes before the name, but it's used as a description of the person rather than as the person's title.

WORDS TO GO . . . WORDS TO GO . . . WORDS TO GO

An **appositive** renames or explains the word following it.

It was now up to the FBI's special agent Blake Daniels to solve.

In this example, *the FBI's special agent* is used as a title in apposition to a personal name.

If a common noun is part of a proper noun naming something specific, then the common noun is capitalized, too:

library	*but*	Library of Congress
avenue	*but*	Park Avenue
university	*but*	New York University
airline	*but*	American Airlines
cape	*but*	Cape Cod
falls	*but*	Grand Falls

SEE ALSO Chapter 8, "Capitalization"

Count Nouns

Count nouns identify people, places, and things that, simply put, can be counted. These nouns are able to appear in both singular and plural forms.

COUNT NOUNS

Single Form	Plural Form
leaf	leaves
kitten	kittens
dog	dogs
cup	cups
lady	ladies
copy	copies
amoeba/ameba	amoebas *or* amoebae
loggia	loggias *or* loggie
medium	mediums *or* media

Let's look at some examples:

The ladies broke six cups while playing with the dog.

In this first example, the count nouns are *ladies*, *cups*, and *dog*.

When used as the subject of a sentence, the count noun's singular form takes a singular verb:

The kitten is cute.

Kitten is the singular count noun. And the word *is* is the singular verb.

The parallel holds true for plural count nouns. Plural count nouns take plural verbs:

The horses are fast.

Horses is the plural count noun, and *are* is the plural verb.

Mass Nouns

Unlike count nouns, mass nouns (which also may be called noncount nouns) name things that generally are not counted, either because they reference a group of people or things or because they are abstract. Also in contradiction to count nouns, mass nouns do not usually take the plural form.

MASS NOUNS

Single Form		
advice	flour	sand
chaos	honesty	series
cowardice	literature	time
data	nitrogen	water
earth	rice	

It's important to remember that the addition of numbers alone is not how to quantify mass nouns. Here are some examples of what *not* to do:

Joan had three cowardices.
Ron's actions caused fourteen chaoses.
Come and get your six rices.

Obviously, these examples are purposefully flawed. They do not read properly and don't really make a whole lot of sense. To provide a measurement or classification of a mass noun, the prepositional word *of* is a great little helper. Let's take a look at those poor examples in another way:

Joan had three forms of cowardice.
Ron's actions caused fourteen kinds of chaos.
Come and get your six bags of rice.

Now the quantifications and meanings are clear and the mass nouns retain their singular forms.

Here's another clue to identifying a mass noun: The word *much* can be used as a modifier for mass nouns.

> How much time do we have?

As usual, the mass noun remains in its singular form.

When serving as the subject of a sentence, a mass noun usually takes a singular verb. However, when the parts that form the group (the people or things) are being emphasized instead of the group itself, a plural verb can be used.

> The Delta Three team was taking precautions in the jungle.

In this example, *team* is the mass noun. *Was* is the plural verb. When it is important to reference the members of a group (team) as a single unit, it is okay to use a singular verb (was).

If we wanted to switch this example up and make the emphasis on the individual team members, here's what we would have:

> The Delta Three team were the best-trained jungle reconnaissance military force.

In this instance, it should be clear from the use of the plural verb (were) that we are saying that "each member of the team"—all without using the extraneous wordage.

1.2 COMPOUNDS

Compound Nouns
Hyphenated Compounds
Solid Compounds
Open Compounds

Compound words, as the name suggests, are words formed by joining two or more words. The joined words then function as a single word unit, most often possessing a new meaning. Compound words can take three forms: open, solid, and hyphenated. In this subchapter, I cover compound nouns and the three compound word forms.

WORDS TO GO . . . WORDS TO GO . . . WORDS TO GO

A **compound word** is a new single unit word made of two other words.

SEE ALSO 6.9, "Hyphens, Dashes, and Slashes"

SEE ALSO 10.1, "Spelling"

Compound Nouns

Compound nouns are the combining of two words to form a new noun. Often, but not always, the meaning of the compound noun bears no resemblance to the meanings held by the separate, uncombined words.

knucklehead knuckle head	jackrabbit jack rabbit
headline head line	

Conversely, some compound words retain the same meaning regardless of the form in which they are presented.

anytime any time	awhile a while

In these examples, the word *anytime* is actually defined as *at any time whatsoever*. As for the use of *awhile* versus *a while*, this gets a bit more tricky. Whenever used as a single word unit, this compound word should be able to take on an understood, but not necessarily written out, "*for*" preceding it.

I'm going out (for) awhile.

I'm going out for a while.

In these examples, whether the word is written as one word or two, the meaning remains the same: *for a while*.

Another use of *a while*, and a way to make sure that this should be written as two separate words, is when there is no way to include the word *for*.

They called again after a while.

As you can see from the use in the example, there is no way to place *for* preceding this use of *a while*—whether written or simply understood as part of the meaning. So that's a handy test: If the word *for* won't work in front of *a while*, you know you need to present them as two words.

Hyphenated Compounds

When two or more words are connected by one or more hyphens, the result is a hyphenated compound. Some compound words are hyphenated to avoid being misread or ambiguous.

mind-set	white-footed mouse
wire-puller	shout-out
well-being	T-shirt
hoof-and-mouth disease	nine-year-old

Hyphenated compounds that would never be joined except to avoid a misread will be discussed later in the chapter on hyphens.

SEE ALSO 6.9, "Hyphens, Dashes, and Slashes"

Solid Compounds

When forming compound words, your first inclination might well be to simply insert a hyphen between two words and be done with it, and sometimes you are correct doing that, as outlined in the preceding section.

However, the practice of using a hyphen to form compounds has become less common as solid compound words become more readily accepted by the collective consciousness and the single-meaning concepts of these words are generally understood. As the American-English language evolves, hyphens that were once relied upon are now being deleted. Compound words are increasingly being closed up as solid, or closed, compounds.

breakfast	rollback
hardback	slingshot
needlepoint	wellspring
otterhound	whatever
restroom	

Open Compounds

Sometimes no hyphenating or closing up is necessary to form a compound. Open compounds are words that are used as a single unit of meaning but are still written separately as two words.

first aid	near miss
wind chime	wet nurse
roller coaster	ostrich fern
Welsh terrier	sleeping bag
mug shot	

Very often it is the placement and use of a compound word within a sentence that determines whether it is required to be hyphenated, solid, or open.

common sense	noun
commonsense	adjective
first aid	noun
first-aid	adjective
roller coaster	noun
roller-coaster	adjective

The use of some words, such as these, can be completely altered simply with a slight change in form.

SEE ALSO 6.9, "Hyphens, Dashes, and Slashes"

1.3 PRONOUNS

Pronouns and Antecedents

Pronoun Classes

A **pronoun** is a word that replaces either a noun or another pronoun. Pronouns are used to avoid repeating the same word.

> *Without pronouns:* The boy told the boy's sister that the boy was going to run away.
>
> *With pronouns:* The boy told his sister that he was going to run away.

Pronouns can also be used in place of a noun that has already been identified and is understood without repeating it or replacing it.

WORDS TO GO . . . WORDS TO GO . . . WORDS TO GO

Pronouns are substitution words used in place of the nouns and noun phrases they represent.

The following table lists some common pronouns.

Pronouns

all	hers	no one
another	herself	nobody
any	him	none
anybody	himself	one
anyone	his	oneself
anything	hisself	other
both	I	our
each	it	ours
either	itself	ourself
everybody	many	ourselves
everyone	me	self
everything	mine	she
few	my	some
he	myself	somebody
her	neither	someone

continues

continued

Pronouns		
something	this	whom
somewhat	those	whomever
such	thou	whomso
that	thyself	whomsoever
thee	us	whose
their	we	whoso
theirs	what	whosoever
theirselves	whatever	you
them	whatnot	you-all
themselves	whatsoever	yours
these	which	yourself
they	who	yourselves
thine	whoever	

Pronouns and Antecedents

A pronoun gets its identity and definition from its **antecedent**, the noun for which it fills in. Regardless of whether both the pronoun and its antecedent appear in the same sentence, both must be unmistakable, or the meaning won't be clear to the reader. The antecedent and its pronoun must agree in all ways, particularly in number.

Thinking in terms of a stage production: The noun is the star who mysteriously "trips" down the staircase after the lights go out. The pronoun is the understudy ... who just happens to run down those same stairs moments later—ready to jump in and take over the part!

WORDS TO GO . . . WORDS TO GO . . . WORDS TO GO

An **antecedent** is the noun for which a pronoun substitutes.

There's an exception to every rule, though. Some pronouns never or rarely need antecedents:

I As the first-person pronoun, *I* does not require an antecedent.

> I have no idea what you are talking about.

you Where preceding antecedents are concerned, this second-person pronoun can take 'em or leave 'em.

SEE ALSO 1.4, "Noun and Pronoun Properties"

> You must be kidding.
>
> David, you must be kidding.

it Oftentimes, when used as an expletive pronoun, *it* does not need an antecedent.

> It is cold in here.

who, what, which These words, used as interrogative (question) pronouns, do not need antecedents.

> Who called?
>
> What did they want?
>
> Which?

what As a relative pronoun, *what* never needs a preceding antecedent.

> What a kid!

they The ever popular *they* is very commonly used, but often it is left vague and undefined. This is especially true when the foundation of our argument is coming up short and we resort to supplementing our position with an unsubstantiated assertion.

> They say so all the time.

Pronouns are used for a couple of reasons. The first is to avoid repeating the same word over and over, again and again …

> *Without pronouns:* The boy told the boy's sister that the boy was going to run away.
>
> *With pronouns:* The boy told his sister that he was going to run away.

Making use of pronouns allows a clear understanding of what's happening without annoying and distracting repetition.

Pronouns can also be used in place of a noun that has already been identified and is understood without repeating it or replacing it.

With that in mind, you know that …

> Jerry, did you feed the dogs?

can easily be replaced with …

Did you feed the dogs?

without any misunderstanding. And within the response of …

It wasn't my turn!

the *it* is readily understood to mean *feeding the dogs*.

Pronoun Classes

Pronouns can be identified by the various pronoun classifications. Which class a pronoun falls into is determined by the function and meaning of the pronoun within a given sentence. A pronoun can easily appear in more than one classification.

Style manuals cite varying numbers of pronoun classes; some list six, while others list the traditional eight or more. In this section, I cover all of these:

- Personal
- Demonstrative
- Interrogative
- Relative
- Indefinite
- Adjective
- Reflexive
- Intensive
- Reciprocal

Personal Pronouns

A personal pronoun is used to make reference to a specific person or group. The personal pronouns are: *I*, *it*, *he*, *she*, *they*, *us*, *we*, and *you*.

They want it more than she does.

Demonstrative Pronouns

Demonstrative pronouns are used to identify, set apart, point out, and specify. The demonstrative pronouns are: *that*, *these*, *this*, and *those*.

Those are useless, but this book will help.

Interrogative Pronouns

Simply put, the interrogative pronouns ask questions. The interrogative pronouns are: *what*, *which*, and *who*.

Which do you want?

Relative Pronouns

A relative pronoun is a connecting word that introduces a subordinate clause and provides a link from one clause to another clause. The relative pronouns are: *that*, *what*, *whatever*, *which*, and *who*.

The happy laughter that made me smile came from the three-year-old who lives next door.

SEE ALSO 3.3, "Forms of Modifiers"

SEE ALSO 3.4, "Dangling and Misplaced Modifiers"

Indefinite Pronouns

Indefinite pronouns typically indicate an unspecified, even generic, person or thing. The indefinite pronouns are: *all*, *any*, *each*, *few*, *many*, *none*, *one*, *some*, and *such*.

Few make it to the final callbacks.

Adjective Pronouns

Adjective pronouns, which also may be referenced as *pronominal adjectives*, serve as noun modifiers. Almost all pronouns can be used as adjectives.

Those dogs were having a very good time.

I wonder if that error will cost us the game.

A few notable exceptions cannot perform this adjectival function: personal pronouns, *who*, and *none*.

Reflexive Pronouns

A reflexive pronoun refers to the subject of the sentence, clause, or phrase in which it finds itself. Reflexive pronouns include: *herself*, *himself*, *itself*, *myself*, and *themselves*.

Marie takes care of herself.

Intensive Pronouns

An intensive pronoun is used to add emphasis to a preceding personal pronoun. Such constructions are a bit rare and uncommon, especially given the current trend toward succinctness. Intensive pronouns include: *myself*, *themselves*, and *ourselves*.

I myself rarely write this way.

Reciprocal Pronouns

A reciprocal pronoun is used when those referenced are expected to bear an equal relationship with one another. The reciprocal pronouns include: *each other* and *one another*.

Maybe someday we will learn to help each other.

Now that we've discussed the definition of the classifications of pronouns, it should be clear that it's really all about location, location, location.

1.4 NOUN AND PRONOUN PROPERTIES

Noun and Pronoun Case

Gender

Person

Number

Nouns and pronouns share the same four properties: case, gender, person, and number. Implementation of these properties as regards the nouns and pronouns in a sentence conveys to the reader all of the details the writer intended regarding the function and form of the words.

Noun and Pronoun Cases

Case is the form a noun or pronoun takes to indicate its relationship with the other words in a sentence. A word's case shows whether the word functions as the subject, as the object, or in another capacity.

Three main cases exist: nominative case, possessive case, and objective case. In the nominative case, a noun fills the role of subject; in the possessive case, it's a modifier; and in the objective case—you guessed it—the noun is an object within a sentence or phrase.

Plain and Possessive Case

As mentioned, the form that a noun or pronoun takes indicates its function within a given sentence. All nouns can manage the following two cases: plain and possessive. A **plain-case noun** (*Rick, doctor*) doesn't change form unless its function changes and it needs to transform into the possessive case (from *Superman* to *Superman's*). The plain-case noun can perform all functions within the parameters of a noun in a sentence.

WORDS TO GO . . . WORDS TO GO . . . WORDS TO GO

Nouns found in the dictionary are **plain-case nouns.**

The **possessive case**, also called the genitive case, indicates ownership or a relationship. The most common way to denote possession—and how it's done for single nouns—is to add an apostrophe and an *s*.

Superman's cape is red.

Nora Roberts's books all hit *The New York Times* list.

To show possession for plural nouns that end with *-s* or *-es*, only an apostrophe is needed at the end of the word.

The bears' cave appeared to be empty.

The Jones' dog ran away three times.

Sometimes, however, possession is shown with a greater change in form.

Their dog bit the postman.

Your room is a mess.

Check the plain-case noun in a good dictionary if you aren't sure how to show possession. Any greater changes than the addition of an *–s* will be included with the word definition.

Pronouns: Nominative, Objective, and Possessive Cases

Both nouns and pronouns can show possession, but pronouns have a third case: the nominative case (also known as the subjective case).

The nominative case, or form, of a noun or pronoun is used when the pronoun is the subject of a sentence or clause, the complement of a subject, or an appositive identifying a subject.

The following table breaks down and identifies pronouns by case (nominative, objective, and possessive) and by person (first, second, and third).

PRONOUN PROPERTIES

	First Person	Second Person	Third Person
Nominative Case (Subjective Case):			
Singular	I	you	he, it, she
Plural	we	you	they
Objective Case:			
Singular	me	you	her, him, it
Plural	us	you	them
Possessive Case:			
Singular	mine, my	your, yours	her, hers, his, its
Plural	our, ours	your, yours	their, theirs

Gender

All nouns and pronouns are classified as one of three genders: feminine, masculine, or neuter.

Feminine	Masculine	Neuter
she	he	it
her	him	its
hers	his	cat
hen	rooster	fowl
sister	brother	sibling
aunt	uncle	family
queen	king	royalty
woman	man	gelding

Gender is mainly based on the sex of the noun or pronoun in question. And although most inanimate objects fall under the neuter category, some are frequently referenced as feminine: ships, cars, and countries, just to name a few.

The gender for pronouns presented in succession should be the same for all when referring to the same antecedent.

Incorrect: The duck flapped its wings and then he hopped off the barn.

Correct: The duck flapped its wings and then it hopped off the barn.

Person

Person indicates whether the subject or object referenced is doing the speaking (first person), being spoken to (second person), or being talked about (third person). Personal pronouns (and verbs) change their forms to show a variance in person.

Let me tell you, Brian, Stephen doesn't know what he is doing.

Here, *me* is in the first person, *you* is in the second person, and *he* is in the third person.

SEE ALSO 2.3, "Verb Properties"

Number

Number is the form of a noun or pronoun that indicates whether the word is singular (one) or plural (more than one). Nouns and personal pronouns change to show a difference between singular and plural forms of a word. (Verbs and demonstrative adjectives do so also, but that's for another chapter.)

child
children

dog
dogs

piano
pianos

As mentioned earlier, some words indicate a group of something that can be used as singular or plural.

amount
number
quantity
majority
preponderance
total

On some occasions, the use of such a word is meant to indicate the whole of the group, while other uses focus on the individual members of the group.

Focus (group): <u>The number</u> of bills is overwhelming.

Focus (group members): <u>A number</u> of them are fairly inexpensive.

When the word is preceded by *the*, it's a good bet that the word is being used in its singular context. If the word is preceded by the article *a*, it's being used in its plural form.

2

VERBS

2.1 Verbs

2.2 Verb Forms

2.3 Verb Properties

2.4 Subject and Verb Agreement

2.1 VERBS

Helping Verbs
Linking Verbs
Regular Verbs
Irregular Verbs
Transitive Verbs
Intransitive Verbs

A *verb* is a word or a group of words used to indicate something about the subject of a sentence, such as an act or action (*ran*, *hate*, *change*); an occurrence (*become*, *happen*); or a state of being, including emotions (*be*, *seem*). Some verbs indicate action (*walk*, *run*, *shout*, *whisper*, *soar*); other verbs indicate something more (*fear*, *daydream*, *exist*, *hope*, *trust*).

She ran to the beach.
I hate the beach.

A verb is one of the basic parts of speech that combines with other words to create clauses or sentences. The verb within a clause or a sentence is called a predicate in relation to the subject of the clause or sentence.

SEE ALSO 5.1, "Basic Sentence Structure"

A verb is a unique part of speech because it can fully communicate a whole host of meaning all by itself. It is rare that any other part of speech can completely communicate a fully expressed thought or command on its own, but certain verbs used on their own—often accompanied by the appropriate punctuation—can do it.

Stop!	Run!
Help!	Enjoy!

There is an understood "you" preceding the verbs in these examples of imperative commands. This verb form on its own really doesn't require the *you* to be overtly stated for the meaning to be clear.

While such verbs can stand alone, other verbs—compound verbs, for instance—are complete only when they are combined with the various forms of auxiliary words, such as *be*, *can*, *have*, *do*, and *will*.

Other verbs, **helping** or **linking verbs**, relate the subject of a sentence with its predicate. The most common linking verbs are the various forms of the word *be*, which are words that connect to the senses (seeing, hearing, feeling, tasting, and smelling). *Become*, *appear*, and *seem* are helping verbs.

> Al Gore is a Democrat.
>
> The house smells yummy.

WORDS TO GO . . . WORDS TO GO . . . WORDS TO GO

> **Helping verbs**, or auxiliary verbs, relate subjects with their predicates to identify tense. Helping verbs can also identify voice, person, number, or mood.
>
> **Linking verbs** connect the subject to another word in the sentence. That connected word can be a predicate noun, pronoun, or adjective.

Helping Verbs

The following table lists some common helpers.

Helping Verbs		
am	does	ought
are	done	shall
be	had	should
been	has	was
being	have	were
can	is	will
could	may	would
did	might	
do	must	

A helping verb, also called an auxiliary verb, is used with a **main verb** to create a verb phrase. One helping verb or multiple helping verbs can be used in conjunction with the main verb in the verb phrase. All the verbs found in the dictionary can be combined with helping verbs.

Verb Phrase	Helping Verb
will drive	will
has been driving	has been
could have been driving	could have been
could have driven	could have

WORDS TO GO . . .WORDS TO GO . . .WORDS TO GO

The **main verb** is the infinitive, present participle, or past participle in all verb phrases that carries the main meaning.

The helping verb identifies tense.

She has driven.
She had driven.
She will have driven.

When joined with the various forms of the word *be* (*am*, *are*, *be*, *been*, *being*, *is*, *was*, *were*) and hooked up with a main verb, certain helping verbs (*did*, *do*, *does*, *had*, *has*, *have*, *shall*, *will*) can indicate both time and voice.

She will run.
The windows were closed.
He had run.
Wild mustangs have been seen.
They did not want cookies.
The cat was startled.

When joined with main verbs, other helping verbs (*can*, *could*, *may*, *might*, *must*, *ought*, *shall*, *should*, *will*, and *would*) show a sense of necessity, obligation, permission, or possibility.

She could dance.
I might ask her again.
You must not.

When the different sorts of helper verbs come together, they can create verbal phrases that are more complex than when they're used on their own.

She might have said something before now.
She would have been too late anyway.
They ought to have been three hours earlier.

Linking Verbs

Linking verbs connect or link the subject to another word in the sentence, its **complement**. That connected word can be a predicate noun, a pronoun, or an adjective. Two types of linking verbs exist: the various forms of the word *be* (meaning "to be") and the sensory-related intransitive verbs (such as *feel*, *look*, *seem*).

Ralph <u>is</u> a truck driver.

She <u>looks</u> beautiful.

They <u>are</u> teachers.

WORDS TO GO . . .WORDS TO GO . . .WORDS TO GO

A **complement** is a word or group of words that helps to give a completeness to the understanding of the meaning of a subject, an object, or a verb.

If a linking verb is followed by a subject complement, the linking verb must be able to stand in agreement with its subject, not with the complement. Whenever a linking verb is followed by a subject complement, the verb tense must agree with its subject instead of with the noun or pronoun that's functioning as the subject complement.

True <u>love</u> <u>is</u> a <u>horse</u>.

In this example, *love* is the subject, *is* is the linking verb, and *horse* is the complement.

<u>Merry's barn and fields</u> <u>are</u> her <u>escape</u>.

Here, *Merry's barn and fields* is the subject, *are* is the linking verb, and *escape* is the complement.

Regular Verbs

Most verbs are regular verbs. They're able to take on their past-tense and past participle forms simply by adding *-d* or *-ed* to their infinitive state. The past-tense and the past participle forms are identical in how they're formed. If one takes the *-d*, the other will also, and vice versa. The same goes for the *-ed* addition. The following table shows some examples of regular verbs in their past-tense and past participle forms.

SEE ALSO 2.2, "Verb Forms"

Infinitive	Past Tense	Past Participle
hope	hoped	hoped
love	loved	loved
trust	trusted	trusted

continues

continued

Infinitive	Past Tense	Past Participle
agree	agreed	agreed
walk	walked	walked

Whenever you need confirmation of a verb's form, dig out your trusty dictionary. The verb form found in the dictionary is the infinitive form. If no other form options are listed, the verb is a regular verb.

Irregular Verbs

Some verbs do not follow the system for regular verbs. These are *irregular verbs*, for which the past-tense and past participle forms are created in ways other than adding *-d* or *-ed*. Some irregular verbs form their past-tense and past participle versions by making a change in an internal vowel, as shown in the following table.

Infinitive	Past Tense	Past Participle
begin	began	begun
come	came	come
ring	rang	rung
sing	sang	sung

Some irregular verbs not only make an internal vowel alteration to create their past-tense form, but they also add an *-n* to the past participle—and they can be all over the place with the internal vowels. Sometimes they revert back to the infinitive form with just the added *-n* for their past participle forms.

Infinitive	Past Tense	Past Participle
break	broke	broken
draw	drew	drawn
grow	grew	grown
throw	threw	thrown

Other irregular verbs can have the same form in all three forms.

Infinitive	Past Tense	Past Participle
bid	bid	bid
burst	burst	burst

Infinitive	Past Tense	Past Participle
let	let	let
set	set	set

So how do you know when to use what? You can always check a dictionary. You can also memorize a list of the forms. I've provided a list of some of the most common irregular verbs here.

COMMON IRREGULAR VERBS

Infinitive	Past Tense	Past Participle
arise	arose	arisen
become	became	become
begin	began	begun
bid	bid	bid
bite	bit	bit, bitten
blow	blew	blown
break	broke	broken
bring	brought	brought
burst	burst	burst
buy	bought	bought
catch	caught	caught
choose	chose	chosen
come	came	come
cut	cut	cut
dive	dived, dove	dived
do	did	done
draw	drew	drawn
dream	dreamed, dreamt	dreamed, dreamt
drink	drank	drunk
drive	drove	driven
eat	ate	eaten
fall	fell	fallen
find	found	found
flee	fled	fled
fly	flew	flown
forget	forgot	forgot, forgotten

continues

continued

Infinitive	Past Tense	Past Participle
freeze	froze	frozen
get	got	got, gotten
give	gave	given
go	went	gone
grow	grew	grown
hang	hanged, hung	hanged, hung
hear	heard	heard
hide	hid	hidden
hold	held	held
keep	kept	kept
know	knew	known
lay	laid	laid
lead	led	led
leave	left	left
let	let	let
lie	lay	lain
lose	lost	lost
pay	paid	paid
prove	proved	proved, proven
ride	rode	ridden
ring	rang	rung
rise	rose	risen
run	ran	run
say	said	said
see	saw	seen
set	set	set
shake	shook	shaken
sing	sang, sung	sang, sung
sink	sank, sunk	sank, sunk
sit	sat	sat
sleep	slept	slept
slide	slid	slid
sneak	sneaked, snuck	snuck
speak	spoke	spoken

Infinitive	Past Tense	Past Participle
spring	sprang, sprung	sprung
stand	stood	stood
steal	stole	stolen
swim	swam	swum
take	took	taken
tear	tore	torn
think	thought	thought
throw	threw	thrown
wear	wore	worn
wind	wound	wound
write	wrote	written

Whenever you encounter an irregular verb in a dictionary, you'll see its alternate forms, indicating past-tense and past participle forms, included with the original infinitive form. If the dictionary provides only the infinitive and one alternate form, you know that the past-tense and the past participle forms are one and the same.

Transitive Verbs

A transitive verb conveys action that requires an object. The word *convey*, for instance, is a transitive verb. To successfully get across the meaning of this and all other transitive verbs, a direct object must be present as well.

The volcanic <u>eruption</u> <u>decimated</u> the <u>land</u>.

Here, *eruption* is the subject, *decimated* is the predicate transitive verb, and *land* is the direct object.

<u>I</u> <u>shot</u> the <u>sheriff</u>.

In this example, *I* is the subject, *shot* is the predicate transitive verb, and *sheriff* is the direct object.

Intransitive Verbs

Intransitive verbs do not take on direct objects; in fact, they *can't*. The intransitive verbs clearly and completely communicate without a direct object. The intransitive verb can take on a prepositional phrase, although it isn't necessary.

Subject	Intransitive Verb (No Direct Object)	Prepositional Phrase (Optional)
Their preacher	lied.	
The sheriff	died.	
The old man	cried	on his shoulder.
Our kitty	scurried	into the house.

In this section all manner of verbs—helping, linking, regular, irregular, transitive and intransitive—have been examined. This basic part of speech is truly unique in that it provides all of the action for our sentences and can also often clearly express a full gamut of thought or emotion when used solo.

2.2 VERB FORMS

Infinitive

Past Tense

Past Participle

Present Participle

The *-s* Form

All verbs (except for *be*) have five verb forms: infinitive, past tense, past participle, present participle, and the *-s* form. The first three—infinitive, past tense, and past participle—are the keys to the various tenses.

Infinitive

The infinitive, or plain, verb form is used to show that the verb action takes place in the present tense. When using the infinitive form, the subject of the sentence is either a plural noun or one of four pronouns: *I*, *we*, *you*, or *they*.

Dogs frighten him.
They believe in Santa Claus.

The infinitive form is the main-entry form of the verb found in the dictionary.

Past Tense

The past-tense form of a verb shows that the action in question took place in the past. The past-tense verb generally is formed by simply adding *-d* or *-ed* to the infinitive form.

They believed in Santa Claus.
Dogs frightened him.

As discussed in the earlier chapter, irregular verbs (*cut*, *dream*, *flee*, *go*) form their past-tense version in other ways.

SEE ALSO 2.1, "Verbs"

SEE ALSO 2.3, "Verb Properties"

Past Participle

The *past participle* shows that the work of the verb has been completed. Generally, the past participle ends in *-ed*. The past participle is the form of the verb that's used …

- With the helping verbs *have*, *has*, or *had*.

  She had climbed to the peak.

- In the passive voice, with a form of the verb *be*.

  The cake was baked.

- By itself to modify nouns and pronouns.

  His sliced bread was soggy.

SEE ALSO 2.3, "Verb Properties"

With the exception of the irregular verbs, the past participle is written the same as its past-tense form.

They had gone to town.

Present Participle

The present participle shows that the verb is currently in action or that the action is not yet completed. Generally, the present participle is formed by adding *-ing* to the infinitive form of the verb.

The present participle is able to …

- Modify nouns and pronouns.

  The running water flowed out of the tub.

- Function as a noun, as a **gerund**.

  Walking takes forever.

WORDS TO GO . . . WORDS TO GO . . . WORDS TO GO

A **gerund** is a word that ends with *–ing* and can function as the subject of a verb, the object of a verb, a predicate nominative or complement, or the object of a preposition.

- Join with various versions of the *be* verb to show that the verb's action is ongoing.

  She is writing.

The *-s* Form

The *-s* form is used when the action of the verb is happening in the present time. This form of the verb ends in *-s* or *-es*.

begs	learns	teases
has	leaves	tries
hopes	rides	
is	shows	

There are eight forms for the verb *be*. Most other verbs have only five forms (infinitive, present participle, past participle, present tense, and past tense), but the verb *be* also has additional present and past forms.

Infinitive: be
Present participle: being
Past participle: been
Present tense: am, is, are
Past tense: was, were

Verb forms have a great deal of variety, but when deciding on the correct form, the best place to begin—especially for irregular verbs—is a reliable dictionary.

2.3 VERB PROPERTIES

Conjugation

Tense

Mood

Voice

Person

Number

In this next section, we take a look at the properties of verbs, including the conjugation of verbs as well as a review of identifiers for verb tense, mood, voice, person, and number.

Conjugation

Verbs need to change inflection to be in sync with the subject of a sentence in regard to form, tense, mood, voice, and agreement/number. This change in inflection is called **conjugation**.

> ***WORDS TO GO . . .WORDS TO GO . . .WORDS TO GO***
>
> **Conjugation** of verbs is the altering of the verb form to denote changes in form, tense, mood, voice, person, and number.

A verb has seven forms related to conjugation:

- Present indicative
- Present participle
- Present subjunctive
- Past indicative
- Past participle
- Past subjunctive
- Imperative

Each has its own rules for conjugation, as outlined in the following sections.

Let's look at some examples, starting with the conjugation of the verb *to know* in the present tense with the active voice and the indicative mood:

I know	We know
You know	You know
He/She/It knows	They know

Conjugation of verbs is the altering of the verb form to denote changes in voice, mood, tense, person, and number.

Here's the conjugation of the verb *do*:

I do	we do
you do	you do
he/she/it does	they do

A verb has seven forms related to conjugation: the present indicative, the present participle, the present subjunctive, the past indicative, the past participle, the past subjunctive, and the imperative.

Present Indicative

The present indicative form is used for all singular and plural persons in the present tense. The only notable exception is the third-person singular. With the third-person singular, *-s* is added to the **verb stem**. If the stem ends with *-o* or *-y* that transforms into *-i*, an *-es* is added.

First/Second Person	Third Person
create	creates
deserve	deserves
dry	dries
go	goes
hope	hopes
travel	travels
want	wants

WORDS TO GO . . .WORDS TO GO . . .WORDS TO GO

A **verb stem** is the most basic form of a verb. The verb stem is the form of the verb that's generally listed first in a dictionary.

SEE ALSO 1.4, "Noun and Pronoun Properties"

Present Participle

To form the present participle, *-ing* is added to the verb stem. If the verb stem ends with *-ie*, that generally changes to *-y* before the *-ing* is added. For words with a concluding silent *-e*, the *-e* is usually dropped before the *-ing* addition. For all single and plural persons and numbers, the present participle is written the same.

First/Second Person	Third Person
I am creating	They are creating
I am deserving	They are deserving
I am drying	They are drying
I am going	They are going
I am hoping	They are hoping
I am traveling	They are traveling
I am wanting	They are wanting

Present Subjunctive

The present subjunctive tends to use a past-tense verb to express or imply some sort of doubt or impracticability.

First/Second Person	Third Person
If I were creative	If they were creative
If I were to deserve	If they were to deserve

Past Indicative

The past indicative form adds *-ed* to the end of the verb stem for all regular verbs. For irregular verbs, the past-tense form can be created in many different ways. A reliable dictionary such as *Merriam-Webster's Collegiate Dictionary*, 11th edition, is a researcher's best friend and provides the indicative forms for irregular verbs.

REGULAR VERBS

Present	Past
create	created
deserve	deserved
dry	dried
hope	hoped
lock	locked
travel	traveled
want	wanted

IRREGULAR VERBS

Present	Past
cut	cut
dream	dreamed, dreamt
flee	fled
go	gone, went
lose	lost
shake	shaken
tear	torn

SEE ALSO 2.1, "Verbs"

Past Participle

Like the past indicative, the past participle form adds *-ed* to the end of the verb stem for all regular verbs. This is the same process as is used for the past indicative, so the verbs in either of these two forms are always presented exactly the same.

Having completed the task, she moved on to the next.

For irregular verbs, the past participle form is not always the same as the past indicative form. For confirmation of the past participle form of the verb, reach for a copy of *Merriam-Webster's Collegiate Dictionary*, 11th edition.

Past Subjunctive

The past subjunctive form takes the past-perfect verb to convey a mood of uncertainty. The past-perfect tense indicates that an action was or will be completed before some other time or action.

If it had been changed …

If we were fooled …

If it had been delivered …

Imperative

The imperative mood has the verb stem being used to issue a command, make a request, or utter an exclamation. In these imperative instances, the understood subject is an "understood" ***you***.

Hurry!	(You) hurry!
Help!	(You) help!

Run!	(You) run!
Stop!	(You) stop!
Hold on there.	(You) hold on there.
	Hold on there (you).
Come over here.	(You) come over here.
	Come over here (you).

Tense

Verb tense identifies the time of the verb's action with the time when the writer writes about the action. The tenses show that a verb's action or state of being is in either the present tense, the past tense, or the future tense.

Present Tense

The present tense is the infinitive verb stem, which is also referenced as the present indicative form. For the third-person singular in the present tense, *-s* is added at the end of the verb.

First/Second Person	Third Person
I run	She runs
You work	He works
I write	She writes
You return	He returns

Past Tense

Past tense takes its form through the addition of inflections that create the past indicative structure. An *inflection* is a change in the form of a word in order to indicate distinctions such as case, gender, number, tense, person, mood, or voice.

First/Second Person	Third Person
I ran	She ran
You worked	He worked
I wrote	She wrote
You returned	He returned

Future Tense

The future tense is achieved simply by adding *will* or *shall* (for the first person) to precede the verb's basic dictionary spelling. Within the first person, *shall* can be substituted for *will*. This addition shows that the action is anticipated.

First/Second Person	Third Person
I will run	She will run
You will work	He will work
I will write	She will write
You will return	He will return

Perfect Tense (Present, Past, and Perfect)

The perfect tense shows that a verb's action was or will be completed before some other time or when some action takes place. The helping verb *have* is added to a verb's past participle to form the perfect tense.

Present Perfect	Past Perfect	Future Perfect
I have stopped	I had stopped	I will have stopped
Renee has walked	Renee had walked	Renee will have walked

Infinitives

The infinitives are the regular citation of a verb, the version found in the dictionary, often preceded by the word *to*. Remember that the infinitive form (or plain form) is the main-entry or dictionary form of the verb. This is the form used to show that the verb action takes place in the present. When using the infinitive form, the subject of the sentence is either a plural noun or one of these pronouns: *I*, *we*, *you*, or *they*.

to dance	to live
to drive	to pray
to hunt	to return
to listen	to run

Mood

The *mood* of the verb form indicates the feeling or attitude the writer is trying to convey. This verb form shows whether the action or state it indicates is an actual fact or a command, or a possibility or a desire.

Indicative

The *indicative mood* is the form of a verb that gives an opinion, reports on a fact, or asks a question.

Opinion: They <u>need</u> more money.

Fact: They <u>start</u> close to the ice cream guy.

Question: How <u>does</u> he <u>work</u> there?

Imperative

The *imperative mood* is the form of a verb that gives voice to commands or provides direction.

Command: <u>Get</u> more money.

Direction: <u>Go</u> to the bank.

Subjunctive

The subjunctive mood is the form of a verb that states a necessity, desire, or suggestion. The subjunctive mood could also name a condition that appears contrary to the current facts.

Necessity: It must <u>be</u> in single-spaced pages.

Desire: I hope I <u>can earn</u> that right.

Suggestion: He asked that she <u>walk</u> only on the chairs.

Contrary: If she <u>were</u> to fail, her friends would worry.

Voice

When transitive verbs have objects they are connected to, the verb identifies whether the subjects are the ones in action or the ones the action is directed toward.

Active Voice

When using the active voice, the subjects are the ones performing the action.

<u>Rhoda</u> <u>wrote</u> the <u>letter</u>.

Here, *Rhoda* is the subject, *wrote* is the active-voice verb, and *letter* is the object.

Passive Voice

In the passive voice, the verb takes an object. The object or receiver of the action is identified. The subject of passive sentences does not instigate or execute the action specified by the verb; rather, it is acted upon.

The <u>letter</u> <u>was written</u> <u>by Rhoda</u>.

In this example, *letter* is the subject, *was written* is the passive-voice verb, and *by Rhoda* is the prepositional phrase. With the change in voice from active to passive, the subject from the active voice perspective moves out of that position and into the position of a prepositional phrase.

Person

The person qualities of a verb distinguish between whether the verb's action or state of being is …

- That of the speaker, which would mean it's in the first-person form (*I*, *we*).
- That of the person spoken to, which would mean it's in the second-person form (*you*).
- That of the person (or thing) being talked about, which would mean it's in the third-person form (*he*, *she*, *it*, *they*).

SEE ALSO 1.4, "Noun and Pronoun Properties"

Number

A verb's number quality indicates whether it's singular or plural. That number has to match the number of the noun or pronoun being used.

The second-person verb always takes the plural form. It doesn't matter whether there's one person or more than one person spoken to.

> You <u>are</u> such a nice guy.
> You <u>are</u> all such nice guys.

The third-person present indicative singular verb changes its form to convey person and number.

> You <u>write</u>.
> She <u>writes</u>.
> They <u>write</u>.

Now you have the rules of conjugation and those for identifying and properly using conjugation to present a verb's correct tense, mood, voice, person, and number and know how the inflection of verbs can be used to present agreement and clarity with regard to form, tense, mood, and voice.

2.4 SUBJECT AND VERB AGREEMENT

Agreement with Third-Person Subjects

Agreement with Separated Subjects and Verbs

Agreement with Linked Subjects

More Agreement Rules of Thumb

Agreement is the consistency in form between subjects and verbs. Readers' ease of comprehension is aided and increased when there is agreement within the pages they are reading. A subject and verb must always match up.

<u>Stacy</u> rarely <u>raises</u> a ruckus.

Here, both the subject (*Stacy*) and the verb (*raises*) are presented in their third-person singular forms.

This section deals with the kinds of agreement, including agreement with third-person subjects, agreement with separated subjects and verbs, and agreement with linked subjects.

Agreement with Third-Person Subjects

Third-person singular subjects need verbs that end with *-s* or *-es*. When making the noun plural, simply adding *-s* or *-es* to the noun does the trick.

Singular Agreement	Plural Agreement
The girl sits.	The girls sit.
The horse grazes.	The horses graze.
The book falls.	The books fall.

There are exceptions, of course, due once again to those pesky irregular plurals that are formed by nouns.

Agreement with Separated Subjects and Verbs

When going for subject-verb agreement, the sentence's subject and verb(s) might have other words separating them within the sentence and not always sit right next to each other. Still, they have to agree. Forcing the verb to agree with the noun closest to it isn't always correct and can result in an ungrammatical mess. Be sure you match the verb with its true subject, not just the noun nearest the verb.

The schedule of delivery dates and procedural requirements often scares new writers.

The subject in this example is *schedule*, and the verb *scares* must be in agreement with the subject instead of the closer *requirements* noun.

Agreement with Linked Subjects

The subject of a sentence can be made up of more than one thing. Depending on the situation, the multiple subjects will be connected by either the conjunctions *and* or *or/nor*.

and When a sentence has more than one subject and those subjects are linked by the conjunction *and*, to reach subject-verb agreement, the verb is almost always plural in form.

Snickers *and* Kodi were my favorite dogs.

SEE ALSO 4.3, "Conjunctions"

There can be exceptions to the "and" methodology. When the parts of the subject are uniform in a solitary concept or perhaps actually reference just one person or thing, a singular verb is used.

Peanut butter *and* banana was Elvis's favorite sandwich.

or/nor Whenever the subject's parts are singular and connected by the conjunctions *or* or *nor*, the accompanying verb is singular. When the subject's parts are plural, the verb is plural as well.

Singular: Mary *nor* Taylor truly understands what they have done.
Plural: The cheetahs *or* the lions have attacked again.

More Agreement Rules of Thumb

The following additional information should prove helpful in negotiating subject-verb agreement:

Indefinite pronouns tend to be singular in meaning and, therefore, take singular verbs.

Something is wrong.

Some indefinite pronouns can be either singular or plural, so picking out the right verb takes a bit more consideration. This is determined by the ultimate meaning of the nouns or pronouns in question.

All of the flour is being used.

Each time the dogs escape, all go right for the door.

SEE ALSO 1.3, "Pronouns"

Collective nouns (*army*, *audience*, *committee*, *crowd*, *family*, *group*, *number*, *office*, *team*) can take either singular or plural verbs—it really just depends whether the meaning of the noun is singular or plural.

The group loves these get-togethers.

SEE ALSO 1.1, "Nouns"

Plural-form nouns (*athletics*, *economics*, *mathematics*, *measles*, *mumps*, *news*, *politics*, *physics*, *statistics*) that have singular meanings take singular verbs.

Politics is something I could have lived without.

Titles of works from books or movies use singular verbs, as do words that are being discussed or defined simply as words.

Dreamgirls is back on Broadway.

Dudes is a word that has been misused and overused.

It's usual for the subject and verb within the same sentence to have agreement with regard to what person the sentence is presented. This is even necessary when the subjects and their verbs are not overtly connected. Or even when there are more than one subjects.

3

MODIFIERS

3.1 Adjectives

3.2 Adverbs

3.3 Modifiers: Regular, Dangling, and Misplaced

3.1 ADJECTIVES

Descriptive Adjectives
Limiting Adjectives
Adjectival Articles
Participle Adjectives
Proper Adjectives
Attributive Adjectives
Predicate Adjectives

An adjective is a word used to modify—describe, restrict, or somehow qualify—nouns and pronouns. Adjectives modify only nouns and pronouns; they do not modify other adjectives, verbs, or adverbs. (That's what adverbs are for.)

His brother was the serious student.

Here, *serious* is the adjective describing the noun *student*.

That was me … silly me.

In this example, *silly* is the adjective describing the pronoun *me*.

Some adjectives are simple and common, single-syllable words.

bad	left	true
bright	new	weird
dark	old	wrong
dumb	right	young
false	strange	
good	stupid	

Colors can be used as adjectives, too.

black	green	teal
blue	purple	white
brown	red	yellow

Many adjectives are created simply by adding certain suffixes to words that were previously nouns or verbs.

Noun or Verb	Suffix	Adjective
revive	*-able*	revivable
fiction	*-al*	fictional
legend	*-ary*	legendary
lead	*-en*	leaden
beauty	*-ful*	beautiful
collect	*-ible*	collectible
Arab	*-ic*	Arabic
self	*-ish*	selfish
repress	*-ive*	repressive
seam	*-less*	seamless
lady	*-like*	ladylike
pore	*-ous*	porous
win	*-some*	winsome
sun	*-y*	sunny

Now let's look at specific types of adjectives and how they are used for modification.

Descriptive Adjectives

Descriptive adjectives more definitively and fully identify a characteristic of a noun.

The cold floor
A beautiful girl

In these examples, without the addition of the adjective, the reader would still know that a floor and a girl were being discussed. However, the addition of an adjective provides a better idea of what sort of floor and girl are being discussed.

Limiting Adjectives

Limiting adjectives narrow the scope of a noun to some degree. This classification includes the following kinds of adjectives:

Possessive adjectives show possession or ownership: *my*, *her*, *his*, *our*, *their*, *your*.

This is my book.

Numbering adjectives identify number or amount: *many*, *nineteen*, *several*, *three*.

Sixteen girls at the party had brown hair.

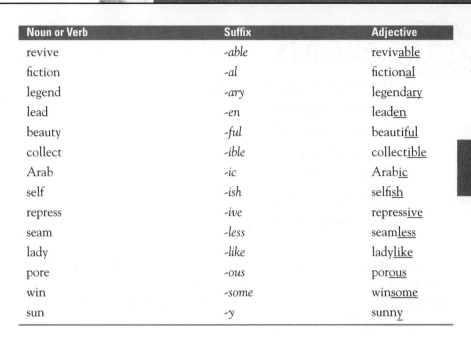

Demonstrative adjectives distinguish one from another: *that*, *these*, *this*, *those*.

Hand me those candles, please.

Interrogative adjectives ask a question: *what*, *which*, *who*, *whose*.

Whose idea was that?

Adjectival Articles

The articles *a*, *an*, and *the* are also limiting adjectives. When an article comes before a noun or a phrase, it clarifies whether the "something" to follow is definite (*the*) or indefinite (*a*, *an*). When an article is used, another adjective can also be used between the article and the noun itself.

They went down the road.
She was born a working girl.

For a series of coordinate nouns, an article must be added before each noun.

The doctor and the dentist ran toward the exit first.

If the list of nouns has a single thread of an idea, there's no need to repeat the article.

The cat and mouse appeared to be in a dance to the death.

When an *a* or *an* is required and one doesn't work for both examples, just use them both as appropriate.

He recommended that I see a dentist and an orthodontist.

When the named things have one plural noun governing them, the definite article should not be repeated for each modifier.

He ran for president during the second and third semesters.

Participle Adjectives

The participle adjective is a participle being used to modify a noun. A present participle is a verb with the *-ing* suffix added.

living	This is a living testament.
loving	What a kind, loving woman.
drawing	The drawing board fell off of the wall.

A past participle is a verb with the *-ed* suffix added.

beloved	Her beloved sister died tragically.
twisted	The twisted tie fell off the bag.
completed	He turned in his completed assignment.

An irregular past participle is a verb with the *-en* suffix added.

graven	Do not worship graven images.
craven	The craven fool ran out blindly.
earthen	She bumped the table and the earthen pot fell.

SEE ALSO 2.1, "Verbs"

Proper Adjectives

Proper adjectives are derived from proper nouns and are almost always capitalized.

She was supposed to be an English expert.
Warm, crusty French bread is yummy smeared with butter.
They stole a priceless Elizabethan watch.

Attributive Adjectives

When an adjective is adjacent to the noun being modified, it is considered an *attributive adjective*.

The fun was over when the blue sky turned gray.
No one in the room had red hair.
There was a clear sky.
They could see the full moon shining bright.

Predicate Adjectives

Adjectives are considered *predicate adjectives* when they are placed to follow a linking verb.

The sky is blue.
The ship is large.
The hopes are high.

As demonstrated in this section, adjectives assist the writer by providing more description options than the bare bones of a subject-and-predicate sentence.

3.2 ADVERBS

Adverbs **modify**—describe, restrict, or in some way qualify—verbs, adjectives, or other adverbs. Adverbs can also modify clauses, phrases, and entire sentences. Adverbs indicate the *how*, *when*, *where*, and *what* (*extent*) of something.

How: She'll run there quickly.
When: I'm going to go today.
Where: Bring that book here.
What (extent): She was fully immersed in the water.

WORDS TO GO . . .WORDS TO GO . . .WORDS TO GO

To **modify** means to restrict the meaning of.

Let's look at some examples:

The ballerina delicately danced across the stage.

Delicately is the adverb here describing the verb *danced.*

How could the only four people to survive go missing?

Here, the adverb *only* modifies the adjective *four* and the noun *people.*

He quite seriously questioned the superintendent's methods.

In this example, *quite* is the adverb modifying the adverb and verb *seriously* and *questioned*, respectively.

We arrived just after they left for the airport.

Here, *just* is the adverb modifying the clause *after they left.*

They walked closely to the edge of the lava flow.

Closely is the adverb here, modifying the phrase *to the edge.*

Thankfully, he reached them just in the nick of time.

Here, *thankfully* is the adverb modifying the rest of the sentence.

Most adverbs are formed by adding the suffix *-ly* to adjectives, but you can't count on the *-ly* alone to identify adverbs. Some adjectives also use *-ly* (*fatherly*, *lonely*, *motherly*). And while adverbs can modify verbs, adjectives, and other adverbs, adjectives modify nouns and nouns alone. With that in mind, when you see an *-ly* modifier in a sentence, you can identify whether it's an adjective or an adverb based on what it's modifying.

Her fatherly uncle
Her fatherly old uncle

As with adjectives, the addition of suffixes helps create and identify adverbs. In this instance the suffix added is *-ly*.

Word	Suffixes	Adverb
bad	*-ly*	badly
lucky	*-ly*	luckily
poor	*-ly*	poorly

In this section, I covered the manner in which adverbs work with other parts of speech (verbs, adjectives, and even other adverbs), clauses, phrases, and even whole sentences, to provide modification. That modification provides greater description of what's being modified. By understanding the way in which adverbs are used, you can decipher and more clearly present the *how*, *when*, *where*, and *what* (*extent*) of what is being modified.

3.3 MODIFIERS: REGULAR, DANGLING, AND MISPLACED

Regular Forms of Modifiers

Dangling Modifiers

Misplaced Modifiers

Limiting Modifiers

Modifiers add specificity to whatever is being elucidated. In this section I review the three regular forms of modifiers: the positive form, the comparative form, and the superlative form.

Regular Forms of Modifiers

Modifiers, whether adjectives or adverbs, tend to have three forms: the positive form, the comparative form, and the superlative form.

The *positive form* is the basic dictionary version of a descriptive word. In this form of modification, there is no comparison; the word is simply the word (*cold, hard, hot, soft*).

The *comparative form* compares what is modified with something else (*colder, harder, hotter, softer*).

The *superlative form* compares what is being modified with at least two other things—or perhaps even more (*coldest, hardest, hottest, softest*).

	Positive	Comparative	Superlative
Adjectives	good	better	best
	bad	worse	worst
	little	little, less	littlest, least
	some, much	more	most
Adverbs	well	better	best
	badly	worse	worst

The comparative and superlative forms of adjectives and adverbs have to be used correctly for proper understanding.

Positive: He spoke <u>righteously</u>.

Comparative: He spoke more righteously than she did.

Superlative: He spoke most righteously of everyone.

Dangling Modifiers

A dangling modifier is a modifying word or phrase that either doesn't link up well with its object or links with another word that's been left out.

Dangling: Having arrived early, the meeting had not yet begun.

Corrected: Having arrived early, we discovered that the meeting had not yet begun.

Corrected: Because we arrived early, we found that the meeting had not yet begun.

Most danglers happen because some modifying words or word phrases come before the sentence's main clause. The problem words and phrases don't have subjects, so the reader assumes the noun that comes after the modifier is its object. When modifiers don't describe the noun that follows, they are dangling. A dangler can be fixed fairly easily with just a bit of a rewrite of the sentence.

Dangling participial phrase: Being very tired, the sun failed to interrupt Gail's sleep.

Reworked: The sun failed to interrupt Gail's sleep because she was so very tired.

Dangling infinitive phrase: To rise and shine, an enormous effort was required.

Reworked: An enormous effort was required for her to rise and shine.

Dangling prepositional phrase: Upon rising, a good breakfast was the key to starting the day.

Reworked: A good breakfast upon rising was the key to starting the day.

Dangling elliptical clause: Until wide awake, cooking was not possible.

Reworked: Cooking was not possible until she was wide awake.

Misplaced Modifiers

A misplaced modifier is one that's placed too far from the word or words it's supposed to modify. A misplaced modifier seems to modify the wrong part of a sentence or isn't clear what part of the sentence is meant to be modified. Often interrupting prepositional phrases or subordinate clauses get in the way of correct modifier placement.

With Prepositional Phrases

Prepositional phrases are often the cause of misplaced modifiers. Be sure to place prepositional phrases in the best location to clearly modify the intended object.

If you stick a prepositional phrase in the wrong place, hilarity may well ensue.

Misplaced modifier: Christie gave cookies to the kids on paper towels.

It's unlikely that the kids were on the paper towels when Christie gave them the cookies, but from this construct, that's what it sounds like. Here's a better setup:

Christie gave the kids cookies on paper towels.

With Subordinate Clauses

Just as with prepositional phrases, it is important for subordinate clauses to be properly placed with modifiers, so that correct modification is a clear certainty, or else they may appear to simply modify whatever is nearest to them in the sentence.

Misplaced modifier: According to the media, many starlets are stalked by paparazzi who party all night.

With this setup, it seems like the paparazzi party all night, when in fact, it is the starlets. This version is clearer:

According to the media, many starlets who party all night are stalked by paparazzi.

Limiting Modifiers

Limiting modifiers modify the expressions placed directly after them in a sentence. You can often identify a limiting modifier by one of the following words:

almost	just	scarcely
even	merely	simply
exactly	nearly	
hardly	only	

Only is a commonly misused limiting modifier:

Dan *only* dated Chris after high school.

Did Dan only date Chris? As opposed to doing exactly what with Chris? Or was Chris the only girl he dated after high school? Correct modifier placement clears up the confusion:

Dan dated *only* Chris after high school.

This chapter covered all forms of adjectival and adverbial modification, including all manner of adjectives—descriptive, limiting, adjectival, participle, proper, attributive, and predicate—and the *how*, *when*, *where*, and *what* focus of adverbs. And by knowing about regular modifiers, you can avoid dangling modifiers and misplaced modifiers.

4

PREPOSITIONS AND CONJUNCTIONS

4.1 Prepositions

4.2 Prepositional Phrases

4.3 Conjunctions

4.1 PREPOSITIONS

Terminal Prepositions

To Capitalize or Not to Capitalize?

A preposition is a word or phrase that functions as a connector, uniting a noun (or a word or a group of words functioning as a noun) or a pronoun with another word in the sentence. The noun being connected is called the object of the preposition.

Dolphins live in water.

Here, *Dolphins* is the noun, *in* is the preposition, and *water* is the object of the preposition.

Similar to nouns, prepositions can be either simple or compound. The simple preposition is a single, often monosyllabic word (*as*, *in*, *to*, *with*). Compound prepositions have more than one syllable and very often are two or more words. Compound prepositions can be joined to form a new word (*onto*, *outside*, *throughout*, *within*) or remain individual words that are used together (*according to*, *apart from*, *instead of*). The following table lists some common prepositions.

Prepositions			
about	at	due to	next to
above	athwart	during	of
according to	because of	except	off
across	before	except for	on
after	behind	excepting	on account of
against	below	for	onto
along	beneath	from	out
along with	beside	in	out of
amid	between	in addition to	outside
among	beyond	in spite of	over
apart from	by	inside	owing to
around	concerning	instead of	past
as	considering	into	pending
as to	despite	like	regarding
aside from	down	near	respecting

Prepositions

round	till (to)	unlike	with
since	to	until	within
through	toward	unto	without
throughout	under	up	
til/'til (until)	underneath	upon	

Unlike nouns, pronouns, and verbs, prepositions never take alternate forms. What you see is what you get.

Terminal Prepositions

Most every teacher and book on grammar will instruct you to avoid ending a sentence with a preposition. Generally, that's a good rule to follow—except when it makes better sense to break the rule to make your writing easier for your reader to understand.

> This is the sort of bloody nonsense up with which I will not put.
> —Winston Churchill

As demonstrated in Churchill's famous response to criticism of his use of a preposition at the end of a sentence, avoiding terminal prepositions can result in stiff, convoluted sentence structures. While prepositions generally don't conclude a sentence and usually precede their objects, these aren't hard-and-fast rules.

> "What do you want to talk about?" Christie asked.

Here, *What* is the object and *about* is the preposition.

> Danny pointed to the boathouse he lives in.

Boathouse is the object here, and *in* is the preposition.

It's important to remain flexible with words. Making sure the placement fits the context is more important than following somewhat archaic rules that might leave your reader confused or frustrated.

To Capitalize or Not to Capitalize?

When you're including prepositions within titles, knowing when to capitalize them and when to lowercase them can be confusing. There are a few ways you can go.

Capitalize everything—including prepositions, conjunctions, and articles.

The Chicago Manual Of Style

Capitalize everything except prepositions, conjunctions, and articles.

"Everything I've Got in My Pocket"

"Lie to Me"

Capitalize everything except the prepositions, conjunctions, and articles that have four or less letters.

"Looking for a Kiss"

"You Were Right About Everything"

This last option is the general rule of thumb in use today—and is my own preference.

SEE ALSO 8.1, "Capitals"

4.2 PREPOSITIONAL PHRASES

Punctuating Prepositional Phrases

A prepositional phrase is the preposition plus its object and any modifiers.

Dolphins frolic in the ocean.

Dolphins is the noun here, *in* is the preposition, and *ocean* is the object of the preposition. Together, *in the ocean* is the prepositional phrase. It's important for prepositional phrases to be placed where they clearly modify the intended word or words. Avoid ambiguity.

Ambiguous: She served tea to the ladies in china teacups.

Clearer: She served the ladies tea in china teacups.

Prepositional phrases usually serve as adjectives, but they're also able to function as nouns and adverbs.

Adjective: The picture in the frame is an old one.

Noun: Through the field is the shortest route.

Adverb: We ran to the corner first.

Punctuating Prepositional Phrases

A prepositional phrase that introduces a sentence is usually set off with punctuation, often a comma. However, when the prepositional phrase introducing the sentence is short, following punctuation is not always used. Authors generally choose a style approach for each work and stick with it.

With punctuation: Instead of waiting to get confirmation, the *Chicago Daily Tribune* printed the story with the infamous "DEWEY DEFEATS TRUMAN" headline.

Without punctuation: In the year 2000 many news sources made a similar error.

When a prepositional phrase interrupts or ends a sentence, it is *not* set off with punctuation *if it restricts the meaning of the word or words it's modifying.*

Everything about her is a delight.

He is never in the way.

However, when the prepositional phrase simply adds information to a sentence and *does not restrict the meaning*, punctuation—usually a comma or two—is added to set it off.

> North Korea, according to reports, has begun testing their nuclear weapons.
>
> Madonna is not adopting a child from Africa, according to her representatives.

It's important to note that a preposition and its objects should not be separated by the inclusion of commas. This is demonstrated in all of the examples provided in the preceding section.

SEE ALSO 6.3, "Commas"

4.3 CONJUNCTIONS

Coordinating Conjunctions
Correlative Conjunctions
Subordinating Conjunctions

Conjunctions are words that link and form a relationship between two phrases or parts of a sentence. The most commonly recognized conjunctions are *and*, *but*, and *or*.

If you're familiar with Schoolhouse Rock's "Conjunction Junction," the lyrics might still be familiar to you, or at least part of the chorus:

> Conjunction Junction, what's your function?
> Hooking up words and phrases and clauses ….
> I got "and," "but," and "or,"
> They'll get you pretty far.

The learning visual of a train conductor using conjunctions to link up various railway cars was dead on.

> *phrase + phrase = sentence.*
>
> The "+" is where the conjunction goes.

Three types of conjunctions exist: coordinating, correlative, and subordinating.

Coordinating Conjunctions

Coordinating conjunctions link words or word groupings that have equal grammatical status within the sentence—two nouns, two verbs, two clauses, etc. The list of coordinating conjunctions is short, and like prepositions, they do not change form.

and	nor	so
but	or	yet
for		

And, *but*, *nor*, and *or* link like words or word groupings—nouns with nouns, verbs with verbs, adjectives with adjectives, adverbs with adverbs, word phrases with word phrases, clauses with clauses (subordinate with subordinate, main with main).

The firemen *and* policemen worked together to save the dog.

The radio was blaring, *but* the television was louder.

For and *so* are able to connect only main clauses. *For* implies a cause, while *so* indicates a result.

Renee left the house, *for* she had many errands to run.

Peter was the ADA in charge, *so* he filed the necessary forms personally.

It is also noteworthy to mention that although *yet* can be an adverb, it also functions as a coordinating conjunction, indicating contrast, much like *but* would.

Jerry kept a close eye on the new puppy, *yet* it escaped the yard almost daily.

Some coordinating conjunctions always connect words or word groups of the same type (nouns, verbs, adjectives, adverbs, phrases, or clauses). *And*, *but*, *nor*, and *or* are such coordinating conjunctions.

Madeline *and* Annabelle will be thrilled to see their names.

Writing is exciting *but* challenging.

She worked day *and* night, *but* she still could never seem to meet the deadlines.

Starting a Sentence with a Conjunction

Some English teachers frown on beginning sentences with conjunctions, but that once hard-and-fast rule has become very relaxed in recent years.

Review your sentences to make sure the structure is what you intended. If it isn't, you'll want to make adjustments. But if it is, leave it alone.

Beginning a sentence with a coordinating conjunction could result in a sentence fragment, though, so be careful.

Conjunctions and Compound Sentences

If a compound sentence is made of multiple clauses that have considerable length, are complicated, or have punctuation within the clauses themselves, use a semicolon as well as a coordinating conjunction to separate the clauses. Doing so allows the integrity of each clause to remain intact and makes the whole sentence more readable.

I dedicate this to my agent, Jacky, who knew this project, though terrifying for me, was a challenge I had to face; and to my friends and family, who would not let me fail.

If the subject of a sentence is made of two or more **substantives** and connected by the conjunction *and*, it must use a plural form verb.

The casting of the play and distribution of backstage responsibilities *are* job one at the start of each season.

WORDS TO GO . . . WORDS TO GO . . . WORDS TO GO

A **substantive** is a word or word group that's used as a noun.

Sometimes the connecting conjunction *and* can be replaced with a comma, which holds the same meaning.

The memory of her face, her smile was all he needed.

SEE ALSO 6.3, "Commas"

The connecting *and* can also be omitted between coordinate clauses when they are separated by a semicolon.

The cat climbs the tree; the owner looks everywhere else.

Correlative Conjunctions

Correlative conjunctions—also called correlatives—are pairs of conjunctions used together to link either similar or differing elements.

as … as	not … but
both … and	not only … but (also)
either … or	though … yet
neither … nor	whether … or

Let's look at some examples:

Either you do or you don't.

Neither cats nor dogs were allowed.

The interview indicated she possessed not only the necessary skills but also an easygoing temperament.

Both Steve and Brian made the journey.

It was hard to say whether the cat ran up the tree or under the house.

Either Jessica or Jennifer were going to go first.

Because correlative conjunctions work in pairs, misplacement of the first conjunction violates the necessary parallel form correlatives follow.

Misplacement: The company neither assumes responsibility for health care nor to provide day care for part-time workers.

Corrected: The company does not assume responsibility for providing either health care or day care for part-time workers.

To correct an out-of-sync correlative construction, sometimes a change in the verb of one clause is required.

Out of sync: It occurs not only in greenhouse plants but is generally found throughout all of nature.

In sync: Not only is it found in greenhouse plants, but it is generally found throughout all of nature.

Subordinating Conjunctions

Subordinating, or subordinate, conjunctions join clauses that are not equal in grammatical weight, with the subordinating conjunction linking the smaller, subordinate clause to the larger, main clause structure. The subordinating conjunctions always come at the beginning of the subordinate clauses.

The politicians smiled for the cameras as they lied.

I desperately want to be a writer even though I don't write well.

Subordinating Conjunctions		
after	how	so that
although	if	than
as	in case	that
as if	in order that	though
as long as	inasmuch as	till
as much as	just in case	unless
as soon as	lest	until/'til
as though	like	when
because	now that	whenever
before	once	where
by the time	only if	whereas
even if	provided (that)	wherever
even though	rather than	whether
every time	since	while

Subordinating conjunctions indicate the following relationships:

Time *after*, *as*, *as long as*, *before*, *since*, *until*, *when*, *while*

As we approached, the deer was startled.
The car slid down the hill after the brakes locked.

Place *where*

She found a great spot where she could read quietly.

Manner *as if*, *as though*.

He strode through the garden as if he owned the world.

Comparison *as*, *as far as*, *as much as*, *as well as*, *else*, *otherwise*, *rather*, *than* (*Than* only when it follows comparative adverbs or adjectives or the words *else*, *rather*, *other*, or *otherwise*.)

Are cats more independent than dogs?
As far as my lapdog is concerned, yes.

Condition *except*, *if*, *once*, *though*, *unless*, *without*

Once they agreed on a location for the wedding, they began planning the details.
You don't want it unless someone else has it.

Reason *although*, *as*, *because*, *for*, *inasmuch as*, *once*, *since*, *though*, *why*

She wanted an answer because she had to leave.
Although he wanted to say yes, he couldn't.

Purpose *that*, *in order that*, *so that*, *such that*

She raised her hand so that he could see her.
It rained so hard that the gutters backed up.

Appositions *and*, *or*, *that*, *what*

The doctor detailed what was involved with the treatment.
They recalled everything that had been special.

Indirect questions *when*, *whether*, *why*

She could not tell them whether to go north or south.
He shouldn't go when there are people coming.

The subordinating conjunctions *as* and *while* can be used to indicate multiple adverbial relationships such as time and comparison; *while* can also indicate concession. It's important that writing be clear and unambiguous. If an *as* or *while* sentence seems ambiguous, it may be necessary to recast the sentence with another word to eliminate any confusion.

> *Ambiguous:* As I was praying, the bombs were falling.
>
> *Clear:* The bombs were falling even though I was praying.
>
> *Clear:* Because she was sick, she could not perform.

In this chapter, I discussed prepositions and conjunctions. We looked at terminal prepositions and learned that it is okay to remain flexible with language and writing and use prepositions at the end of sentences if it makes sense to do so. And when to capitalize and when not to capitalize prepositions within titles should no longer be a question. In addition to prepositions and prepositional phrases, this chapter also focused on conjunctions and examined the coordinating, correlative, and subordinating conjunctions and how those linking parts of speech form connections between other words and phrases.

5

SENTENCE STRUCTURE

5.1 Basic Sentence Structure
5.2 Types of Sentences
5.3 Parallelism
5.4 Figures of Speech
5.5 Stylistic Devices

5.1 BASIC SENTENCE STRUCTURE

Subjects and Predicates

Identifying Subjects

The English language has standard rules that are commonly accepted by all and are used in most written and spoken communications. It's important to master the basics of English and apply these rules to your writing. These tried-and-true rules may conflict with how many of us actually speak; however, if your sentences don't conform to these general standards, your writing could confuse or mislead your reader. Once you have mastered the basics, then you can branch out into your own personal writing "style" with greater confidence.

Sentence structure is an especially important area for writers to pay attention to. To understand sentence structure and to recognize and correct any problems, you need to understand and incorporate the basics.

Subjects and Predicates

Think about young children who are just learning to speak. They make basic sentences by pairing a few words.

> Jack walk.
> Bird fly.

The same structure that applies to these simple sentences applies to longer, more complicated sentences. That's because every sentence in English is composed of a **subject** and **predicate**.

WORDS TO GO . . . WORDS TO GO . . . WORDS TO GO

A **subject** is the word (or words functioning as a unit) that's the focus of the action or state of the predicate within a sentence or clause.

A **predicate** is a part of each sentence that's neither the subject nor its modifiers. It must contain a verb and may include objects and modifiers of the verb.

The subject and predicate can also be described as the topic and the comment: what's being talked about (the subject) and what's being said about it (the predicate). In the preceding example sentences, *Jack* and *bird* are the subjects, and *walk* and *fly* are the predicates.

Each sentence component can be characterized by three general traits: its position in a sentence, its grammatical construction, and its meaning. The subject is usually located at or near the beginning of the sentence (position), consists of a noun phrase (construction), and indicates the topic at hand (meaning). The predicate typically follows the subject, begins with a verb showing action or state of being, and comments on the subject.

Types of Subjects

The subject is usually a noun or pronoun—the person, place, or thing—that acts, is acted on, or is described in the sentence. Three types of subjects exist:

Simple subject A noun or pronoun.

I	flower
she	spoon

SEE ALSO 1.1, "Nouns"

SEE ALSO 1.3, "Pronouns"

Complete subject A noun or pronoun with its modifiers.

the pretty flower	her red bandanna
the greasy spoon	

Compound subject Two or more subjects joined by a conjunction.

he and I	Shelley and Ari
the spoon, fork, and knife	

Types of Predicates

The predicate is the action or description that occurs in the sentence.

Three types of predicates exist:

Simple predicate A complete verb (a verb and any helping verbs).

jog
was standing
could have gone

Complete predicate A simple predicate plus all its modifiers.

jog in the park
was standing proudly
could have gone with the others

Compound predicate Two or more predicates with the same subject.

We were jogging in the park and listening to headphones.
He was standing proudly and smiling infectiously.
I could have gone or could have stayed.

To be a predicate, a verb that ends in *-ing* must have a helping verb with it. An *-ing* verb without a helping verb cannot be a predicate in a sentence.

SEE ALSO 2.1, "Verbs"

Identifying Subjects

If you're having trouble identifying the subject of a sentence, you can test your sentences to find the subject by changing your sentences into yes-or-no questions. When in the question form, subjects are more easily identified.

All squares are rectangles.

Now turn it into a yes-or-no question.

Are all squares rectangles?

In forming the question, the verb *are* moves around the subject *all squares*.

Sometimes more words are needed to form a yes-or-no question.

The cat sat on the mat.

Change *sat* to *did sit* to form the verb that moves around the subject *cat* to create the question.

Did the cat sit on the mat?

The subject and predicate may not always appear together or fall in the normal order. Prepositional phrases and adverbs may separate them, and in a question, the order may be reversed or the subject may separate the complete predicate.

The pigeons in the park will peck at the food.

In the park is the prepositional phrase.

In the park, the pigeons will always peck at the food.

Here, *always* is an adverb.

Will the pigeons peck at the food?

Sentence structure may ultimately be composed of many parts, but remember that the foundation of each sentence is the subject and the predicate. The subject is a word or a group of words that function as a noun; the predicate is at least a verb and possibly includes objects and modifiers of the verb.

5.2 TYPES OF SENTENCES

Simple Sentences
Compound Sentences
Complex Sentences
Compound-Complex Sentences
Questions
Exclamations
Commands
Interjections
Fragments
Run-On Sentences
Comma Splices

They say variety is the spice of life, and sentence variety spices up any piece of writing. By varying the types of sentences you use, you make your writing more natural and engaging.

Simple Sentences

Simple sentences contain only one clause and may be as short as one word. They have a subject and a predicate, and they may include modifiers.

> Eat!
> Cara eats.
> Cara eats pasta.
> Cara from Connecticut eats pasta at the café.
> Ravenously twirling her fork, Cara from Connecticut eats pasta primavera at the café.

As you can see, a simple sentence can be quite long. Each of these sentences has the same simple structure. Length doesn't necessarily impact the structure, although it is often a factor.

We frequently use simple sentences when speaking, but we must use them carefully when writing. On one hand, simple sentences can be effective for adding variety, catching the reader's attention, and emphasizing or clarifying a point.

On the other hand, too many simple sentences can make your writing seem juvenile.

Simple sentences alone are not conducive to expressing complex thoughts. They cannot show relationships or offer qualifying thoughts. Sentences develop as we add to them, by either multiplying the elements of the simple sentence or adding more elements to it. Multiplying elements creates a compound sentence; simply adding more elements creates a complex sentence. Like compound and complex subjects and predicates, compound sentences use conjunctions, and complex sentences use additional structure.

SEE ALSO 5.1, "Basic Sentence Structure"

Compound Sentences

Compound sentences consist of two or more independent clauses (or simple sentences) joined by a conjunction (such as *and*, *but*, *or*, *nor*, *so*, *yet*, and *for*) or a semicolon.

> The United States is the world's wealthiest country, but it has many poor people.

SEE ALSO 4.3, "Conjunctions"

This example is made of two simple sentences joined by the word *but*:

1. The United States is the world's wealthiest country.
2. It has many poor people.

By multiplying the number of simple sentences, you could conceivably continue joining elements together with the word *and*. This is what children often do when they are first learning to connect their thoughts.

> I rode the bus, and I got to school, and I ran to my desk, and I talked to Bobby, and Bobby had a new PlayStation, and he let me play it, and …

Of course, this example exaggerates the way compound sentences are joined, but each element is still its own simple sentence. Using too many compound sentences in your writing, though, may come across as childish or prove to be incredibly confusing for the reader. The most effective way to use a compound sentence is to juxtapose your thoughts to show contrast or to equate your thoughts to show balance.

Manhattan has more art, but Brooklyn has more artists.

The birthstone of April is the diamond, and the birthstone of May is the emerald.

Either Todd stays, or we both go.

Compound sentences can also be joined by a semicolon instead of or in addition to a conjunction.

Manhattan has more art; however, Brooklyn has more artists.

The birthstone of April is the diamond; the birthstone of May is the emerald.

Complex Sentences

A complex sentence consists of an independent clause and at least one dependent clause. A dependent clause, or restrictive clause, is generally introduced by a subordinate conjunction (such as *although*, *because*, or *while*) or a relative pronoun (such as *that* or *who*).

Although I am tired, I can't fall asleep.

Her alarm did not go off because the electricity went out.

It's your new job that we're celebrating.

Jose and Clare went to Bermuda after they were married.

In the first example, the dependent clause (*Although I am tired*) is easy to spot because it is followed by a comma. When the dependent clause follows the main clause, as in the second example, there is no need to separate them with a comma.

Complex sentences are drastically different from simple and compound sentences because they show which of the ideas is most important. Consider the following examples, and notice which part is more important.

Simple: I am tired. I can't fall asleep.

Compound: I am tired, but I can't fall asleep.

Complex: Although I am tired, I can't fall asleep.

In the first two instances, neither clause appears more important. In the third example, the subordinating conjunction *although* at the beginning of the first clause clearly demonstrates that the fact that I'm tired is less important than (or subordinate to) the fact that I can't fall asleep.

Compound-Complex Sentences

Compound-complex sentences consist of two complex sentences or one simple sentence with one complex sentence, joined by a conjunction or a semicolon. They can also be formed by at least two independent clauses and one or more dependent clauses. The words *however* and *consequently* often—although not always—appear in the second part of the sentence.

> The food came promptly, but the waiter vanished before I could ask for salt and pepper.
>
> He enjoyed the meal; however, when the check arrived, he did not leave a tip.

Questions

Questions, or interrogative sentences, ask who, what, where, why, which, or how. Beginning a sentence or independent clause with one of these words is almost always a sure indicator of a direct question.

> Who ate the pie?
>
> What time is it?
>
> Where are you going?
>
> Why did she leave?
>
> Which direction should we take?
>
> How long till we go?

A **declarative sentence**—any statement without qualifiers—can be turned into a direct question simply by adding a question mark. When speaking, a declarative sentence becomes a question by ending with a higher pitch. Consider how you'd say the following as declarative and interrogative sentences when speaking out loud.

> *Declarative:* You're going home.
>
> *Question:* You're going home?

WORDS TO GO . . .WORDS TO GO . . .WORDS TO GO

A **declarative sentence** is the usual sort of simple sentence. The goal of the declarative sentence is to communicate information. Its organization tends to be simple: subject + verb + object (and usually in that order).

The question mark at the end denotes a raised pitch in verbal speech; likewise, the high-pitched verbal ending implies the written question mark. There are several other ways to form questions.

Question marks must fall after the question, even if the question is not at the end of the sentence.

> When did she arrive? he wondered.
>
> Is the sweater available in peach? with stripes? in a larger size?

In the first example, the question mark would never be set at the end of the sentence because "he wondered" is not a part of the question. However, if the meaning would be clearer, the second example could be turned into a series with only one question mark at the end.

> Is the sweater available in peach, with stripes, and in a larger size?

Who, What, Where, Why, Which, and How

Beginning a sentence or independent clause with one of these words is almost always a sure indicator of a direct question.

> Who ate the pie?
>
> What time is it?
>
> Where are you going?
>
> Why did she leave?
>
> Which direction should we take?
>
> How long until we go?

And now for the exception that makes the rule: Indirect questions do not use question marks. An indirect question doesn't ask; instead, it describes a question that is being asked.

> He wondered what time it was.
>
> She asked how he was feeling.
>
> Where he went yesterday doesn't affect where he goes today.

Exclamations

Exclamations are usually expressions of excitement or any other burst of emotion. They are similar to commands and interjections, but they can also be complete sentences. Added for emphasis or enthusiasm, exclamations are usually followed by exclamation points.

Yes!

Fantastic!

A thief broke in and stole everything!

In some cases, sentences that are phrased like questions actually function as exclamations. If the question is rhetorical and emphatic, use an exclamation point rather than a question mark.

How dare you!

What was I thinking!

My advice would be to use exclamation points with cautious deliberateness—too many will make your prose or dialogue seem unrealistic and silly. As noted by F. Scott Fitzgerald:

> Cut out all these exclamation points. An exclamation point is like laughing at your own joke.

Commands

Commands, or imperative sentences, make direct requests and prohibitions. They consist of predicates that are infinitive verbs but have no explicit subjects. The subject *you* is implied. Commands often end in exclamation points, although they certainly don't have to.

Halt!

Use a fork.

Don't go there!

Let's split.

Water the plants and pick up the dry-cleaning.

Call the doctor, please.

The implied subject *you* could be added, but it would likely be redundant when making a direct request.

Don't (you) go there!

(You) call the doctor, please.

Because commands are so commanding, they can be considered rude, so use them with care.

Interjections

Interjections are expressions of emotion, unique in that they're always independent of the overall sentence. Often interjections are single words or short phrases set off by commas within the sentence; sometimes they're on their own with an exclamation point. The stronger the emotion, the more likely the interjection is to use an exclamation point.

Interjections are common in speech and as a result crop up frequently in writing with dialogue. Poetry and works of fiction may also use interjections in the narrative to show humor, irony, disappointment, or a whole host of other emotions.

Although interjections may occasionally show up in some informal writing (e-mails, web logs, etc.), they are uncommon in any type of formal nonfiction writing, unless used in a direct quotation.

> Ouch!
> Wow! Did you see that?
> Shoot, I forgot!
> Oh my gosh, I can't believe it.
> Hey, what's up?
> The fish was, oh, three or four feet long.
> Ordering the pickle martini is, um, strongly discouraged.

Because interjections act independently, various parts of speech can function as interjections. These are often one-word sentences in which the subject *you* is implied.

> *Noun:* Jerk!
> *Verb:* Listen!
> *Adjective:* Awful!
> *Conjunction:* As if!

A few words can be used only as interjections because they form no other part of speech.

> Whoops!
> Whew!
> Shh!

Fragments

Fragments are incomplete sentences. Every sentence must have at least one main clause, which contains an independent subject and verb and expresses a complete thought. Fragments, on the other hand, lack one of these elements. A punctuation change can usually amend a fragment and reconnect it to the main clause. Other times, the fragment can be fixed by adding connecting words or by creating a new sentence.

Jerry wants to go. But can't.
Amanda likes animals. For example, cats, dogs, birds, and bunnies.
I went to the concert. Which is why I have a headache.

In each of these examples, the second "sentence" is a fragment. Each lacks critical elements needed to form a complete sentence, and each can be corrected with some minor revisions.

Jerry wants to go but can't.
Amanda likes animals, such as cats, dogs, birds, and bunnies.
Because I went to the concert, I now have a headache.
Although Jerry wants to go, he can't.
Amanda likes animals. For example, she likes cats, dogs, birds, and bunnies.
I went to the concert. I now have a headache.

Intentional fragments can be used effectively for emphasis, but use them in moderation because they can become distracting.

Shawn danced and sang for the cameras. What a ham!

In works with dialogue, stammering or faltering speech may result in sentence fragments. However, these fragments tend to be stylistic, to show emotion or lapses in time. These should not be corrected because they aren't really grammatical errors; however, too many of them can make your writing seem forced or unfocused.

"Oh, but … you said … I mean, I thought …," he griped.
"What the? How did? You can't be serious!" she exclaimed.
"Toward the border. Go!" he barked.

Fragments should generally be avoided in formal and technical writing.

Run-On Sentences

Run-ons result from two or more independent clauses joined into one sentence that lacks punctuation or conjunctions. Run-ons are sometimes called fused sentences because they fuse clauses that could ordinarily stand on their own. People often speak in run-on sentences, where they are less noticed because the speaker usually pauses and changes his tones in verbal speech. These run-ons cause punctuation problems when speech is transcribed word for word. Considered errors of punctuation, run-ons should always be corrected.

I didn't know what to do I was so confused.

The car is brand-new don't touch it.

Here's how these run-ons should be corrected:

I didn't know what to do; I was so confused.

The car is brand-new. Don't touch it.

Comma Splices

A comma splice is a run-on sentence that's joined by a comma even though stronger punctuation is necessary to correct the sentence.

It's too late, we'll never make it on time.

Comma splices are bad, run-ons are worse.

Correct comma splices by changing the comma to a period or a semicolon.

It's too late. We'll never make it on time.

Comma splices are bad; run-ons are worse.

SEE ALSO 6.3, "Commas"

5.3 PARALLELISM

Parallel Lists

Parallel Numbers

Parallel Correlative Conjunctions

Overall sentence structure requires balance between like elements. The principle of parallelism ensures that corresponding parts of a sentence must also correspond in structure.

Unparallel: The babysitter's responsibilities included making dinner for the kids and to put them to bed.

This sentence lacks parallel structure because the two verb phrases after *included* and joined by *and* use different structures. To correct the sentence, both need to be present participles.

Parallel: The babysitter's responsibilities included making dinner for the kids and putting them to bed.

This principle can be used to fix most unbalanced structures.

Unparallel: The contractor oversees the administration of payroll, the number of workers, and completing the project.

Parallel: The contractor oversees the administration of payroll, the number of workers, and the completion of the project.

Unparallel: Do you think I should go to the movies with Thom or that I should just stay home?

Parallel: Do you think I should go to the movies with Thom or just stay home?

Parallel Lists

Items in a list should always be parallel in structure. Whether the list is shown as a series within the sentence or as a bulleted list, the elements should be structurally identical.

Unparallel: Some of Kenny's duties include ringing up purchases, cleanliness of store shelves, and greeting customers.

Parallel: Some of Kenny's duties include ringing up purchases, cleaning store shelves, and greeting customers.

Unparallel: Kenny's job description includes the following:

- operating the cash register
- stocking the shelves
- customer service

Parallel: Kenny's job description includes the following:

- operating the cash register
- stocking the shelves
- managing customer complaints

Parallel Numbers

Numbers joined within a sentence should follow the parallel principle as well. This applies not only to usage of digits versus spelled-out numbers, but also to types of numbers, such as percentages and fractions.

Unparallel: More than half of the people surveyed agreed, but only 34 percent disagreed.

Parallel: More than half of the people surveyed agreed, but only one third disagreed.

Parallel: More than 50 percent of the people surveyed agreed, but only 34 percent disagreed.

Unparallel: Only seventeen out of 1,056 people did not respond.

Parallel: Only 17 out of 1,056 people did not respond.

SEE ALSO 11.1, "Numbers"

Parallel Correlative Conjunctions

Correlative conjunctions are used together to form a complete thought, and both conjunctions must join two parallel structures. The same part of speech should immediately follow the conjunction to create a parallel structure. The most common correlative conjunctions include *either … or*, *neither … nor*, *if … then*, *both … and*, and *not only … but also*, among others.

Unparallel: Joan wants to either go to Hawaii or to go to Aspen.

Parallel: Joan wants to go either to Hawaii or to Aspen.

Unparallel: Greta needs not only a new dress but also needs a new pair of shoes.

Parallel: Greta needs not only a new dress but also a new pair of shoes.

SEE ALSO 4.3, "Conjunctions"

5.4 FIGURES OF SPEECH

Metaphors
Similes
Idioms
Euphemisms
Slang
Colloquialisms
Puns
Clichés
Hyperbole
Personification
Oxymorons
Onomatopoeia

Figures of speech add color, humor, and depth to our language, lending strong images to our communications. These devices help us create mental pictures and let us live in a more dynamic world full of unique expressions.

WORDS TO GO . . .WORDS TO GO . . .WORDS TO GO

A **figure of speech** is a word or phrase used to express something other than its literal meaning.

Many figures of speech are now a familiar part of our lexicon, as they have been used so often that their literal meaning is most often overlooked. For instance, the expression "raining cats and dogs" is now so commonplace that we don't actually visualize cats and dogs falling from the sky.

There any many types of figures of speech, but here we'll look at only the ones used most frequently: metaphors, similes, idioms, puns, clichés, hyperbole, personification, oxymorons, and onomatopoeia.

Metaphors

A metaphor is a figure of speech that compares one concept to another by likening the first to something else. Often the concepts are unrelated but equal, joined by some form of the verb "to be" to create a new or unusual association. Some metaphors have become everyday expressions, while others breathe new life into the language.

She is a rising star.
He is a loose canon.
America is a melting pot.
The eyes are the windows to the soul.

Some metaphors are used so often that their meanings become generic and cliché. (See the later section for more on clichés.)

Metaphors are frequently confused with similes because they have similar uses. They are both used to make comparisons, but they have different structures. For instance, the expression "Ben is a couch potato" is a metaphor, whereas "Ben lounged like a couch potato" is a simile. Continue reading for more on similes.

Similes

A simile is a figure of speech that compares two unlike concepts and joins them by the words *like*, *as*, or *than*. Similes differ from metaphors in that the concepts are not treated as equals. Many similes have become part of our everyday language.

Her skin is as smooth as silk.
He was white as a ghost.
Wendy cried like a baby.
Ron's mouth was drier than a desert.

Comparisons serve to make our language more descriptive to paint a more clear picture. While it is perfectly fine to say "the tires screeched," the image can be much more descriptive by using a simile such as "the tires screeched like a hundred angry monkeys."

Idioms

An idiom is a figure of speech that cannot be understood by the literal meaning of the individual words; instead, the words together form a unique meaning that is understood only because of its specific manner of use. For example, the expression "apple of my eye" makes little sense when examined literally. Someone who knows only the meaning of the words *apple* and *eye* wouldn't understand the expression's actual meaning, which is cherished and proud of, usually said by a parent regarding his or her child. Therefore, idioms are likely to confuse people who aren't already familiar with them. And without some prior experience or knowledge, people may have a hard time readily deducing the idiom's figurative meaning simply from the literal meaning of its words.

Some idioms are peculiar to a certain region or group, and while they serve to spice up our language, they are not essential to communicating ideas.

all thumbs
bend your ear
birds of a feather
break a leg
burning a hole in his pocket
burn your fingers
catching her eye
down in the dumps
down in the mouth
hold your horses
keep an eye on it
no leg to stand on
out on a limb
pay through the nose
pot calling the kettle black
put my foot in my mouth
put the cart before the horse
read between the lines
rub elbows with
step on toes
step up to the plate
take to heart
time out of mind
toe the line
walking papers

Euphemisms

A euphemism is a word, phrase, or expression that has been softened so it is not offensive or disagreeable and is used in place of something that could very well cause offense or indicate some less-than-pleasant reference—or makes a reference that is less than delicate.

Euphemism	Meaning
au naturel	naked
butter up	flatter
chicken ranch	house of prostitution
commode, john	toilet
cross over	die
expecting	pregnant
intoxicated	drunk
love child	illegitimate child, child out of wedlock
memorial park	cemetery
moisture	sweat

Euphemism	Meaning
odor	stink
passed	died
plant food	manure
special	developmentally challenged
ralph, upchuck	throw up
tissue	toilet paper
underprivileged	destitute, poor

Slang

Slang terms are informal, nonstandard words, phrases, or expressions, the use of which indicates everything from colloquialism to illiteracy and may include words changed arbitrarily as well as many variations on figures of speech.

Slang	Meaning
blow his top	lose his temper
C-note	$100 bill
chintzy	cheap
egghead	smart person
hood	neighborhood, thug
mooch	take
posers	fake people
psych	just kidding
sourpuss	grumpy person

Colloquialisms

A colloquialism is a local or regional word or expression that may not be readily understood outside the area. But these sorts of words add uniqueness and "flavor" to our ever-evolving language.

Colloquialism	Meaning
fuss-budget	cranky child/person
shine on	to flatter or tease
sody	soda/carbonated beverage
threads	clothes
well, I'll swan …	well, my goodness …

Puns

A pun, also known as a "play on words," is a figure of speech that intentionally confuses similar words or phrases for rhetorical effect. These clever and usually humorous expressions most often employ homonyms, metaphors, or words with several different meanings.

The magician was so angry he pulled his hare out.

Writing with a broken pencil is pointless.

The cross-eyed teacher couldn't control her pupils.

A warning, though: Bad puns can be predictable and corny.

SEE ALSO 10.1, "Spelling"

Clichés

A cliché is any figure of speech that has become so trite and commonplace that it no longer carries much meaning. Clichés are generic expressions that may have been fresh at first, but with time have been far overused and as a result have become predictable.

as busy as a bee

more than meets the eye

selling like hotcakes

The strongest writing avoids clichés like the plague, although clichés may be used occasionally for humorous effect. In general, when something is described as being "cliché," it has a negative connotation because it lacks imagination or originality.

Hyperbole

Hyperbole is a figure of speech that uses deliberate exaggeration for heightened effect and is not intended for literal interpretation. Hyperbole can be used humorously or seriously.

I'm so hungry I could eat a horse.

He talked a mile a minute.

She cried an ocean of tears.

Personification

Personification is a figure of speech that attributes human characteristics or qualities to animals, inanimate objects, or abstract ideas.

The lion waged war on its helpless prey.
The wind spoke with a soft whisper.
Death arrived in the night and took the old man away.

Oxymorons

An oxymoron is a figure of speech that couples opposite or incongruous terms to create a new meaning. Some of these contradictory terms are meant literally; others are simply meant to be comic.

act naturally	liquid smoke
jumbo shrimp	working vacation

Onomatopoeia

Onomatopoeia is a funny-sounding word for a figure of speech that describes other funny words—the kinds of words we use to name or imitate sounds. Some sounds can be difficult to express in writing, but onomatopoeia helps us put sounds into words.

boing	pop
clack	whirr
ding-dong	zing

Onomatopoeia also lets us express animal sounds with words.

baa	peep
hiss	ribbit
moo	woof

SEE ALSO 9.1, "Italics"

5.5 STYLISTIC DEVICES

Alliteration

Consonance

Assonance

Repetition

Allusion

Symbols

Diction

With the essential sentence structure groundwork laid, you can start to build and shape your language to create a style all your own, using various types of sentences and figures of speech. **Stylistic devices** go beyond figures of speech to refine your word choices and to create a rhythmic, almost musical quality to your language. Stylistic devices are common in poetry and song lyrics, but they can be important and effective tools for emphasis and cadence in regular prose as well.

WORDS TO GO . . . WORDS TO GO . . . WORDS TO GO

A **stylistic device** is the method a writer chooses to convey information by manipulating language in various techniques to achieve differing results.

Alliteration

Alliteration is a stylistic device that repeats the consonant sound at the beginning of two or more words used consecutively or in close proximity.

good as gold
the more the merrier
road rage
the sweet smell of success

Alliteration is a popular device in business and product names, as well as television shows and musical groups.

Coca-Cola
The Beach Boys
Gilmore Girls

Krispy Kreme

"Livin' La Vida Loca"

Too much alliteration, however, can result in a real tongue twister.

Sally sold seashells by the seashore.

Peter picked a peck of pickled peppers.

How much wood would a woodchuck chuck if a woodchuck could chuck wood?

Tongue twisters may be fun to practice, but an inadvertent string of words used alliteratively will be distracting for the reader and could prove difficult to speak aloud.

Consonance

Consonance is a stylistic device that repeats the consonant sound in a series of words. Consonance differs from alliteration in that the repeated sound can be anywhere within the word, although it is most often located at the end.

The jerk kicks rocks.

She is gorgeous but self-conscious.

A burst of bright light lit the apartment.

Sibilant sounds (those created by the *s* and *sh*) create a very noticeable type of consonance, which is called sibilance.

The hissing and slithering snakes scared Sarah's sister.

Slowly she swam south toward shore.

Steve assessed the storm while shoveling the snow.

Assonance

Assonance is a stylistic device that provides for a similar sound within multiple syllables or words. These similar sounds—usually repeating vowel sounds without the repeating of consonants—tend to be close to each other at the beginning of the words (alliteration) or within the word, but do not tend to be placed at the end of the words.

The Rat Pack laughed when Sammy ran past.

Emily expects everyone to emulate her energy.

Jane made rainy days okay.

No showboating goes unnoticed by Tony.

We meet new people each week.

Repetition

Repetition is a stylistic device that replicates individual words for greater effect. The words can be repeated at the beginning or ending of a phrase and within the same sentence or in consecutive sentences.

> "What lies behind us and what lies before us are tiny compared to what lies within us." (Ralph Waldo Emerson)
>
> She shook her head and said, "Shame, shame, shame."
>
> Gently, gently he lowered himself into the water.

Allusion

Allusion is a stylistic device that intentionally references an idea, person, or happening that exists outside the current context. Making an indirect reference to a work of art or a historical or cultural event can add greater meaning to your statement or comparison because the image is shown concisely.

> She looked up to the sky, feeling like it was morning again in America.
>
> Molly fingered her engagement ring and thought, *My precious*.
>
> Kevin wore a Cosby sweater to the party.
>
> He expected shock and awe but got only dismay and despair.

Some allusions are used so frequently they have become clichés, such as "Big Brother" and "fifteen minutes of fame." Most biblical and mythological references, such as "David and Goliath" and "Achilles' heel" are commonly understood but have become clichés as well.

It is important to note that very esoteric allusions may be lost on most people. If the reference isn't recognizable, the reader will not understand its intended meaning, so use allusions wisely.

Symbols

A symbol is a stylistic device that represents something other than itself, especially a visible sign representing something invisible. Symbols help us ground abstract ideas in real, tangible objects that represent that idea each time we encounter it.

For example, black typically symbolizes bad and white often symbolizes good. Evil characters may be dressed in black clothing or a black cat may portend something bad about to happen; good characters may live in a white house or a white flower may represent hope. Also, a white dove symbolizes peace, while a black raven can represent death and despair.

Likewise, a swastika is a symbol of Hitler and the Holocaust and the atrocities of World War II. And the aptly named peace symbol represents antiwar sentiments and the desire for world peace.

Symbols can be used in writing to show concepts in concrete form. Cliché symbols include red roses representing love and lions representing courage; however, a key could symbolize possibility and Oprah Winfrey could symbolize success and the American Dream.

Diction

Diction is a stylistic device that includes not just vocabulary, but the choice of specific words over others and the emotions associated with them. For example, to describe a person as "assertive" can imply several different meanings. To some readers, it could be an insult, meaning "pushy" or "aggressive." To others, it could be a compliment, meaning "confident." Likewise, to describe a situation as "wild" can convey contradictory meanings. On the positive side, it may mean "fun" and "exciting"; but on the negative side, it could be "chaotic" or "uncivilized." Therefore, we must carefully consider the words we choose to avoid ambiguity. Using strong words with definite meanings can portray clearer images.

When used effectively, all these stylistic devices help us convey our ideas more clearly; clarify our meanings; and add color, humor, and description to our words.

6

PUNCTUATION

6.1 Use of Punctuation

6.2 Periods

6.3 Commas

6.4 Question and Exclamation Marks

6.5 Ellipses

6.6 Colons and Semicolons

6.7 Quotation Marks

6.8 Apostrophes

6.9 Hyphens, Dashes, and Slashes

6.10 Parentheses and Brackets

6.1 USE OF PUNCTUATION

Punctuation is a set of universally accepted, standardized marks such as periods, commas, and question marks that help clarify the meaning of a sentence or structural portions of writing. You'll use many types of punctuation marks in your writing; the most common are shown in the following table.

Punctuation Marks

.	period
,	comma
?	question mark
¿ ?	Spanish question marks (open and close)
!	exclamation mark
¡ !	Spanish exclamation marks (open and close)
...	ellipsis
:	colon
;	semicolon
’	apostrophe
‘ ’	single quotation marks (open and close)
“ ”	double quotation marks (open and close)
-	hyphen
–	en dash
—	em dash
/	slash
\	backslash
( )	parentheses (open and close)
[ ]	brackets (open and close)
{ }	braces (open and close)

Whenever a sentence is treated one way (usually roman) but punctuation precedes or follows a word or small group of words that are set apart with special treatment (bolded, italicized, underlined), the punctuation should match style with the whole of the sentence instead of the special-treatment word(s).

The only exception to this rule is when using the exclamation mark. When an exclamation mark is used, followed by a close quotation mark, the exclamation mark will take the special treatment but the close quotation mark will stand with the treatment of the rest of the sentence.

6.2 PERIODS

With Sentences

With Abbreviations

With Names and Initials

With Acronyms and Shortened Words

Periods are used to provide conclusions to sentences. They are also used within abbreviations as well as with names and initials. And sometimes periods are used with acronyms, but not always.

With Sentences

A period indicates the conclusion of a sentence. The sentence can be a statement, a mild command (lacking the excitement or strength indicated by an exclamation mark), or an indirect question.

SEE ALSO 5.2, "Types of Sentences"

A statement can be the reporting of facts or opinions, a declaration, a remark, or an assertion.

> *Gilmore Girls* used to be my favorite TV show.
>
> In November 2006, the Republicans lost control of both the Senate and the House of Representatives.
>
> We bought the condo for a song and sold it for a huge profit just before the market went soft.

A mild command is a sentence that directs authoritatively or gives an order. Generally, it does not have the same level of strength behind it that an actual command holds. If you're unsure whether to use an exclamation point or a period after a command, use the period.

> No smoking allowed.
>
> Change the channel.
>
> Make a sharp left turn.

SEE ALSO 6.4, "Question and Exclamation Marks"

An indirect question repeats a question that someone else has asked, but the recitation is not presented as a direct quotation. For these sorts of questions, a period is used at the conclusion of the sentence instead of a question mark.

The officer asked why the doctor was speeding.

The children asked how Santa Claus could be in every child's house during the same night.

After 9/11, everyone had to ask what was coming next.

SEE ALSO 6.4, "Question and Exclamation Marks"

With Abbreviations

Periods are used quite often with abbreviations. Although there's been a recent attempt to do away with the use of periods with certain abbreviations, many such uses remain steadfast.

Dr. = doctor

Mrs. = missus

Mr. = mister

M.D. = doctor of medicine

M.E. = managing editor or medical examiner

Ph.D. = doctor of philosophy

Now for the exceptions: *miss* and *ms*. Although other personal address words have abbreviated forms, *Miss* has no alternate form when used in this manner. Likewise, *Ms*. is just "Ms." There's no definitive etymology for this term, which first came into popularity around the mid-1900s. The best guess is that it's a combination of *Mrs*. and *Miss*, as it's used mainly when a woman's marital status is not established.

Whenever an abbreviation naturally concludes a sentence, only one period is used. There's no need to retain the abbreviation's period and add another period to show the end of the sentence.

Incorrect: I'm studying for my Ph.D..

Correct: I'm studying for my Ph.D.

Incorrect: We're heading down to D.C..

Correct: We're heading down to D.C.

The same cannot be said for other forms of punctuation that follow the periods in abbreviations. When a period is a necessary part of an abbreviation, it can be used with any punctuation.

I have a Ph.D., sir.
You have a Ph.D.?
Yes, I have a Ph.D.!

With Names and Initials

Periods are used whenever a person's name is abbreviated as initials, but periods are not used when a person is referenced simply by a shortened form of his or her name.

Benjamin:	*John Paul Smith:*
Wrong: Ben.	*Wrong:* J.P. Smith
Right: Ben	*Wrong:* JP Smith
Right: Benj.	*Right:* J. P. Smith

With Acronyms and Shortened Words

As discussed in subchapter 5.2, acronyms are words formed by joining the first letter of each of the words in a full name. Acronyms most often go without adding periods.

Acronym	What It Means
ABC	American Broadcasting Company (U.S. television and radio network)
ERA	Earned Run Average or Environmental Risk Assessment or Equal Rights Amendment
FedEx	Federal Express
NFL	National Football League
UPS	United Parcel Service
USA	United States of America
USPS	United States Postal Service

As you can see from the examples, the trend for acronyms nowadays is to go without adding period punctuation.

***SEE ALSO* 6.1, "Use of Punctuation"**

***SEE ALSO* 10.2, "Abbreviations"**

6.3 COMMAS

Serial Commas

Comma Splices

With Clauses and Phrases

With Nonrestrictive and Restrictive Elements

With Dates, Locations, and Numbers

With Abbreviations

With Quotations

A comma is a punctuation mark used as a separator within sentences, allowing for a short pause. The comma is the punctuation mark with the smallest break value within a sentence's structure. Commas fulfill technical uses as well, including mathematical and bibliographical uses. Commas also provide separation for a string of related words.

Using commas correctly enables your readers to grasp your material with ease. Writers must remain vigilant and judicious about the use of commas.

Serial Commas

Serial or series commas are used to separate three or more items in a list when the last two items are joined by a conjunction. Serial commas help avoid confusion or ambiguity.

> They asked for dolls, trucks<u>, and</u> electric trains for Christmas.
>
> Take a left, a right<u>, and</u> another left to get there.
>
> Barbara ran for the door, I ran for the phone<u>, and</u> Kitty just ran around in circles.

If the items in the series are each linked by conjunctions, it's not necessary to add commas to separate the elements. However, the commas can be added if they would help provide clarity, particularly when the elements are long or involved.

> From that distance, it could have been <u>black or blue or purple</u>.
>
> You could call from the corner store that's down at the end of the street, or you could take a quick left to call from the Wash and Dry over by that burned-out car<u>, or</u> you can probably call from the gas station up Main Street.

Comma Splices

As mentioned in subchapter 6.2, a comma splice occurs when a sentence has two main clauses set apart by a comma but lacks a coordinating conjunction linking them. The comma splice can be corrected easily with a slight change in sentence structure by one of the following methods: keeping the comma but adding a coordinating conjunction, replacing the comma with a semicolon, or replacing the comma with a period and creating a second sentence out of the second part of the original comma-splice sentence.

> *Comma splice:* The day was short, it held many useless activities.
>
> *Coordinating conjunction added:* The day was short, but it held many useless activities.
>
> *Semicolon added:* The day was short; it held many useless activities.
>
> *Two sentences:* The day was short. It held many useless activities.

Occasionally, commas are used between short main clauses to show a grammatical parallelism.

> He was not a father, he was a monster.
>
> She was a girl, she was innocent.

SEE ALSO 5.2, "Types of Sentences"

With Clauses and Phrases

Commas often follow adverbial or participial phrases that start sentences. This is particularly true when the intention is for a short pause. That said, the comma isn't necessary if the starting word or short phrase offers no chance of a misread—or if the comma would be too intrusive in context.

With comma:

> Oh, is that what you are talking about?
>
> For Topher, the role of Eric was a perfect fit.

Without comma:

> Yes sir.
>
> Oh no!

Absolute Phrases

An absolute phrase includes a noun (or pronoun) and a participle, and is not linked to the rest of the sentence by a connecting word. This sort of phrase modifies an entire clause or sentence rather than just one word. Absolute phrases are always set off from the rest of a sentence with punctuation of some sort, usually one or more commas.

They seek a local girl, all things being equal.

Windshield busted, wheels flattened, sides dented in, the car looked beyond repair.

The carnival came through town, bears, elephants, and acrobats galore.

Clauses

Clauses, whether main or subordinate, use commas as well as connecting words to link them with the rest of the sentence. Clauses are able to stand on their own as a sentence because they are a group of words that hold both a subject and a predicate.

Subordinating Words		
after	if	unless
although	in order that	until
as	once	when
as if	rather than	whenever
as though	since	where
because	so that	wherever
before	than	while
even if	that	who
even though	though	

Because I ran away, there was no going back.

I paid the money, even though the car was expensive.

Although her project was nearly at an end, she abandoned it.

With Nonrestrictive and Restrictive Elements

A nonrestrictive element provides supplemental information about the word or words it references, but it's not a limiting component. These elements can easily be deleted from a sentence without changing the sentence's basic meaning. For this reason, nonrestrictive elements are always set off by punctuation, usually commas.

Her husband, David, was working late again tonight.

The car, a Porsche 550 Spider race car, lunged toward James Dean's date with death.

Restrictive elements limit—restrict—the meaning of the word or words to which the restrictive elements apply. Because of this restriction, no punctuation can be used.

Her brother Brian called.

This use is restrictive, hence no commas. She has more than one brother.

With Nonrestrictive Appositives

Appositives are words or a group of words that rename the word or group of words that precede it. Generally, appositives are nouns renaming other nouns. Certain words or groups of words are used to introduce appositives, including *for example*, *in other words*, *or*, *such as*, and *that*. As with all nonrestrictive elements, appositives that do not restrict the meaning of the word or words they reference are set off by punctuation, usually one or more commas.

The house, an old Victorian, sold for a cool million.

With Parenthetical and Transition Expressions

Parenthetical expressions serve as explanations or transitions and are often set off by commas. They are not essential to the sentence and could be cut out, leaving the sentence understandable but perhaps less defined.

Any warm body, therefore, would do.

Regardless, Mel Gibson remains a top box-office draw.

With a vampire in hot pursuit, she made tracks, of course.

Transitional Words and Phrases

a description of	also
above	although
accordingly	altogether
adjacent to	an illustration of
after a while	and
after all	and then
afterward	and yet
again	as a result
all in all	as has been said

continues

continued

Transitional Words and Phrases

as long as
at last
at length
at that time
because
before
below
besides
but
but at the same time
consequently
despite
despite that
earlier
elsewhere
equally important
even
even so
even though
farther on
finally
first
for all that
for example
for instance
for this purpose
formerly
further
furthermore
hence
here
however
immediately
in addition
in brief
in conclusion
in contrast
in fact
in other words
in particular
in short
in simpler terms
in spite of
in summary
in the first place
in the meantime
in the past
in the same way
indeed
irregardless
it is true
last
lately
later
likewise
meanwhile
moreover
near
nearby
nevertheless
next
notwithstanding
now
of course
on the contrary
on the other hand
on the other side
on the whole

Transitional Words and Phrases

opposite to
otherwise
presently
regardless
second
shortly
similarly
simultaneously
since
since then
so far
soon
specifically
still
subsequently
that is
then
there
thereafter
therefore
thereupon
though
thus
to illustrate
to put it differently
to summarize
to the east/west/etc.
to the left/right/etc.
to this end
too
truly
until
until now
when
with this object
yet

With Dates, Locations, and Numbers

Commas are used for separation notations of the various parts of dates and locations, and for numbers in the thousands or greater. If the date or location is placed within a sentence and appropriately punctuated with a comma, it also always has a concluding comma.

> She remembered a day late that August 21, 2006, was Merry and Jerry's thirtieth anniversary.
>
> Her best and worst memories were of Winfield, Missouri, her hometown during her teen years.
>
> The house cost $16,500 when they bought it in 1976.

Within addresses, commas are used before and after information regarding apartment, floor, suite, etc., but they are not used between state names and zip codes.

> The shop is located at 999 Greenwood Avenue, Suite 111, Brooklyn, New York 11218.

With Abbreviations

Abbreviations may have a comma precede and follow them when used in a sentence. This is specifically the case for *etc.* (*et cetera,* Latin for "and so on") when the abbreviation falls at the conclusion of a series. If the abbreviation lands at the end of a sentence, no concluding comma is needed.

Red, green, blue, etc., are all colors of the rainbow.

The pet detective specialized in recovery of dogs, cats, birds, etc.

Note: Etc. is generally replaced in more formal writings with *and other things, and so forth, and so on,* or *and the like.* When these other phrases are used instead of *etc.*, the phrase should follow the same comma styling as *etc.* and take commas at the front and end of the phrase.

With Quotations

Use commas with quotations and to introduce or conclude speech set within quotation marks. If explanatory information is interjected between a quote, commas can be used to set it off, start to finish.

"Stop playin'," she said.

He did stop, but he whispered, "No."

"I mean it," she said, "stop now."

In this section, I have identified serial commas and comma splices and shown how to use commas with absolute phrases and clauses. This section also dealt with one of the more challenging aspects of comma usage: differentiating between nonrestrictive and restrictive elements. And finally, the proper use of commas within citations of dates, locations, numbers, abbreviations, and with quotations was covered.

SEE ALSO 6.1, "Use of Punctuation"

6.4 QUESTION AND EXCLAMATION MARKS

Question Marks

Exclamation Marks

Question marks are used to indicate … you guessed it: questions. Exclamation marks are used to express an emphasis of some sort. When used following Spanish-language questions and exclamations, these marks require a like mark to be inverted and placed before the first word of the sentence.

Question Marks

Question marks are the concluding punctuation for direct questions. (An indirect question takes a period as the concluding punctuation.) Question marks should not be combined with other punctuation marks, although occasionally writers take liberties and combine question marks and exclamation marks for emphasis.

> Who will help her?
> How do we get there from here?
> How is that possible?!?

SEE ALSO 6.1, "Periods"

Exclamation Marks

An exclamation mark is used to demonstrate an emphatic statement, an interjection, or a command.

> Yay! We won!
> Oh no!
> Stop!

Mild commands or interjections take commas or periods, as appropriate, instead of exclamation points. As mentioned previously, it's a good idea to remain prudent and selective with the use of exclamation marks. Too many can make your writing look unprofessional.

SEE ALSO 5.2, "Commands"

SEE ALSO 6.1, "Use of Punctuation"

In this section, we've looked at question marks and exclamation marks and their uses.

6.5 ELLIPSES

Ellipses, three equally spaced periods (…), are used to show a pause or an omission of a word or multiple words. When using ellipses for omitted words, it's important for the meaning to remain clear. Enough text should remain that the reader can understand what's left.

Simple sentence: Stop … think about what you're doing.

Dialogue: "I'm not sure … three?"

Quote: "… [I]t should be renamed Black-and-Blue Friday."
—*The New York Times*

If the ellipsis follows the conclusion of a complete sentence, the ellipsis follows the concluding period. It'll look like you have four dots, but in reality, the first "dot" is a period and the rest are the ellipsis. In such an arrangement, the period takes its place closed up with the last letter of the last word of the sentence, and the ellipsis periods are equally spaced—including the one that comes before the first letter of the first word of the next sentence. When the ellipsis follows other punctuation, the same rules and placement apply for the three ellipses marks.

"'Do not judge, or you too will be judged. … Why do you look at the speck of sawdust in your brother's eye and pay no attention to the plank in your own eye?'"—Matthew 7:1–3

Ellipses can also be used to indicate a trailing off of thoughts.

Gee, I don't know….

Well, …

Are you sure? …

SEE ALSO 6.1, "Use of Punctuation"

Just as with exclamation marks, you should be judicious in your use of ellipses. Otherwise, your writing could be jerky … and uneven … creating a difficult read.

6.6 COLONS AND SEMICOLONS

Colons

Semicolons

Colons and semicolons are addressed in this section. From the material presented here, you will see that colons carry greater weight of division than semicolons.

Colons

The colon is used to introduce explanations (formal or long), extracted quotations, summaries, statements introduced by the words *the following* or *as follows*, concluding appositives, and series listings. Whenever what follows the colon is a complete sentence, the first letter of the first word of that sentence should be capitalized. If it isn't a complete sentence, then what follows the colon will all be lowercase.

> The following is a group of examples for colon uses:
>
> Refer complaints to: www.blahblahblah.com.
>
> As Charles Dickens wrote: "It was the best of times, it was the worst of times."
>
> She can't pay her rent bills or her car insurance: She has no money.

A colon is also used to separate subtitles from titles, establish time divisions, and identify the chapter and verse in biblical and literary citations.

> *Anyway: The Paradoxical Commandments: Finding Personal Meaning in a Crazy World*
>
> 7:33 P.M.
>
> John 3:16

Semicolons

Semicolons are used to separate main clauses that are not linked with a coordinating conjunction. The semicolon offers less pause than a period but more than either a comma or a coordinating conjunction. A semicolon provides a sense of expectation in the reader that doesn't come with a comma or a coordinating conjunction.

> I am going away; I intend to stay gone.

If elements in a series have punctuation within their parts or are overly involved or long, the parts should be separated by semicolons.

> You have your choice of fruit sorbet; strawberry, vanilla, or chocolate ice cream; and cheesecake.

Occasionally, writers take creative license and use a comma between relatively short, closely parallel main clauses. This is particularly the case when dealing with quoted speech.

> Mr. Khule said, "The girls sit on the right, the boys sit on the left."

SEE ALSO 6.1, "Use of Punctuation"

In this section, we've reviewed the uses of colons and semicolons, two of the most commonly misunderstood and misused marks of punctuation.

6.7 QUOTATION MARKS

Double Quote Marks

Single Quote Marks

Use with Titles

The main function of quotation marks (also referenced as "quote marks") is to envelop direct quotations, whether from spoken or written word. Quote marks must always be used in pairs, regardless of whether the quote marks are doubles or singles. If there's an open-quote mark, there must be a close-quote mark.

Double Quote Marks

Double quote marks (" ") are used to enclose a direct quotation.

> As Mel Brooks is noted to have said, "Anybody can direct, but there are only eleven good writers."

Single Quote Marks

Single quote marks (' ') are used to hold a quote within a quote.

> And then she said, "As Mel Brooks is noted to have said, 'Anybody can direct, but there are only eleven good writers.'"

As you can see here, if there is concluding punctuation followed by single quotes and double quotes, the sequence is: punctuation, then single quotation mark, then double quote mark. Between each there is only a small space left. This spacing is often referenced as a *hair space*.

Use with Titles

Song titles, book chapter or section titles, article titles within newspapers and magazines, and the titles of episodes of television or radio programs are all treated in roman type within quotation marks. As long as it isn't a quotation within a quotation, these titles are in double quotation marks.

Title	Type
"Copacabana (At the Copa)"	Song title from *Ultimate Manilow*
"Punctuation"	Chapter title from *Grammar and Style at Your Fingertips*

continues

continued

Title	Type
"Graphic Novels' New Readers"	Newspaper article from the *New York Times*
"The Next Act"	Magazine article from the *New Yorker*
"Sales Resistance"	Television program episode from *I Love Lucy*

SEE ALSO 6.1, "Use of Punctuation"

In this section, we covered double and single quotation marks and the uses of each.

6.8 APOSTROPHES

Possessive Apostrophes
With Compound Words
With Sole and Joint Possession
With Omissions

Apostrophes are punctuation marks used to form the possessive for nouns and pronouns; to identify omissions within contractions; and to create plural versions of letters, numbers, and words as words.

Possessive Apostrophes

The possessive case indicates an ownership or possession of something by something or someone. The owner or possessor can be either singular or plural. If singular, the apostrophe is attached at the end of the word and followed by -*s*—including singular words that end in -*s*. When plural, the apostrophe is attached at the end of the word and followed by -*s* unless the word itself ends in an -*s*.

> Nora Roberts's best-selling novels keep hitting number one.
> The girl's doll was creepier than the boys' toys.

In the second example, note both singular possessive (*girl's*) and plural possessive (*boys'*) are shown.

SEE ALSO 1.4, "Properties"

With Compound Words

To form the possessive for compound words, add -'s to the last word or the last word in a word group.

> Her mother-in-law's new plan is to move into her spare bedroom.
> The senate page's name was withheld.
> My Russian grey's a pill at around three in the morning.

With Sole and Joint Possession

Whenever more than one owner or possessor is mentioned and you want to show that each one holds ownership or possession independently, add -'s to each name or word. To show that the multiple names share joint possession, add -'s to only the last name or word.

Merry's and Jerry's brothers arrived within minutes of each other.

Merry and Jerry's dog ran after the truck.

In the first example, both Merry and Jerry have a brother or brothers who were arriving. In the second example, the dog belongs to both Merry and Jerry. There's only one dog.

With Omissions

Apostrophes are used in contractions to show the omission of at least one letter, number, or word.

am not = ain't	is not = isn't
are not = aren't	it is = 'tis
cannot = can't	madam = ma'am
class of 1966 = class of '66	they are = they're
did not = didn't	was not = wasn't
do not = don't	were not = weren't
does not = doesn't	who is = who's
has not = hasn't	you are = you're
have not = haven't	

SEE ALSO 10.1, "Spelling"

Be on the lookout and avoid misplacing apostrophes in personal pronouns such as *its*, *their*, *your*, and *whose*.

SEE ALSO 1.3, "Pronouns"

SEE ALSO 6.1, "Use of Punctuation"

6.9 HYPHENS, DASHES, AND SLASHES

Hyphens
En Dashes
Em Dashes
Two- and Three-Em Dashes
Slashes

Rules and uses for hyphens, dashes, and slashes are reviewed in this section. As you will see from the materials provided here, each of these punctuation marks has its own uses and requirements.

Hyphens

Hyphens are punctuation marks used to divide compound words, various elements of words, or numbers.

With Compound Words

Hyphens are used with hyphenated compound words and names. Whenever in doubt about whether or not to use a hyphen, the first resource is, of course, your dictionary. More and more often hyphens are being removed and the words are being re-formed as closed compounds.

> 2- and 3-em dashes
> post-Einsteinian
> non-Indo-European

SEE ALSO 1.2, "Compounds"

For Syllabic Division

Hyphens are used to provide syllabic breaks in words that fall at the end of lines. For compound words, the division should be made only between the words that create the compound or at the fixed hyphens that create the compound.

> There were many people in town with concentrated and deter-
> mined sales resistance.
>
> Many other people in town thought this was the most-
> determined sales force ever.

Single-syllable words should not be broken, no matter where they fall. If a single-syllable word won't fit on a line, the type should be reflowed or rearranged to fit.

If you are uncertain where a word's syllables break properly, please check your dictionary.

For Letter-to-Letter and Numbers Separation

Hyphens are used whenever words are supposed to be spelled out letter by letter.

> l-e-t-t-e-r
>
> "Pronouncing is one thing, but please at least spell my name correctly: L-a-r-a."

Numbers use hyphens to separate numbers that aren't inclusive. Some of these sorts of numbers are ISBNs (International Standard Book Numbers used for books), Social Security numbers, and telephone numbers.

> *ISBN:* 978-1-59257-657-9
>
> *Social Security number:* 123-XXX-XXXX
>
> *Phone number:* 1-800-XXX-XXXX

En Dashes

En dashes are lines that are larger than hyphens but smaller than em dashes. The en dash can be used to mean "to," "up to and including," or "up to and through," and is most often used to join numbers, dates, and words.

> His years as principal: 1986–1996
>
> Isaiah 40:1–5
>
> Reference pages 343–376
>
> Bob Smith (1946–)

When a spread of information is introduced with the word *from*, use *to* and not an en dash to demonstrate the spread.

> He was principal from 1986 to 1996.

En dashes can be used with compound words that are not equal on both sides of the dash. One of the elements of the compound word might be a compound in itself and the other not. Or both sides might be carrying compound words. In either case, an en dash is used instead of a hyphen.

> As soon as we entered the post–Cold War era …
>
> State University of New York–Stonybrook

Em Dashes

Em dashes are very versatile in their use. They can be used within a sentence to indicate an aside or to further explain something not directly in line with the rest of the sentence.

> My boss was in a less than jolly mood—he had just been told to fire three people.
>
> Bob—her truest of true loves—died in a tragic accident.

With Sudden Breaks

Sudden breaks in dialogue, thought, or other sentence structure should be indicated by an em dash.

> "I can't go until—" The immediate silence that followed instantly caused grave concern.

With Other Punctuation

Em dashes can be used with exclamation marks or question marks, but not with any other punctuation.

> "Hey! Stop—!"

Two- and Three-Em Dashes

The two- and three-em dashes are used to show that a word, a big part of a word, or a name is missing. When a two-em dash is used to replace a word, be sure a space separates the dash from the text on both sides. However, when a two-em dash replaces letters within a word, it should be closed to the surrounding text.

> Her stream of —— words embarrassed even the sailors.
>
> Gnarls B——y [Barkley?] …

Three-em dashes, often used in bibliography citation to indicate a missing name or a repeat of the preceding author, should be closed to the following period.

> ———. *Today, Tomorrow, and Forever*. New York: Berkley Books, 2007.

Slashes

Slashes are used between two or more words that are alternating options.

> This is a pass/fail class.
>
> That was a yes/no question.

Slashes are also used to show the separation of poetry or song lines that are placed within text. Note that the slashes are separated from the surrounding text with spaces.

> The saddest poem "Please God, let me see the sunset. / Please God, let me see another morning. / Please God, let me see my friend again / with both eyes intact / and no gaping holes in his body." Was cited simply as being by "A Soldier."

SEE ALSO 6.1, "Use of Punctuation"

6.10 PARENTHESES AND BRACKETS

Parentheses

Brackets

In this section, we will take a look at what parentheses and brackets really are and how they're used.

Parentheses

Parentheses are punctuation marks used to isolate elements within sentences that are not exactly necessary but that add to the reader's understanding. These parenthetical expressions include examples, explanations, facts, and digressions.

> She loved her first brand-new car <u>(a 2000 Ford Escort ZX2)</u> and ignored those who would mock her choice.
>
> The population growth rate dropped (–0.3 percent) in 2006.

Parentheses can also be used to enclose numbers or letters in listings within sentences—or as a design element for list extracts.

> They decided <u>(1)</u> to stop watching TV and <u>(2)</u> to stop staying up late at night.

Brackets

Brackets are used within quotations to identify and separate your own commentary from the words that come from the one being quoted.

> Once in awhile [*sic*] even she misspelled an easy word or two.

Brackets can also be used within parentheses, just as when single quotes are placed within double quotes.

> Sometime before (before the race [to the top of the volcano] began), he had already decided to lose.

SEE ALSO 6.1, "Use of Punctuation"

Throughout this chapter, we've looked at all manner of punctuation, from the basics of periods, commas, question marks, and exclamation marks to the more intricate uses of other punctuation marks. At this point, you should now know how to use everything from a period at the end of simple sentence to the proper placement of punctuation with single quotation marks within double quotation marks and bracketed commentary placed within parenthetical notations—and everything in between.

7

PLURALS AND POSSESSIVES

7.1 Plurals

7.2 Possessives

7.1 PLURALS

Exceptions

Plural Letters and Abbreviations

Plural Numbers

Plural Proper Nouns

Plural Compound Words

Plural Italicized Words

Plural means "more than one." And much like the name, plural words have more than one rule. Most of the time, nouns are made plural by simply adding *-s* after the last letter of the root word.

cat	=	cats
house	=	houses
noun	=	nouns

If the root word ends with *-ch*, *-j*, *-s*, *-sh*, *-x*, or *-z*, add *-es* instead of *-s*.

boss	=	bosses
fox	=	foxes
wish	=	wishes
stretch	=	stretches

When the word ends with *-y*, to form the plural, that *-y* usually transforms into *-ies*. This isn't a hard-and-fast rule because the last letter of these words isn't the ultimate determiner. It's necessary to look at the letter preceding the concluding *-y*, too. If the letter preceding the concluding *-y* is a vowel, add *-s*; if the letter preceding the concluding *-y* is a consonant, drop the *-y* and add *-ies*.

boy	=	boys
key	=	keys
mystery	=	mysteries
baby	=	babies

Exceptions

As with most rules, there are exceptions to the preceding plural rules. Difficulties can arise when the rules don't apply. There's no easy way to learn all of the exceptions, but the following exceptions help you navigate through plurals.

Words Ending with *-f* or *-fe*

Words ending in *-f* or *-fe* can go both ways—sometimes ending with *-s*, sometimes changing the *-f* to *-v-* and adding *-es* at the end.

roof	=	roofs
fife	=	fifes
wife	=	wives
self	=	selves
hoof	=	hooves

Words Ending with *-o*

Nouns that end with *-o* can go both ways, too—sometimes adding just *-s*, sometimes adding *-es*. Typically, if the letter before the concluding *-o* is a vowel, or if the word is of foreign origin or in a shortened form, only *-s* is added.

burrito	=	burritos
folio	=	folios
typo	=	typos
hero	=	heroes
potato	=	potatoes

Irregular Plurals

Irregular plurals come in innumerable variations. Some change in the middle to form the plural from the singular spelling.

man	=	men
goose	=	geese
mouse	=	mice

Other words add, change, or remove letters from their endings.

memorandum	=	memoranda
minutia	=	minutiae
radius	=	radii

And still other words remain exactly the same as their singular form.

deer	=	deer
craft	=	craft (as in boats, aircraft, spacecraft)
cannon	=	cannon (as in large weapon)

Because there is no strict rule for each and every one of the irregular plural exceptions, the best place to look to verify a plural spelling is a good dictionary. Most dictionaries include irregular plurals along with the singular form of the word. If the dictionary offers more than one plural spelling, such as for *appendix* (offers both *appendixes* and *appendices*), the best bet is to use the first spelling listed. Just be sure the different spellings do not also have different uses or meanings. For example, the plural forms of the word *louse* are *lice* and *louses*. *Louses* refers to a group of disagreeable people, but *lice* refers to an infestation of insects. Obviously, there's a big difference in meanings for these words. Choose wisely!

Plural Letters and Abbreviations

Plural forms of capital letters used as words and abbreviations without periods need only *-s* at the end.

the four Cs	your ABCs
both URLs	a dozen MREs

When discussing grades given in school, simply add *-s* to form the plural.

Carlos earned three As, two Bs, and one C.
The teacher was notorious for giving Fs.

For plurals of lowercase letters, add an apostrophe plus the *-s*, to make it *-'s*.

p's and q's
dot the i's and cross the t's

Abbreviations with periods are handled similarly to plurals of lowercase letters. Because abbreviations with internal or terminal periods may look awkward as plurals, an apostrophe is added to avoid confusion.

two Ph.D.'s
too many etc.'s and et al.'s
a handful of legal asst.'s

Some plural abbreviations add the *-s* before a period; others have no *-s*.

ed.	=	eds.
f.	=	ff.
p.	=	pp.

Many common abbreviations are listed in the dictionary, so it's good practice to double-check there if you have any questions. The general rule is to make abbreviations plural by adding *-s*, unless they include periods or lowercase letters—in that case, add *-'s*.

SEE ALSO 10.2, "Abbreviations"

Plural Numbers

To form the plural of numerals, simply add *-s* after the numeral.

in the '60s
since the 1800s
no more 9/11s

Whenever numbers are spelled out, they are pluralized following the general rules for noun plurals. For most numbers, just add *-s* or *-es*. For numbers ending in *-y*, change it to *-ies*.

Jonathan was in the terrible twos phase.
She'd been swimming since her twenties.
The dice rolled perfect sixes.
They say things always happen in threes.

SEE ALSO 11.1, "Numbers"

Plural Proper Nouns

Proper nouns are made plural simply by adding *-s*. If the word already ends with *-s*, add *-es*.

the Millers
Tuesdays with Morrie
several Mr. Darcys
both Kansas Citys
the Forbeses

The plural form of a family name should never be created by adding the possessive form -'s, such as the Anderson's. Regular nouns seldom require apostrophes in the formation of their plurals. The same holds true for proper nouns.

There are always exceptions: proper names that end in a silent *-s* should remain in a singular construction even when used as a plural. Or they can be rewritten to prevent the plural use entirely. Always be sure to double-check for the correct pronunciation, though, because sometimes the same name is pronounced differently.

Original: Both Albert Camus, the writer and the philosopher, exhibited beliefs of existentialism.

Better: Both sides of Albert Camus, the writer and the philosopher, exhibited beliefs of existentialism.

Same spelling but with the -s pronounced: The Camuses, both Raoul the conductor and his wife, Amy, the cellist, love classical music.

Some names that end in a pronounced *-s* simply do not lend themselves well to being pluralized. The best bet in such cases is to reword the sentence.

the Rodgers family (better than the *Rodgerses*)

the Smothers brothers (better than the *Smotherses*)

Plural Compound Words

For many compound words, the end word takes the plural form. In general, both closed and open compounds use the standard plural forms ending in *-s*, *-es*, or *-ies*.

Closed Compounds

When two words are fused into one word to form a closed compound, the ending takes the plural.

bookcases	raincoats
racecars	wineglasses

A rare exception to this style is the plural form of the word *manservant*, which becomes *menservants*. In this case, both words in the closed compound become plural. Here are a few other irregular compounds:

Singular: mother-in-law

Plural: mothers-in-law (*not* mother-in-laws)

Singular: Passerby

Plural: passersby (not passerbys)

Open Compounds

When two or more closely related words form a single thought in an open compound, only the end word becomes plural.

clock radios	sales assistants
dining rooms	vice presidents

Hyphenated Compounds

Some notable exceptions exist for hyphenated compounds in which the root word forms the plural. In some cases, hyphens are not used even though the compound is treated as one unit.

attorneys-at-law
fathers-in-law
ladies-in-waiting

SEE ALSO 1.2, "Compounds"

Plural Italicized Words

If a title that's ordinarily set in italics is used in the plural form, the added *-s* is not italicized. Because the *-s* isn't part of the italicized term, it's treated as regular text.

a stack of *Vogue*s on the table
the leftover *New York Post*s

For ease of use and to avoid awkward construction, rephrasing the sentence to avoid the plural form may be necessary.

a stack of *Vogue* magazines on the table
the leftover copies of the *New York Post*

Similarly, for words used as words and letters used as letters, do not set the plural ending in italics.

Your sentence uses too many *that*s.
The common abbreviation for *World War I* uses two capital *W*s and one capital *I*.

For foreign words and phrases, the plural forms are usually made as part of the root word; therefore, the *-s* becomes italic.

Students in France are called *étudiants*.
The paella recipe calls for two *merlozas*, or hake fish.

SEE ALSO 9.1, "Italics"

7.2 POSSESSIVES

Possessive Proper Nouns
Possessive Letters and Numbers
Possessive Pronouns
Possessive Gerunds
Possessive Compounds
Possessive Appositives
Possessive Attributive Nouns
Holiday Possessives
Possessive Italicized Words
Other Possessive Uses

In general, possessives require nothing more than an apostrophe and sometimes an additional *-s*. For all singular words, add *-'s* to the end. Even if the word ends in *-s*, *-x*, or *-z*, the most common usage adds *-'s* to the ending.

my father's car	the kitten's claws
the gas's odor	the ax's blade
jazz's historical significance	

For plural words that don't end in *-s*, add *-'s*.

four children's books	the people's choice
the oxen's trail	the women's shoes

For plural words that do end in *-s*, add only the apostrophe.

five cops' badges	the science teachers' labs
the auto mechanics' shop	three girls' dresses

For nouns that are plural in construction but singular in use, add only an apostrophe. The same is true for expressions using a *for … sake* construction in which the noun in the middle ends in *-s* or with an *s* sound.

a species' survival	for goodness' sake
for appearance' sake	politics' dark side

SEE ALSO 1.4, "Noun and Pronoun Properties"

Possessive Proper Nouns

The same rules outlined earlier apply when using proper nouns. If the proper noun is singular, add *-'s*. If it's plural and ends in *-s*, add only the apostrophe.

Brian Williams's newscast
Iowans' farms
James's house
Kansas's capitol
Ms. Davis's car
New York's nightlife
Rosie Perez's voice
St. Moritz's ski resorts
the Callahans' children
the Joneses' family reunion

For ancient and religious names ending in *-s*, add only the apostrophe. The same is true for proper nouns that are plural in construction but singular in use, and any word whose last syllable has an *eez* sound.

Achilles' heel
Euripides' writings
Jesus' love
Kew Gardens' new curator
Moses' laws
the Ganges' source
the United States' success

For proper nouns that end with a silent *-s*, add only an apostrophe. However, be sure to double-check the pronunciation of the words, as often they are of foreign origin.

Arkansas' capitol
François' accent

Possessive Letters and Numbers

Add *-'s* to create the possessive form for letters, abbreviations, and numbers.

CNN's news coverage
the 1990s' tech boom
2006's midterm elections
Louis XIV's chateau

Possessive Pronouns

Possessive pronouns can be a bit trickier. They don't have the telltale apostrophe, and you don't always have to add the *-s*. Some possessive pronouns—*my*, *your*, *his*, *her*, *its*, *our*, *their*, and *whose*—function to modify nouns.

his bike
your sister
their guitars
our integrity

Each possessive pronoun has a corresponding independent form that can be used without a noun. These stand-alone possessive pronouns include *mine*, *yours*, *his*, *hers*, *its*, *ours*, *theirs*, and *whose*.

this bike of his
that guitar of theirs

Which is mine?

The Possessive of *Its*

Its is a unique construction because this possessive word quite frequently gets mistaken for its cousin *it's*. To keep the meanings straight, you need to remember just two things:

- Possessive pronouns don't have apostrophes.
- *It's* is a contraction meaning "it is." Try substituting *its* or *it's* with the words *it is* or *it has*, and see if the sentence still makes sense. If it doesn't, you know not to use the apostrophe.

It's a beautiful butterfly.
It is a beautiful butterfly.

Its wings are gold and blue.
It is wings are gold and blue.

In the first example, the substitution works, so you know *it's* is correct. In the second example, substitution does not work because the pronoun is possessive.

SEE ALSO 10.1, "Spelling"

The Possessive of *Whose*

Like *its*, the word *whose* is often confused with the contraction *who's*. You can use the same substitution trick as mentioned earlier for *it's/its*. *Who* is a pronoun just like *it*, and the *who* possessive doesn't take an apostrophe, either. Whenever you see *who's*, remember that it's a contraction and then try substituting *who's* and *whose* for *who is* or *who has*.

Whose drink is this?
Who is/has drink is this?

Who's drinking from my glass?
Who is drinking from my glass?

In the first example, the substitution doesn't make sense because the pronoun is possessive. In the second example, substitution works because it's obviously a contraction and not a possessive construct.

SEE ALSO 1.3, "Pronouns"

Possessive Gerunds

Gerunds are present participles that are used as nouns and end with an *-ing*. Gerunds can function as the subject of a verb, the object of a verb, a predicate nominative or complement, or the object of a preposition. The *-ing* throws a wrench into the sentence, though, because it looks like a verb; but if you can substitute the *-ing* word with a noun without changing the meaning of the sentence, then the preceding word is possessive.

> Courtney regretted his losing.
>
> Courtney regretted his loss.

Substitution works here because the gerund is a noun, not a verb. It's tempting to write this as *Courtney regretted him losing*, but that's wrong. By looking at *losing* as a noun, as we do with *loss*, you can see that the possessive *his* is correct.

> Billy's crying broke her heart.
> Billy's tears broke her heart.
>
> As much as she tried, she couldn't prevent his leaving.
> As much as she tried, she couldn't prevent his departure.

Substitution works in the first example because the *-ing* word is a noun, not a verb. And substitution works in the second example because the gerund is a noun, not a verb.

If the *-ing* word is functioning as a verb, however, then the possessive is incorrect.

> She saw Billy walking away.

Here you can't substitute *walking* for a noun, so it is *not* possessive.

Possessive Compounds

Possessive compounds are compound words and sentences used in the possessive form. They have a few rules all their own.

Possessive Compound Sentences

If two nouns operate as one compound unit and the element of possession is shared by both, only the last noun shows the possessive construction.

> my mom and dad's dog
>
> Rachel and Fred's apartment

But if the nouns have individual possession, they each use the possessive form.

my mom's and dad's cooking
Rachel's and Fred's mothers

SEE ALSO 5.2, "Sentence Types"

Possessive Compound Words

In a compound noun or phrase, the last element usually takes the possessive *-'s*.

the coffeepot's handle
the editor in chief's decision
the sous-chef's recipes

However, sometimes a plural compound makes an awful possessive construction, and it's best to recast the phrase.

Recast: the attorneys-at-law's offices
Better yet: the offices of the attorneys-at-law

Possessive Appositives

An appositive is a word or phrase that renames or explains a noun and is often set off between commas. When one follows a possessive noun, the *-'s* is attached to the appositive rather than the noun. In this construction, the commas that would normally surround the appositive are removed.

My oldest brother Tim's Jeep is red.
Loretta Beam the director's decision was sound.

These constructions should be used frugally, though, as they're usually awkward and difficult to understand. If the expression doesn't look or feel right to you, rephrase it using the preposition *of*.

The Jeep of my oldest brother, Tim, is red.
The decision of the director, Loretta Beam, was sound.

However, if the appositive is used at the end of the sentence and is included only for clarification, the noun uses the possessive construction.

The red Jeep is my brother's, Tim.
The decision was Loretta Beam's, the director.

Possessive Attributive Nouns

An attributive noun is a noun that modifies another noun and usually acts as an adjective. This construction can be prickly, though, when that attributive noun ends in *-s* because it may be difficult to distinguish the intended meaning. In the examples that follow, the first uses the word *Steelers* as a plural along with *quarterback* to both modify *Ben Roethlisberger*; the second uses the possessive form of *Steelers* to modify *quarterback*, with *Ben Roethlisberger* as an appositive.

Steelers quarterback Ben Roethlisberger was injured.
The Steelers' quarterback, Ben Roethlisberger, was injured.

If you can add another modifier between the word ending in *-s* and the noun, it's likely to use the possessive form.

The Steelers' (new) quarterback, Ben Roethlisberger, was injured.

***SEE ALSO* 1.1, "Nouns"**

Holiday Possessives

Several American holidays are possessive in construction, for both singular and plural usage, with a few notable exceptions that are not possessive.

All Souls' Day
April Fool's Day
Father's Day
Mother's Day
New Year's Day
Parents' Day
Presidents' Day
St. Patrick's Day
Valentine's Day

Exceptions:

Christmas Eve
Martin Luther King Jr. Day
Veterans Day

Possessive Italicized Words

If a word or title ordinarily set in italics is used in the possessive form, the -'s is not italicized. Because the -'s is not part of the italicized term, it's treated as regular text.

in *Vogue*'s health and beauty section
the *New York Post*'s sports coverage

***SEE ALSO* 9.1, "Italics"**

7.2

Other Possessive Uses

Occasionally, other possessive constructions crop up. One is the genitive case of the plural possessive, in which the word *of* is implied. The genitive case is the possessive form used in constructions when the *of* is omitted. This is a much more common structure in other languages; in English, there are only a few usages.

with one week's notice
the Hundred Years' War
three hours' sleep

Another uses the word *of* to show possession but also uses the possessive construction.

a friend of Mike's
a shirt of mine

The occasional double possessive construction that uses two or more possessive words or phrases consecutively is probably unavoidable. Watch out for them, though, and rewrite when you can.

Janice's mother's home
Frank's friends' freezer

Within this chapter, we have reviewed the rules and exceptions governing plurals and possessives. The plural section provided rules for creating regular and irregular plurals for words (regular, proper, and all manner of compounds). Also covered was the pluralization of letters, abbreviations, and numbers. In the section regarding possessives, we covered how to create the possessive from nouns, pronouns, letters, and numbers.

8
CAPITALIZATION

8.1 Personal Names and Titles
8.2 Proper Nouns

8.1 PERSONAL NAMES AND TITLES

Personal Names
Personal Titles
Kinship Names
Academic Titles
Civil, Military, Royal, and Religious Titles

Capitalization has a lot of rules—and exceptions to the rules. Still, there are some very basic rules of thumb for capitalization:

- Capitalize the first word of a sentence.
- Capitalize the pronoun *I*.
- Capitalize the interjection O (a variant of the interjection *oh*).
- Capitalize proper nouns and proper adjectives.
- Capitalize common nouns when they're essential as parts of proper nouns.
- Capitalize trademarked names.
- Use capitalization for emphasis.
- Full-word capitalization within e-mails, instant messaging, and other online postings generally indicates that the writer is shouting the words.
- Avoid excessive and unnecessary capitalization.

Personal Names

Personal names are the names of people and should be capitalized. If a person includes or goes by their initials, those should be capitalized as well. When two or more initials are used in place of part of the person's name, and if those initials carry periods, the initials should be spaced equally with each other and the first/last name. If the initials are used without periods, they should be closed, with no spaces.

J. D. Robb	F. Scott Fitzgerald
John Smith	George W. Bush
W. E. B. Griffin	RFK

One can find confirmation for the treatment for famous folks' names—living or dead, real or fictional—with a variety of resources: A rather extensive biographical listing can be found at the end of *Merriam Webster's Collegiate Dictionary*, 11th edition. There is also *Merriam Webster's Biographical Dictionary*, and *Encyclopedia Britannica Online* which are both far more extensive.

John Smith
e. e. cummings
George W. Bush
J. D. Robb
W. E. B. Griffin

When there are two or more initials used in place of part of the person's name, and if those initials carry periods, then the initials should be spaced equally with each other and the first/last name.

If the initials are used sans internal periods, then they should be closed up.

W. E. B. Griffin *but* RFK

When a person's surname includes particles—articles and prepositions such as *d'*, *de*, *de la*, *della*, *du*, *l'*, *le*, *les*, *ten*, *van*, *van der*, and *von*—there's much debate regarding whether the particles should be capitalized. The general rules dictate that the particles are capitalized for names that originate in the United Kingdom and the United States. However, these same sorts of naming elements are historically lowercased (as long as a forename or a title precedes the name) if the name is French, Italian, Spanish, Portuguese, German, or Dutch.

Andrea del Sarto
Blount DeMille
Dame Daphne du Maurier
Eugen Francis Charles D'Albert
John Le Carré
Leonardo da Vinci
Li Hung-chang
Ludwig van Beethoven
Martin Van Buren
Pierre-Charles L'Enfant
Vincent van Gogh
W. E. B. Du Bois
Willem de Kooning

French names come with additional capitalization rules: the particles *L'*, *La*, *Le*, and *Les* are generally capped, and *d'* and *de* are lowercase.

The particles retain the same capitalization or lowercasing treatment when used with the last name only—without the full name. The exception to this is when the particle starts a sentence; in those cases, the particle always takes a cap.

You can find confirmation for the treatment for famous folks' names—living or dead, real or fictional—from a variety of resources. *Merriam Webster's Collegiate Dictionary*, 11th edition, contains a rather extensive biographical listing. *Merriam Webster's Biographical Dictionary* and *Encyclopedia Britannica Online* are both far more extensive. A person's official website is probably a reliable source for the spelling and treatment.

Personal Titles

Capitalize a personal title—*Mr.*, *Miss*, *Mrs.*, etc.—when it precedes a personal name or when it's used alone, without the person's name. When the personal title alone is used in direct address, it should be spelled out. The only exception for this is *Miss*, which has no alternate version.

Miss Jackson	Mrs. Blanche Kelly
Mr. Koontz	Ms. Greenville

Miss: Would you step this way, Miss?

Mrs.: I need to show Mrs. Kelly first.

Mr.: Don't you love Mr. Koontz's books?

Ms.: They were looking for Ms. Greenville.

Kinship Names

Kinship names identify relatives according to their genealogical relationships.

Kinship List

aunt	grandfather	mother-in-law
brother	grandmother	nephew
cousin	great-aunt	niece
daughter	great-great-grandmother	stepbrother
daughters-in-law	half sister	uncle
father	mother	

Kinship names are lowercased except when they directly precede the person's name or when they are used in direct reference instead of the person's name. Lowercase kinship names when they follow a pronoun, regardless of whether the personal name follows the kinship name. In such instances, the kinship is used in apposition before the personal name, or when the kinship name is used as a description and not as part of the name.

Was that Mother on the phone?

Do you mean my mother or your mother?

I don't know what to tell you, Mother; it just didn't work out.

The Olsen twins will be bizillionaires by the time they hit twenty-one.

Tell your uncle John to get ready. Tell Cousin George, too!

SEE ALSO 1.3, "Pronouns"

Terms of endearment or pet names are always lowercased, except when they start a sentence, of course.

Come over here, sweetheart.

Oh, darling, that's superb!

References to the kinship terms for religious positions follow the preceding rules, too.

It was clear that Mother Superior had little appreciation for the prank.

Did you appeal to Father Joe? The father has always been fair.

Those sisters are young enough to remember how mischief can be made without intending to do so.

Academic Titles

Academic titles are capitalized only when they precede the person's name or are used directly. Otherwise, those titles should be lowercased.

the professor	the department chair
a professor emeritus	the chair of the department
Professor Joe Shelton	the president
President George Smith	the president's office
Joe Shelton, professor of psychology	Bob Derryberry, senior professor, SBU Department of Communication

Civil, Military, Royal, and Religious Titles

Capitalize a person's civil, military, royal, or religious title when his or her proper name follows it. If the title follows the proper name or is used alone instead of the person's name, lowercase the title, as it's being used in apposition to the name and not as a part of the name itself.

President Bill Clinton	the president
Senator Hillary Clinton	the senator
Baron De La Warr	the baron
Queen Elizabeth II	the queen
Pope John Paul II	the pope
Director of Thus and So	the director; Jane Doe, director of Thus and So

If the professional title is used alone in direct address, in place of the personal name, capitalize the title.

We aren't certain yet, Mr. <u>President</u>.

Have you offered an opinion, <u>Senator</u>, as to what we should do?

What happened here, <u>Officer</u>?

<u>The first officers</u> on scene are standing over there, <u>Detective.</u>

Civil Titles and Offices

the president; presidency; the president of the United States; President William Jefferson Clinton

the vice president; the vice presidency; the vice president of the United States; Al Gore, vice president of the United States

the secretary of state; secretary of state; the secretary; Secretary of State Condoleezza Rice

senator; the senator; the senator from Missouri; U.S. Senator Edward Kennedy of Massachusetts; Iowa state senator

the congressman; the congresswoman from Oregon; the representative; Representative Neil Abercrombie of Hawaii; Congressman Vernon J. Ehlers

Speaker of the House of Representatives; the Speaker; Thomas P. "Tip" O'Neill, Jr., former Speaker of the House

the mayor; the mayor of New York; Michael R. Bloomberg, mayor of New York; Mayor Mike

the chief justice; the chief justice of the United States; John G. Roberts, Jr., chief justice of the United States; the justice; Justice Ruth Bader Ginsburg; Sandra Day O'Connor, former associate justice

the ambassador; John Danforth, former ambassador to the United Nations; the embassy; Russian Foreign Minister Lavrov; the foreign minister

the governor; the governor of Ohio; Governor Bob Taft; governor of the state of Ohio

the prime minister; Tony Blair, prime minister of the United Kingdom

member of Parliament (M.P.)

Military Titles and Offices

the commander in chief

the general; General Ulysses S. Grant

the admiral; the commander of the fleet; Fleet Admiral; Fleet Admiral Chester W. Nimitz

the captain; Captain James T. Kirk

the sergeant; Sergeant Schultz

the chief petty officer; the chief; Master Chief Petty Officer Charles W. Bowen

Royal Titles and Offices

the queen; the queen of England; Queen Elizabeth II, queen of England; the dowager queen; Dowager Queen Mary; *but* the Queen Mother

the king; the king of England; King Henry VIII; the prince; the prince consort; *but* the Prince of Wales

the emperor; His Imperial Majesty Akihito, the 125th emperor of Japan; Her Imperial Majesty Michiko, empress of Japan

the earl; the earl of Perth; John Stuart, Earl of Bute; the baron; Baron Walpole; Sir Horatio Walpole; the count; Count Dracula

the duke; Prince Philip, duke of Edinburgh *(sometimes this honorary title is capitalized)*

Royal or Honorific Titles of Address

His (Her) Majesty

His (Her) Royal Highness

His (Her) Eminence

lord; lady; Lord Whosit; Lady Whatsit

madam; sir

my lord; my lady

Your Excellency; Excellency

Your Honor

Religious Titles and Offices

the papacy; the pope; Pope John Paul II

the mother superior (*but* Mother Superior *in direct address*)

the cardinal; Cardinal Francis Eugene George

continues...

(continued)

Religious Titles and Offices
the bishop; the archbishop; the archbishop of Canterbury; the bishop of St. Louis; diocese
the rabbi; Rabbi Hananiah
the minister; the reverend; the Reverend J. T. Smith; Rev. J. T. Smith; the rector; the rector of XYZ Church

8.2 PROPER NOUNS

Peoples, Nationalities, and Languages

Days and Holidays

Time Zones

Historical Happenings and Items

Building Names and Geographical Terms

Governmental and Political Agencies and Terms

Religious Terms

Medical Terms

Odd but True

All proper nouns naming specific people, places, and things require initial capitalization. "People" includes their nationalities and languages, as well as their personal names. "Things" includes the names of holidays, companies, organizations, and trademarks.

Peoples, Nationalities, and Languages

Capitalize all official references to races or other groups of persons linked by a united culture or kinship, generally sharing common language or beliefs. References made with regard to skin tone should be written in lowercase.

African-American
Afro-American
American Indian
Arab
Asian
black
Caucasian
Chicana/Chicano
European
Highlander (Scottish)
Hispanic
Indo-European
Latina/Latino
Mongol
Muslim
Native American
Nordic
white

Capitalize all references made to nationalities and languages.

American
British
English
French
German
Latin
Native American
Neapolitan
Spanish

Days and Holidays

Capitalize the names for the days of the week and the months. In addition, capitalize all holidays and days of special observation (generally religious or governmental).

U.S. Holidays

New Year's Day
Bank Holiday
Martin Luther King Jr. Day
Holocaust Memorial Day
Chinese New Year
Al Hijra (Islamic New Year)
Groundhog Day
Accession Day
Lincoln's Birthday
St. Valentine's Day
President's Day
Washington's Birthday
Ash Wednesday
St. Patrick's Day
Spring Equinox
All Fools Day
Palm Sunday
Passover
Good Friday
Easter
Earth Day
May Day
National Day of Prayer
Nurses' Day
Mother's Day
Armed Forces Day
Ascension Day/Holy Thursday
Memorial Day
Shavuot (Feast of Weeks)
Flag Day
Father's Day
Summer Solstice
Independence Day (Fourth of July)
St. Swithin's Day
Parents' Day
Air Force Day
Coast Guard Day
Friendship Day
Assumption of the Blessed Virgin Mary
Labor Day
Grandparent's Day
Patriot Day
Citizenship Day
Rosh Hashanah
Autumn Equinox
Ramadan
Yom Kippur
National Children's Day
Columbus Day
Bosses' Day
Sweetest Day
United Nations' Day
Mother-in-Law Day
Navy Day
Halloween
All Saints' Day
Election Day
Marine Corps Day
Veterans Day

U.S. Holidays

Thanksgiving Day
Advent Sunday
Pearl Harbor Remembrance Day
Winter Solstice
Christmas Eve
Christmas Day
Kwanzaa
New Year's Eve

Time Zones

Capitalize time zones and their acronyms.

Daylight Saving Time (DST)

A time zone is a geographic region in which the same time is used. There are obviously multiple time zones in the world. The following list identifies these terms.

North American Time Zones

Newfoundland Standard Time (NST)
Newfoundland Daylight Time (NDT)
Atlantic Standard Time (AST)
Atlantic Daylight Time (ADT)
Eastern Standard Time (EST)
Eastern Daylight Time (EDT)
Central Standard Time (CST)
Central Daylight Time (CDT)
Mountain Standard Time (MST)
Mountain Daylight Time (MDT)
Pacific Standard Time (PST)
Pacific Daylight Time (PDT)
Alaska Standard Time (AKST)
Alaska Daylight Time (AKDT)
Hawaii-Aleutian Standard Time (HAST)
Hawaii-Aleutian Daylight Time (HADT)

Historical Happenings and Items

Capitalize historical periods, movements, artifacts, and documents.

Bill of Rights
California Gold Rush, the

Civil Rights Movement, the
Civil War, the
Declaration of Independence
Great Depression, the; Depression, the
Hellenism
Middle Ages
Prohibition
Romanesque
World War I, World War II (*also* WWI, WWII)

Building Names and Geographical Terms

Capitalize names for buildings and other specific constructions, especially those that are historically or architecturally notable. Capitalize common nouns like *bridge*, *mountains*, *dam*, *river*, etc., when they're used as part of a proper name. If *the* precedes the name, the common noun is lowercase.

Big Ben
Brooklyn Battery Tunnel
capital, the (a city)
capitol, the (a building)
Capitol, the (national)
Eiffel Tower
Empire State Building
Golden Gate Bridge
Jefferson Memorial
Panama Canal
Radio City Music Hall
Statue of Liberty
Washington Monument
White House, the

Capitalize geographical regions, locations, and terms.

Appalachian Trail
Arctic Circle
Beacon Hill
East, the
eastern
Easterner
Eastern Hemisphere
Midwest, the
Midwestern
Midwesterner
Mount Everest
North, the
Northern
Northerner
North Pole
Ozark Mountains
Rattlesnake Mountain Range
Rocky Mountains
South, the
Southern
Southerner
South Africa
South America
West, the
western
Westerner

When geographical words are presented as simple direction or destination references, they remain in their lowercase forms. Should you have questions about whether to capitalize or not, a quick look in *Merriam-Webster's Collegiate Dictionary*, 11th edition, will give you guidance.

Capitalize the proper names of bodies of water.

English Channel, the
Lake Eerie
Mississippi River
Niagara Falls, the

Governmental and Political Agencies and Terms

Capitalize all specific references to governmental and political agencies and terms.

New York City Administration for Children's Services
Democratic Party, Democrats
Court of Appeals
Socialist
Pentagon

Religious Terms

Capitalize most references to specific religions and to many religious icons.

Baptist
Bible
Buddhist
Catholicism
Christianity
Crucifixion
Hinduism
Last Supper, the
Nativity
New Testament
Pentateuch
Resurrection

Medical Terms

Generally, medical references to diseases, symptoms, syndromes, procedures, and so on are lowercase. However, if a proper name is included in the term, that portion is capitalized.

Achilles tendon
gastroesophageal reflux
Gestalt psychology
Parkinson's disease
shin splints
tuberculosis

Odd but True

Automat, *Dumpster*, and *Laundromat* are known as service marks or trademarks and should always be capitalized.

> The mugger threw the lady's empty purse in the <u>Dumpster</u> before disappearing down the dark alley.

The capitalization of trademark terms in text identifies that the trademark exists. In running text, it is never necessary to add any trademark symbols to words or phrases that are service marks, trademarks, or even registered trademarks.

SEE ALSO 12.1, "Trademarks"

9

SPECIAL TYPE TREATMENT

9.1 Italics

9.2 Boldface

9.3 Small Capitals

9.4 Serif versus Sans Serif

9.5 Underlining

9.1 ITALICS

Titles and Names

Emphasis and Identification

Pretty and elegant, italic is a slanted type treatment akin to cursive script. All forms of writing have several common usages for italics.

Titles and Names

Titles of works that appear within the main text or in any type of citation are customarily treated differently from the surrounding text. In most cases, the title is set in italics. If the text is already italic, the title should be set roman to stand out.

Book, Play, and Essay Titles

Set book titles, including novels and textbooks, italic. Longer works such as plays, novellas, and book-length poems and essays are italic as well.

Angela's Ashes
The Joy of Cooking
Much Ado About Nothing
The Iliad

Religious and Governmental Texts

Religious works and governmental texts are set in regular (roman) type.

the Bible, the Koran, and the Talmud
books of the Bible, such as Genesis and Luke
the Magna Carta
the Constitution
the Bill of Rights

Subtitles

Subtitles are the second part of a title, often included to explain the main title or to give more information about it. Subtitles are also italicized as part of the book's complete title. The two titles are joined with a colon.

Tropical Truth: A Story of Music and Revolution in Brazil
The Audacity of Hope: Thoughts on Reclaiming the American Dream

Titles Within Titles

Titles within titles remain italicized but are set off with quotation marks.

War Themes in "Lord of the Flies"
The Manual for "Romeo and Juliet"

Parts of a Book

Chapter titles, short stories and poems, and individual articles are usually not set in italics. Instead, they are set in regular roman type and enclosed within quotation marks. Title capitalization follows standard headline style, which generally has initial capitals for all words except for articles, conjunctions, and prepositions that have four or less letters.

The story "Silence" appears in Alice Munro's collection *Runaway*.
Has he read "Emergency" by Denis Johnson?

However, generic names for parts of the book, such as *preface*, *foreword*, *index*, and *bibliography*, are not given any special type treatment and should appear lowercased and in regular text.

Please turn to chapter 4.
The term is defined in the glossary.

Series Names

Series names, unless a part of the book's title, are not set in italics. They should be capitalized in headline style and set in regular text.

The latest book in Simon Brett's Fethering Mystery series just came out in hardcover.
She's read everything in the Left Behind series.

Tom Clancy's Net Force: *Changing of the Guard*

Articles in Book Titles

If the book title begins with *The*, *An*, or *A*, omit the article if it doesn't fit the syntax of the sentence.

The Handmaid's Tale
A Tree Grows in Brooklyn
She read Margaret Atwood's *Handmaid's Tale*.
He carried a beaten-up *Tree Grows in Brooklyn* hardcover edition.

Plural Construction Within Book Titles

A book's title is always treated as a singular noun within the sentence, even if the title itself uses a plural construction.

The Dubliners is a collection of James Joyce's stories.

Gulliver's Travels was written circa 1726.

SEE ALSO 14.4, "Bibliographies"

Periodical and Journal Titles

Titles of periodicals and journals are set in italics. This includes magazines, newspapers, medical and research journals, literary journals, etc.

The New Yorker

The New England Journal of Medicine

Cat Fancy

The Christian Science Monitor

If the newspaper or periodical title is standing on its own, a preceding article should be italicized if it's a part of the publication's **masthead**. However, within the body of text, the initial *The* can be treated as regular text for simplicity. This rule does not apply to foreign-language publications that use the article in their name.

Refer to articles published in the *New York Times* and *Wall Street Journal*.

She bought Thursday's *Le Monde* at the airport.

WORDS TO GO . . . WORDS TO GO . . . WORDS TO GO

A **masthead** is a publication's name, which is generally presented at the top of the first page (as in a newspaper) or on the cover (as in a magazine). It can also be a list of those involved with putting the publication together.

Titles of Articles, Columns, and Sections

Titles of individual articles are set within quotation marks and use headline-style capitalization. Names of regular newspaper columns and individual sections, however, are capitalized only.

In Maureen Dowd's recent column "Squeaker of the House," she lambastes Nancy Pelosi.

Calvin Trillin, writer of the Deadline Poet column, always inspires thought and laughter.

You can read all about it in the Metro section.

Online Sources

With the advent of the Internet and a whole huge host of electronic media, new rules have come about to treat works that are "published" online and electronically (such as on CD-ROM).

Titles of online sources are generally treated the same as printed works. Electronic books and book-length works are set in italics; shorter works such as articles, poems, and stories are set within quotation marks in regular type.

I read an excerpt of *Freakonomics* online.

The full text of "The Yellow Wallpaper" can be found on the Internet.

She used the CD-ROM version of *Merriam-Webster's Collegiate Dictionary*.

Websites

When listed in full, websites, or URLs, are set in regular type. Search engines, website names, and company names are set in regular type, but names of online publications should appear in italics or quotation marks just as they would if they were published in print. However, if a publication appears in print and online, a distinction should be made between the two sources. If individual pages of a website are titled, they should be set within quotation marks using headline-style capitalization.

Google News can be found at http://news.google.com/.

Online-only magazine: *Slate* is updated several times a day.

Online-only information site: Lots of good information can be found on Wikipedia.

Website: Check out www.comics.com for all the funnies.

Online newspaper: Read the archives on the *New York Times* website.

Company name: Search for a gift on Amazon.com.

Individual page: Visit the "Help" page on www.microsoft.com.

Note that the underlining shown here is for identification only. Web addresses and URLs are never underlined in nonelectronic documents. Commonly used on websites and other electronic documents, underlining signifies a hyperlink and is not related to the treatment of these sites in a printed work.

In general, when citation names include *.com*, they should be set in regular roman type. Titles of online publications should be treated exactly as their print counterparts.

Online-only magazine: "A tour de force. A must-read!" —*The Best Reviews*
Online news website: "An amazing literary feat!"—CNN.com
Online and print newspaper: "Spectacular characterizations."—*USA Today*

Note that **URLs** are not case sensitive, and full web addresses are generally given in all lowercase letters. However, capital letters can be added when necessary to enhance readability or avoid ambiguity, or if the site does require it (this is rare, but some are case-sensitive).

www.save-a-life.org
www.TangoDiva.com

WORDS TO GO . . . WORDS TO GO . . . WORDS TO GO

URL means uniform resource locator; also referenced as the universal resource locator.

SEE ALSO Chapter 13, "Citation"

Film, Television, and Radio Titles

Use italics when writing about movies, TV shows, and radio programs to distinguish them from the rest of the surrounding text.

the cinematic classic *Casablanca*
the sitcom *Friends*
This American Life is on the radio

Set a single episode of a TV or radio program in roman type within quotation marks.

Seinfeld's memorable "Yada Yada" episode
Did you see the "Isabella" episode of *The Sopranos*?

Channels and Network Names

Names of channels and networks as well as their call letters are also set in roman type.

the Independent Film Channel, or IFC
the local PBS affiliate, WHYY
Nickelodeon
Air America Radio shows

Works of Art

Paintings, drawings, photographs, sculptures, and other forms of artwork are set in italics when referred to by name.

Auguste Rodin's *The Thinker*
The Starry Night by Van Gogh

The names of regularly published cartoons and comic strips are also italicized.

The kooky cats of *Get Fuzzy* make me giggle.
Jill adores the *Peanuts* characters.

Works of Music

Titles of musical albums, operas, oratorios, and other long musical compositions are set in italics.

John Coltrane's jazz classic *A Love Supreme*
Two Beatles records are *Revolver* and *Rubber Soul*
Madame Butterfly, written by Puccini

Names of songs are set in regular type and enclosed in quotation marks. They should be capitalized in headline style.

Johnny Cash's hit song "Ring of Fire"
"On My Own" from the musical *Les Misérables*
The instrumental "Green Onions" by Booker T and the MGs

Works of classical music, including symphonies, quartets, and concertos, are generally capitalized but not italicized.

Beethoven's Ninth Symphony
Symphony no. 9
The 1812 Overture by Tchaikovsky

Names of Ships, Aircraft, and Other Vessels

Use italics and capital letters when naming ships, spacecraft, submarines, planes, and trains—but not automobiles.

the *Titanic*	the *Enola Gay*
the space shuttle *Discovery*	a Volkswagen Jetta

Note that the type of airplane and the abbreviations USS and HMS are not set in italics.

the Airbus A380	the USS *Intrepid*
a Boeing 767	

Emphasis and Identification

Italics have other uses that are a little more abstract than for identifying published works. You can use italics to place stress on an individual word or syllable, to show interior monologues or asides, and to highlight foreign or unusual terms or phrases.

Emphasis

In texts that discuss or define new terms or ideas, the first reference is often italicized for emphasis. This first occurrence is often a definition or explanation of the key term, and further references to it are set in regular type. Italicizing the term at its first use signals to the reader that this word or phrase is important and that it will likely recur throughout the text.

A *noun* is a person, place, or thing.
We'll examine two popular types of jazz: *bebop* and *swing*.

In dialogue and narration, italics are often used to emphasize certain words or syllables. This illustrates where we would place stress on a word if we were speaking.

Please, you *must* help me!
He asked you to do *what*?
I said we're evolving, not *de*volving.

Overusing italics in dialogue and narration this way can become distracting or even annoying to the reader. In many cases, the meaning of the sentence is clear without adding the italics. So be prudent, and use italics only to emphasize like this when it's warranted.

Sounds

When expressing the way something sounds with letters on a page, we tend to spell it phonetically and set it italic. This signals for the reader that something different is going on, that a sound is being represented by a word. Some onomatopoeic words are expressed without italics if the meaning is clear.

Marie fell onto the couch with a gentle *ooft*.

The silverware clattered to the floor with a loud *blaang*.

The dog's woof was fierce.

A snowball whirred by his head.

Thoughts

Interior monologue is often critical to understanding a character's motivation. Traditionally, thoughts that are not expressed out loud are shown in italics. You may occasionally see thoughts set in quotation marks or with no special treatment or additional punctuation at all, but these methods may cause trouble for the reader. Setting thoughts in italics clearly distinguishes them from the dialogue and from the narration. Note that words used to express interior thoughts should be in the present tense.

Just keep calm, Joe told himself as he approached the podium.

Betty believed she had fed the cat, but he meowed at her incessantly. *I must have forgotten*, she thought.

Foreign Words and Phrases

Italics are used to distinguish words or phrases in languages other than English. Many foreign words are commonly understood in English and, therefore, don't need to be italicized. Check your dictionary—if the word or phrase appears in the English dictionary, there's no need to set it in italics. If, however, it is a word or phrase that most English-speaking people wouldn't easily recognize, it ought to be set in italics.

Costa Rican people are known locally as *ticos*.

Order the *edamame* appetizer.

The soup du jour is lentil stew.

Carpe diem!

With Quotations

When using direct quotations from other sources, always replicate the quotation exactly as it appears in the original. If emphasis is needed for the sake of your argument, you can add your own italics. If you do this, though, you must also add an editorial note claiming the italicization as your own. The most common way to do this is to include a parenthetical comment after the quotation with the words *emphasis added*, *emphasis mine*, or *my emphasis*. You may also use *italics added*, *italics mine*, or *my italics*. Set this comment within square brackets inside the quotation itself or within parentheses after the quotation, or explain it in a footnote or endnote.

> After two years of waiting, we recoiled at the memory of his words: "It may take a week or maybe even a month, but *no longer than that* [emphasis mine]."

SEE ALSO 14.1, "Footnotes"

SEE ALSO 14.2, "Endnotes"

With Plural Terms

If a term is set in italics within regular text and used in the plural, the plural *-s* is not italicized because it's not part of the italicized term. Treat it as regular text.

> a stack of *Vogue*s on the table
> the leftover *New York Post*s

For ease of use and to avoid awkward construction, rephrasing the sentence to avoid the plural may be necessary.

> a stack of *Vogue* magazines on the table
> the leftover copies of the *New York Post*

SEE ALSO 7.1, "Plurals"

With Possessives

If a term is set in italics within regular text and used in the possessive, the possessive *-s* should not be italicized because it's not part of the italicized term. Treat it as regular text.

> one of *Newsweek'*s reporters
> the *Da Vinci Code'*s detractors

Avoid using the possessive -*s* with songs or other titles that are set within quotation marks. If it absolutely must be done, use -*'s* inside the quotation marks, never outside. Rephrase whenever possible to prevent the awkward construction.

> *Acceptable:* "London Calling's" bass part is hypnotic.
>
> *Preferred:* The bass part in "London Calling" is hypnotic.
>
> *Never: "London Calling"s bass part is hypnotic.*

SEE ALSO 7.2, "Possessives"

Words As Words

When a word or term is used as itself, set it off with italics. This is common when talking about a word rather than using it functionally in the context of the sentence.

> *Queso* means "cheese" in Spanish.
>
> Be careful not to confuse *that* with *which*.

Occasionally, it makes more sense to put these words or terms in quotation marks instead of italics, as demonstrated in the following example, where using italics would seemingly contradict the statement.

> Common phrases such as "joie de vivre" and "modus operandi" are not italicized.

Letters As Letters

When a letter is used to represent itself, italicize it.

> *Lion* begins with the letter *l*.
>
> We were in trouble with a capital *T*.

Two frequently used examples do not use italics and should always use lowercase letters.

> Remember your p's and q's.
>
> Always dot your i's and cross your t's.

When discussing grades as are given in school, use capital letters, set in regular roman type, pluralized with -*s* but no apostrophe.

> Carlos earned three As, two Bs, and one C.
>
> The teacher was notorious for giving Fs.

Letters As Shapes

When a letter is used to represent its shape, do not italicize it.

I pulled a U-turn.

Sophie made an O with her lips and whistled.

Italics Within Italics

If you have a scenario that requires italics to be set within italics, simply reverse the rules presented here. If a term or title needs to be set in italics within a block of text that is already italicized, set it in regular type to make it distinct.

I'd like to see Citizen Kane *because it's a classic*, he thought.

With Punctuation

When the main text of a sentence is treated one way (most often the main text is set roman) but punctuation that precedes or follows a word or small group of words must be set apart with special treatment (be that in bolded, italicized, or underlined text), the punctuation should match style with the whole of the sentence instead of the special-treatment word(s).

The exception is the exclamation mark. When an exclamation mark is used, followed by a close quotation mark, the exclamation mark takes the special treatment but the close quotation mark stands with the treatment of the rest of the sentence

9.2 BOLDFACE

Emphasis

Display

Boldface type is heavier and darker than regular type. Boldface type appears prominently on a page of text, standing out and demanding notice. At times boldface can be used instead of italics, but its use is best limited to display purposes, as too much bold on a page can be distracting to a reader.

Emphasis

In texts that discuss or define new terms or ideas, the first reference is often italicized for emphasis. In some works, though, these words or phrases may be better suited to boldface type. This book uses boldface for terms that are defined in sidebars for example. Sometimes this first occurrence may be a foreign-language term that's already set in italics. In such cases, it would be set bold and italic. Setting the term in boldface at first use signals to the reader that this word or phrase is important and that it will likely recur throughout the text. Further references to the term are set in regular type, unless the foreign term is italicized throughout.

> ***Blomster*** is the Danish word for "flower." Several types of *blomsters* exist.
>
> We'll examine two popular types of jazz: **bebop** and **swing**. Swing enjoyed a popular resurgence in the 1990s, but bebop did not.

There is no precedent for replacing italics with boldface type for titles of works or internal thoughts. In general, though, boldface type should be used sparingly in the body of the main text.

Display

Because boldface type stands out prominently on the page, its primary function is to differentiate display type from regular type. Headings and subheadings may be displayed in bold to introduce a new section. Terms in a dictionary or glossary often appear in boldface, to set them off from their definitions.

> **glossary.** A collection of special terms with their meanings.

SEE ALSO 6.1, "Use of Punctuation"

SEE ALSO 14.3, "Glossaries"

9.3 SMALL CAPITALS

Times and Dates

Signs

Display

Small capitals are exactly that—capital letters set smaller than ordinary capital letters. They are usually used for abbreviations and display type.

Compare SMALL CAPS to FULL CAPS.

Woe is the much beleaguered small capital letter! Time has not been kind to our petite friend, as its many uses are slowly being phased out. Formal writing still tends to rely on the trusty small capital; but for lighter or less formal texts, the small capital has gone the way of *shall* and *whom*. This occurs as more and more funky typefaces are made available for the writer who wishes to express creativity not only in words but also in the lettering itself.

SEE ALSO 9.4, "Serif versus Sans Serif"

Times and Dates

Abbreviations used to distinguish times of day and eras are set in small capitals with periods.

She arrived at 8 A.M.
His flight was scheduled for 6:45 P.M.
Julius Caesar lived from 100–44 B.C.
Christopher Columbus died in A.D. 1506.

Signs

Traditionally, any text that displayed a sign or notice was set off in small capitals to differentiate it from the surrounding text. This style is meant to represent how the words on the actual sign would likely appear, in prominent capital letters.

A BEWARE OF DOG sign hung in the window.
The restaurant door warned NO SHIRT, NO SHOES, NO SERVICE.

However, more recent style calls for initial capitals only, following the standard headline-style method. Longer notices read more easily in quotation style.

A Beware of Dog sign hung in the window.

The restaurant door warned No Shirt, No Shoes, No Service.

The bottom of the receipt declares "Parties of six or more will automatically be charged an 18 percent gratuity."

Either style is considered appropriate, as long as it is used consistently throughout the text.

Display

Because small capitals stand out prominently on the page, they are often used for display type to distinguish the text from regular type. Headings and subheadings may be displayed in small capitals to introduce a new section. Terms in a glossary often appear in small capitals, to set them off from their definitions.

SEE ALSO 14.3, "Glossaries"

9.4 SERIF VERSUS SANS SERIF

Most word-processing programs contain a number of different fonts. This offers flexibility in designing your document, but the two main types have distinctly different uses: *serif* and *sans serif*.

Merriam-Webster's Collegiate Dictionary defines a serif typeface as one with "any of the short lines stemming from and at an angle to the upper and lower ends of the strokes of a letter." Serif fonts are generally considered easier to read because the letters are more recognizable and more closely resemble handwritten letters. Long blocks of text should always be set in serif. For example, the main body of this text is set in a serif typeface.

Conversely, a sans serif typeface is one without serifs (*sans* means "without"). These fonts are usually reserved for headings and other prominent display type, such as an excerpt or some element that needs to be otherwise set off from the main text. Although sans serif fonts frequently appear on the Internet and in e-mails, they should be avoided for long blocks of printed text.

Look at the font examples in the following table—by far not a complete list, but enough to show the variety of standard fonts available on most word-processing programs. Notice how the letters are different sizes and are spaced differently both horizontally and vertically. The spacing between letters is called *leading* in typography terms. These font differences help to determine how your work will appear and ultimately how readable the text is.

Serif Fonts	Sans Serif Fonts
Bodoni	Arial
Celestia Antiqua	**Arial Black**
Century	**Charcoal**
Courier New	Comic Sans MS
Garamond	Franklin Gothic
Goudy	**Impact**
Janson	Lucida Sans
Palatino Linotype	Monaco
Times New Roman	Verdana

The default typeface in most word-processing programs is Times New Roman for its highly readable appearance. (Macs use a nearly identical font called Times Roman, due to licensing and trademark variances.)

Most fonts, both serif and sans serif, also have a distinctive look for italics. The serifs tend to be more elaborate in italics.

Serif Italic Fonts	Sans Serif Italic Fonts
Bodoni	*Arial*
Celestia Antiqua	***Arial Black***
Century	***Charcoal***
Courier New	*Comic Sans MS*
Garamond	*Franklin Gothic*
Goudy	***Impact***
Janson	*Lucida Sans*
Palatino Linotype	*Monaco*
Times New Roman	*Verdana*

9.5 UNDERLINING

Underlines tend to be used either to show emphasis or to show that something is missing.

Emphasis: The turkey was dry, dry, dry.
Fill in the blank: I want to _____.

Occasionally, the font that is being used will not have a traditional italic option, or the ital will be next to impossible to distinguish from the regular font, or there will be no italic option at all. In such cases, it is perfectly acceptable to use underlining (also called underscoring) to indicate the title of a work such as that of a book, journal, newspaper, movie, CD, etc.

His life changed forever with the publication of Helter Skelter.

Throughout this chapter, I've covered the treatment of special type, including italics, boldface, small capitals, serif and sans serif, and underlines.

10

SPELLING AND ABBREVIATIONS

10.1 Spelling

10.2 Word Choices

10.3 Abbreviations

10.1 SPELLING

Word Parts

Contractions

Synonyms and Antonyms

Spelling Challenges

Even if you're a good speller, I encourage you to look up spellings whenever you have the smallest doubt about a word's correct spelling. If you compare the entries of more than one dictionary, you might find spelling variations. Get a good dictionary you can count on (I prefer *Merriam-Webster's Collegiate Dictionary*, 11th edition), and don't be afraid to use it—often.

Word Parts

Words frequently have multiple parts: the root word, prefixes, and/or suffixes. Understanding the roles of these main word parts will be a help to you as you're choosing the right word or tense of the word.

Root Words

A root word is the most basic form of a word. The root word is where the word's **lexical meaning** originates. *Play* is the root word in all of the following words. Although the meanings change from word to word, the root—the lexical meaning—remains the same:

play	player	replayed
playability	playful	replaying
playable	playing	
played	plays	

WORDS TO GO . . . WORDS TO GO . . . WORDS TO GO

Lexical meaning is the basic essential meaning of the root of a word.

Prefixes

A prefix is a standardized group of syllables that is added to the beginning of a word root to cause a change in the word's meaning.

Prefix	Meaning	Root Word	New Word
semi-	half of	annual	semiannual
uni-	having one	cycle	unicycle
counter-	the opposite of	weight	counterweight

Some of the prefixes demonstrate a change in quantity, some show a negation, some show time reference, and others identify a change in direction or position.

Role	Prefix	Meaning
Quantity change	*deca-*	ten
	quad-	four
	milli-	thousand
Negation	*a-*	no, not, without
	de-	the opposite of, remove
	mis-	bad, wrongly
Time reference	*ante-*	before
	pre-	before
	re-	again
Direction/position change	*super-*	above, over
	sub-	below, under
	co-	with

Compound words created with prefixes are usually closed compounds, regardless of whether they're nouns, verbs, adjectives, or adverbs. Hyphens do need to be used to connect the prefix and the word root if the root word is a proper noun and begins with a capital or if the prefix is connected to a numeral.

post-Elizabethan

post-1965

The following table lists most if not all prefixes along with an example for each.

Prefixes

a-	asexual	*hyper-*	hypercharged
ab-	abstract	*hypo-*	hypodermic
ad-	advance	*il-*	illegal
ant-	antacid	*im-*	immoral
ante-	antebellum	*in-*	intact
anti-	anti-American	*infra-*	infrared
be-	bewitch	*inter-*	interplanetary
bi-	biweekly	*intra-*	intradermal
bio-	biography	*ir-*	irregular
centi-	centipede	*kilo-*	kiloton
co-	cohost	*macro-*	macrobiotic
col-	collude	*mega-*	megahit
com-	complete	*meta-*	metaplasia
con-	contrast	*micro-*	microscope
contra-	contrapuntist	*mid-*	midway
cor-	corrode	*milli-*	milliampere
counter-	counterweight	*mini-*	miniskirt
cyber-	cybernaut	*mono-*	monolayer
de-	denote	*multi-*	multihued
dec-	declineation	*neo-*	neoplasm
deca-	decasyllabic	*non-*	nonissue
demi-	demigod	*ob-*	obovate
di-	dioxide	*oct-*	octane
dia-	diameter	*octo-*	octoroon
dicho-	dichogamous	*out-*	outhouse
dis-	disagree	*over-*	overage
em-	embattled	*penta-*	Pentateuch
en-	enthrone	*peri-*	periscope
ex-	exclaim	*photo-*	photograph
exo-	exoskeleton	*post-*	postseason
extra-	extraordinary	*pre-*	preview
hect-	hectare	*pro-*	proventriculus
hemi-	hemisphere	*proto-*	prototype
hepta-	heptameter	*pseudo-*	pseudonym
hexa-	hexagram	*quad-*	quadrangle

Prefixes			
quasi-	quasiparticle	*sym-*	symmetry
quint-	quintuplet	*syn-*	synesthesia
re-	recycle	*tele-*	telephoto
semi-	semiannual	*trans-*	transfix
sex-	sextet	*tri-*	trimonthly
socio-	sociopath	*ultra-*	ultraviolet
sub-	subset	*un-*	unnecessary
super-	supersize	*under-*	underhanded
supra-	supraorbital	*uni-*	unibrow

Suffixes

A suffix is a group of syllables that attach to the end of a word and adjust the meaning. When a suffix changes, the part the word plays changes also. The words become different adjectives, adverbs, nouns, and verbs.

Suffix	Meaning	Root Word	New Word
-ly	like	dry	dryly
-aholic	compulsive need	work	workaholic
-ful	full of	wonder	wonderful

The uses of some suffixes are clear clues to determining the parts of speech for many words. A few of these are identified as follows:

Noun suffixes:

agitation	misery	presidency
casement	nationalist	randomness
discussion	neighborhood	reference
kingdom	operator	socialist
miner	pessimism	

Verb suffixes:

agitate	nationalize
harden	purify

Adjective suffixes:

adoptive	gigantic	presidential
edible	miserable	selfish

fibrous	national	useless
friendly	petulant	wonderful

Adverb suffixes:

friendly	gaily	sweetly

The *-ly* suffix is the only suffix that can be counted on to regularly be adverbial. (If you remember from Chapter 3, though, the *-ly* suffix can also be an adjective.)

SEE ALSO 3.1, "Adjectives"

The following table contains an extensive list of suffixes and examples for each.

Suffixes			
-able	notable	*-cide*	suicide
-ad	triad	*-city*	atrocity
-ade	orangeade	*-cy*	literacy
-age	marriage	*-cycle*	tricycle
-agogy	pedagogy	*-dom*	kingdom
-aholic	workaholic	*-ectomy*	hysterectomy
-al	refusal	*-ed*	cited
-ality	personality	*-ee*	employee
-an	republican	*-eer*	engineer
-ance	annoyance	*-en*	written
-ancy	redundancy	*-ence*	dependence
-ant	pleasant	*-ency*	currency
-ar	liar	*-ent*	permanent
-arch	monarch	*-eous*	courteous
-archy	hierarchy	*-er*	employer
-ard	drunkard	*-ergy*	synergy
-ary	ordinary	*-ern*	Southern
-ate	advocate	*-ery*	nunnery
-athlon	decathlon	*-ese*	legalese
-ation	narration	*-esque*	picturesque
-ative	creative	*-ess*	actress
-atory	lavatory	*-etic*	frenetic
-bound	homebound	*-etics*	phonetics
-centesis	amniocentesis	*-ette*	dinette

Suffixes

-fare	welfare	*-man*	statesman
-ful	beautiful	*-mania*	pyromania
-gnosis	prognosis	*-ment*	development
-gon	pentagon	*-metry*	geometry
-gry	angry	*-mony*	ceremony
-hedron	pentahedron	*-most*	innermost
-hood	neighborhood	*-ness*	likeness
-ia	mania	*-ogram*	cardiogram
-iable	variable	*-ography*	oceanography
-ial	special	*-oholic*	alcoholic
-ian	Iranian	*-oid*	planetoid
-iant	deviant	*-ologist*	archaeologist
-ible	edible	*-ology*	herbology
-ibly	terribly	*-onomy*	taxonomy
-ic	electronic	*-onym*	synonym
-ical	hysterical	*-or*	actor
-id	tepid	*-ory*	sensory
-ier	cashier	*-osis*	psychosis
-ile	textile	*-ous*	disastrous
-ing	ending	*-phobia*	acrophobia
-ion	companion	*-phone*	telephone
-ious	delicious	*-phyte*	neophyte
-ish	selfish	*-s*	reds
-ism	pessimism	*-scope*	kaleidoscope
-ist	socialist	*-script*	manuscript
-ite	graphite	*-ship*	friendship
-itis	gingivitis	*-sion*	delusion
-itude	gratitude	*-some*	threesome
-ity	normality	*-ster*	gangster
-ium	premium	*-t*	dreamt
-ive	reactive	*-th*	eleventh
-ization	categorization	*-tion*	action
-less	hapless	*-ty*	loyalty
-like	childlike	*-uary*	sanctuary
-ly	lately	*-ulent*	virulent

continues

continued

Suffixes

-uous	sensuous	*-ways*	sideways
-vore	herbivore	*-wise*	counterclockwise
-ward	backward	*-word*	afterword
-ware	bakeware	*-y*	cheesy

Contractions

Contractions are succinct versions of combined-word expressions with an apostrophe in place of the letters that have been removed.

ain't = are not, am not, is not, etc.

aren't = are not

didn't = did not

don't = do not

doesn't = does not

can't = can not, cannot

hadn't = had not

hasn't = has not

haven't = have not

he'll = he will

he's = he is

I'm = I am

isn't = is not

it's = it is

'tis = it is

shan't = shall not

she'll = she will

she's = she is

they'll = they will

they're = they are

they've = they have

wasn't = was not

we're = we are

weren't = were not

who's = who is

you're = you are, you were

Synonyms and Antonyms

A synonym is a word that can replace another word. Although there are few instances where the replacement words will have the exact same meaning, these rather interchangeable words manage to take the place of the originals without changing their meaning in a drastic or significant sense. For example, *frigid* is synonymous with *cold*.

An antonym is a word with an opposite meaning. For example, the antonym of *cold* is *hot*.

Word	Synonyms	Antonyms
able	capable, qualified	incompetent, unable
abnormal	odd, peculiar, unusual	average, normal, usual
above	atop, higher than, over	below, beneath, under
absolute	complete, whole	incomplete, limited, partial
absurd	foolish, laughable, ridiculous, silly	reasonable, sensible, sound
abundance	ampleness, copiousness, plenty	dearth, scarcity, want
accept	admit, allow, consent to, receive, take	ignore, refuse, reject
accord	agree, concur	difference, disagreement
adjacent	near, nearby, next to	apart, distant, separate
alarm	dismay, fear, fright	calm, comfort, soothe
amaze	astonish, astound, dumbfound, stun, surprise	bore, disinterest, tire
anguish	agony, distress, misery, pain, suffering	ecstasy, happiness, joy, pleasure
awkward	clumsy, crude, graceless	deft, elegant, graceful, skilled
baffle	confuse, mystify, puzzle	enlighten, inform
banish	dismiss, exile, expel	admit, embrace, receive, welcome
beautiful	attractive, lovely, pretty	homely, ugly, unattractive
begin	commence, inaugurate, initiate, start	end, finish, stop, terminate
blossom	bloom, flower	dwindle, fade, shrink, wither
brazen	bold, brassy, immodest, impudent, insolent, rude, shameless	modest, retiring, self-effacing, shy
broad-minded	liberal, open-minded, tolerant	bigoted, narrow-minded, petty, prejudiced
calm	mild, peaceful, serene	disturbed, roiled, tempestuous
cheerful	cheery, gay, happy, joyful, merry	downhearted, gloomy, morose, sad

continues

continued

Word	Synonyms	Antonyms
coincidence	accident, chance	plan, plant, scheme
come	advance, approach, arrive, near, reach	depart, go, leave, split, take off
confuse	baffle, bewilder, jumble, mislead, mystify, perplex, puzzle	clarify, distinguish, edify, enlighten, illuminate
corrupt	crooked, dishonest, treacherous	honest, scrupulous, upright
curse	ban, oath	benediction, blessing
decide	choose, determine	hesitate, waver
deft	adept, adroit, clever, dexterous, handy	awkward, clumsy, inept, maladroit
dismay	alarm, discourage, dishearten, frighten, scare	encourage, hearten
disrespectful	cheeky, fresh, impolite, impertinent, impudent	courteous, polite, respectful
dreary	cheerless, chilling, depressing, dismal, gloomy	bright, cheery, cheerful, encouraging, hopeful
elegant	choice, cultivated, fine, refined, tasteful	coarse, crude, tasteless, unpolished
enormous	colossal, gargantuan, gigantic, huge, immense, stupendous, vast	diminutive, small, tiny, infinitesimal, slight
expend	consume, exhaust, use	conserve, ration, reserve
fierce	ferocious, furious, savage, violent, wild	gentle, harmless, peaceful
freedom	independence, liberty	bondage, servitude, slavery
friend	acquaintance, chum, companion, crony, mate, pal	enemy, foe
future	approaching, coming, destined, imminent, impending, to come	bygone, former, past, past-tense, post
gather	accumulate, assemble, collect	dispel, disperse, scatter
gay	cheerful, gleeful, happy, joyful, merry	mournful, sad, somber, sorrowful

Word	Synonyms	Antonyms
gracious	courteous, friendly, kind, polite	discourteous, impolite, rude, thoughtless
great	big, distinguished, enormous, gigantic, huge, immense, large	diminutive, insignificant, small, trivial
guilty	blameworthy, culpable, responsible	blameless, guiltless, innocent
haggard	careworn, drawn, worn	animated, bright, bright-eyed, clear-eyed, fresh
headstrong	obstinate, stubborn, willful	amenable, easygoing
healthy	hale, hearty, robust, sound, strong, vigorous, wholesome	ill, sick, unhealthy, unwholesome
honor	character, distinction, esteem, honesty, principle, respect, uprightness	dishonor, disgrace, shame
hungry	famished, starved	full, glutted, sated
identical	alike, indistinguishable, like, same	different, opposite, unalike
improper	inappropriate, unfit, unsuitable	appropriate, fitting, proper
increase	broaden, enlarge, extend, greaten, grow, lengthen, prolong, swell	decrease, diminish, lessen, shrink
intelligent	alert, astute, bright, clever, quick, smart, wise	challenged, dumb, slow, stupid, unintelligent
join	assemble, attach, connect, couple, fit, link, rejoin, unite	divide, separate, split, sunder
juvenile	babyish, childish, puerile	adult, mature
kind	affectionate, friendly, gentle, goodhearted, kindhearted, kindly, mild, tender, warm, warmhearted	brutal, cruel, hardhearted, mean

continues

continued

Word	Synonyms	Antonyms
lack	dearth, need, scarcity, shortage, want	abundance, plentiful, profusion, quantity
lazy	idle, inactive, indolent, slothful, sluggish	active, ambitious, forceful
liberate	deliver, free, loose, release	confine, imprison, jail
light-headed	dizzy, frivolous, giddy, silly	clear-headed, rational, sober
lighthearted	carefree, cheerful, gay, glad, happy, merry	melancholy, sad, serious, solemn, somber
lose	mislay, misplace	discover, find, locate, place
luxurious	deluxe, lavish, rich, splendid	crude, simple, sparse, spartan
male	manly, masculine, virile	female, feminine, womanly
maybe	perhaps, possibly	decidedly, definitely
mingle	blend, combine, mix	separate, sort
moist	clammy, damp, dank, humid, muggy, wet	arid, dry, parched
mutinous	rebellious, revolutionary, unruly	compliant, dutiful, obedient
nasty	dirty, disagreeable, disgusting, filthy, foul, improper, indecent, loathsome, obscene, unpleasant	clean, decent, fair, even-tempered, pleasant, proper, pure
noble	dignified, honorable, honest, upright	base, dishonest, ignoble, lowborn
nourishment	food, nutriment, support, sustenance	deprivation, starvation
object	complain, disapprove of, protest	agree, approve, assent
offend	anger, annoy, displease, irritate, provoke, vex	delight, flatter, please

Word	Synonyms	Antonyms
outrageous	contemptible, disgraceful, gross, offensive, shameful, shameless, shocking	prudent, reasonable, sensible
pain	ache, agony, distress, misery, pang, suffering, torment	comfort, delight, ease, joy
personal	private, secret	general, open, public
pleasant	agreeable, enjoyable, nice, pleasurable, satisfactory, satisfying	difficult, disagreeable, horrid, nasty, sour, unpleasant
poverty	destitution, distress, indigence, need, pennilessness, want	abundance, comfort, fruitfulness, richness, wealth
prudent	careful, discreet, sensible, wise	foolhardy, foolish, rash, reckless
quarrelsome	disagreeable, edgy, irritable, peevish, snappish, testy	even-tempered, genial
quiet	hush, mute, silent, soundless, still	boisterous, loud, noisy
radiant	beaming, bright, brilliant, shining	dark, dim, lusterless
rambling	disjointed, erratic, incoherent	coherent, straightforward
remarkable	extraordinary, noteworthy, special, uncommon, unusual	average, commonplace, ordinary
rude	coarse, crude, ill-mannered, impertinent, impolite, impudent, uncivil, unmannerly	courteous, cultivated, polished
rural	agricultural, backwoods, country, farm, pastoral, rustic	citified, urban
sacred	consecrated, divine, hallowed, holy	blasphemous, profane
serene	calm, peaceful, quiet, tranquil	agitated, stormy, turbulent

continues

10.1

continued

Word	Synonyms	Antonyms
shrill	piercing, sharp	muffled, muted, quiet
spirited	active, animated, energetic, excited, lively, vigorous	indolent, lazy, sleepy
strife	conflict, difference, disagreement, quarrel, unrest	concord, peace, tranquility
sweet	honeyed, sugary	bitter, sour
sympathetic	compassionate, considerate, kind, tender	indifferent, intolerant, unsympathetic
tardy	late, overdue	prompt, punctual, timely
thrive	flourish, grow, prosper, succeed	die, expire, languish
toil	labor, slave, sweat, work	loll, relax
tranquil	calm, peaceful, quiet, undisturbed	agitated, disturbed, upset
triumph	conquest, success, victory	defeat, failure
unassuming	humble, modest, retiring	arrogant, pompous, showy, vain
uncertain	doubtful, dubious, indefinite, questionable, unsure, vague	certain, positive, unmistakable
urge	drive, force, press, prod, push	discourage, dissuade
vacant	empty, stupid, thoughtless, vacuous, vapid	alert, bright, filled, intelligent, occupied
village	hamlet, municipality, town	city, metropolis
voluntary	free, optional, spontaneous	compulsory, forced, required
warm	heated, lukewarm, temperate, tepid	brisk, cold, cool

Word	Synonyms	Antonyms
wealthy	affluent, prosperous, rich, well-to-do	destitute, impoverished, poor, poverty-stricken
wrong	false, inaccurate, incorrect	accurate, correct, right
young	immature, youthful	grown, mature, old
youngster	child, stripling, youth	adult, grownup

Spelling Challenges

A good dictionary is the writer's best friend. But it won't do anyone any good unless you understand how to use it—and actually do use it. When choosing between more than one spelling option for a specific term, the main considerations are for the ease of comprehension and for a consistency of use. Both of these will benefit your audience.

Preferred Spellings

It's important to be consistent with spelling choices throughout the writing of an article, a paper, or a book. In general, always use the preferred spelling option (listed first) in a good dictionary. It's most important that, whatever spelling choices are made, they be used consistently throughout the whole of the piece whenever used.

A brief list of preferred spellings and their secondary spellings follows. Quite often, the secondary spelling is the British spelling style. As always, the best way to confirm the preferred spelling is to check your dictionary.

Preferred Spellings	Secondary Spellings
acknowledgment	acknowledgement
canceled	cancelled
center	centre
color	colour
goodbye	good-bye/good-by
humor	humour
judgment	judgement
realize	realise
theater	theatre
traveled	travelled

Commonly Misspelled Words

A lot of words are commonly misspelled. Whenever you are unsure about a spelling, you can always check your dictionary. Here I've provided a list of some commonly misspelled words.

Correct Spelling	Incorrect Spelling
absorption	asorbtion
abundance	abundence
accessible	accessable
accidentally	accidently
athlete	athelete
athletics	atheletics
brand-new	brand new
bureaucracy	buraucracy
changeable	changable
disastrous	disasterous
eighth	eigth
embarrass	embarass
government	goverment
height	hight
heroes	heros
history	histery
innocuous	inocuous
irrelevant	irrevelent
library	libery
mischievous	mischieveous
manageable	managable
nuclear	nuculer
perform	preform
recognize	reconize
representative	representive
sacrilegious	sacreligious
strictly	strickly
temperament	temprament
twelfth	twelvth
unanimous	unanimus
wholly	wholely
width	with

10.2 WORD CHOICES

A* versus *An

Accept* versus *Except

Affect* versus *Effect

Awhile* versus *A while

Ensure* versus *Insure

Farther* versus *Further

Fewer* versus *Less

Imply* versus *Infer

Indict* versus *Indite

Lay* versus *Lie

Resume* versus *Résumé

-Ward/-Word* versus *-Wards/-Words

Who* versus *Whom

Avoiding Wordiness

Some words are so similar in spelling that they're frequently mistaken and misused for the other. Let's look at some examples and their meanings so you can avoid misusing these, too.

A versus *An*

Each of these articles references one of something. However, the decision about which to use depends on the word following the article. Use *a* in front of all words that start with a consonant sound. Use *an* in front of all words that start with a vowel sound. Note it's the *sound* of the word following the article that matters, not necessarily the first letter of the word itself. This means that for words beginning with a silent *h*—a consonant—you would use *an*.

a kid	an elephant
a horse	an hour

Accept versus *Except*

These words are both pronounced differently and hold different meanings. *Accept* is a verb that means "to receive," "to give admittance or approval," or "to agree with." On the other hand, *except* can be used as either a verb, meaning "to omit," "to exempt," or "to exclude," or as a preposition meaning "other than." When used as a preposition, the word *for* can often be found accompanying the word *except*. Finally, *except* may also be used as a conjunction on occasion. When used as a conjunction, *except* holds these meanings: "unless," "with this exception," or "only."

Accept (verb): He was very willing to accept the offer.

Except (verb): She really wanted all of them except the three in the window.

Except (preposition): I can go anytime except now.

The apartment was great except for the lack of a bathroom.

Except (conjunction): No good awaits except if you repent.

The apartment was unobtainable except with a 25 percent deposit.

She wouldn't accept anything except the very best.

Affect versus *Effect*

These oftentimes confused terms have very different meanings. The word *affect* is almost always used as a verb and means "to influence" or "to cause a response." *Affect* is used as a noun only to identify a psychological term meaning "feeling." On the flip side, the word *effect* can be used as both noun and verb. As a noun, effect means "result" and as a verb it means "to cause."

Affect (verb): The outcome will affect his future.

Affect (noun): The girls showed an amazing lack of affect.

Effect (verb): Low mortgage rates effected the market.

Effect (noun): The effect was minimally invasive.

Awhile versus *A While*

The meaning of *awhile* has an implied *for* preceding it, as in *for awhile*. That's how you can test whether to close *a* and *while* into one word or to keep it as two. If you can add the *for*, keep it as one word.

I have to go to the office awhile.

I already went a while ago.

For awhile works in the first example; it doesn't in the second example. When the *for* is explicitly stated in the writing, there's no need for the implication of it, so the *a* and *while* can remain as two separate words.

Ensure versus *Insure*

Although treated synonymously, *ensure* and *insure* do have their own distinctive uses. Both words mean "to make sure or certain," but *insure* includes the additional meaning of "to guard against loss." Think *insurance*.

I need you to ensure that the package is insured.

Farther versus *Further*

Farther is used to indicate actual, physical distance. *Further* is more conceptual and means "additional." If the discussion deals with actual, physical distance, the choice has to be *farther*. But if I can substitute the word *more*, then I use the word *further*.

She traveled twelve miles farther than he did.
Let me know if you want to discus this further.

Fewer versus *Less*

These two words, *fewer* and *less*, each identify that a comparison is taking place with something that has a greater or larger number, amount, or quantity of some sort.

The word *fewer* is the word to use whenever referencing numbers or countable amounts.

There are fewer mustangs roaming wild these days.
He bought the house with fewer neighbors.

The word *less* is used in other ways: (1) To describe materials, (2) with abstract concepts, and (3) with matters involving degree or value.

(1) There is less MSG in Chinese food these days.
(2) Politicians show less concern for the people.
(3) Four is less than five but more than three.

Imply versus *Infer*

Imply is used to indicate that something is only hinted at and isn't stated explicitly. The word *infer* means that a conclusion is being drawn from statements, evidence, or circumstances.

I infer from what you imply that you aren't happy.

Indict versus *Indite*

Although pronounced the same, the meanings of these two words are very different. *Indict* is a verb that means "to accuse or legally charge with an offense or a crime." *Indite* is a verb that means "to write or compose."

> The court allowed the DA to **indict** the forger and plagiarizer for brazenly daring to **indite** and sell a poem as if he had the right.

Lay versus *Lie*

Lay means "to set" or "to place," while *lie* means "to recline."

> I need to lay that down before I lie down.

The *lay* tenses include *lay*, *laid*, *laying*. The tenses for *lie* are *lie*, *lay*, *lain*, *lying*.

Resume versus *Résumé*

Resume means "to start again." If you add the accents, you get *résumé*, which means "a summary."

> Let's resume the review of the résumés.

-Ward/*-Word* versus *-Wards*/*-Words*

The preferred style for these suffixes is to not have the *-s* tagged on at the end.

afterward	backward	frontward
afterword	foreword	toward
awkward	forward	upward

Who versus *Whom*

The rules for deciding between *who* and *whom* are fairly basic: *Who* is presented as the subject of a verb, while *whom* is used as the object of a verb or preposition.

> I don't know who that is.
> The call was for whom?

Who is overtaking *whom* in today's common language. Very often, when *whom* would be more correct, *who* is being used because it sounds and seems more natural as *whom* is considered to be far too formal.

Avoiding Wordiness

If less is indeed more, then the challenge for each writer is to convey his or her meaning without using an excess of words. Study the following list to avoid wordiness in your writing.

Unnecessarily Wordy	Succinct
a span of time	time
planning in advance	planning
am/is/are going to	will/shall
am of the opinion	believe
as a result of	because
if and when	if
at the present time	now
before very long	soon
by the time	when
meet up with	meet
due to the fact that/in as much as/insofar as/ in view of/the fact that	since
in order to	to
in the event that	if
I would appreciate it	please
with undefined specifics	indefinite

10.3 ABBREVIATIONS

Title and Degree Abbreviations

Time and Date Abbreviations

Other Everyday Abbreviations

Biblical Abbreviations

Geographical Abbreviations

Acronyms

Shortened Forms

An **abbreviation** is the shortened form of a word or a word phrase and can be used instead of the word itself.

In order to clearly communicate the meaning of the abbreviation, it is very helpful for the writer to provide the actual word or words for the first mention. To complete the identification, the abbreviation that will substitute from that point on can be placed within parentheses and placed directly following the full word or phrase.

Abbreviations are very often used to avoid cluttering up a section of writing with the repetition of especially unwieldy words or phrases. This is particularly true where space is at a premium, such as within bibliographies, endnotes and footnotes sections, and lists and columns.

Abbreviations can be treated in many ways. As mentioned, the full word often is used at the first mention of the word or words. The abbreviation can substitute from that point on. And although the trend seems to be to do away with periods and any special treatment of abbreviations, the preference of this book is to hold strong and continue to present in the traditional form—with periods.

Title and Degree Abbreviations

Many specific abbreviations are universally accepted. The following examples are almost always used in their abbreviated forms. This is true especially when attached to a personal name.

Abbreviation	Meaning
B.A.	bachelor of arts
D.D.S.	doctor of dental surgery
Dr.	doctor
D.V.M.	doctor of veterinary medicine
Ed.D.	doctor of education
Esq.	esquire
Gen.	general
Hon.	honorable
H.R.H.	her royal highness
Jr.	junior
M.A.	master of arts
M.D.	doctor of medicine
M.P.	military police or member of Parliament
Mr.	mister
Mrs.	missus
Ms.	miz
Msgr.	monsignor
Ph.D.	doctor of philosophy
Prof.	professor
Rep.	representative
Rev.	reverend
Sen.	senator
Sr.	senior
St.	saint

Time and Date Abbreviations

There's a long history and strong tradition of treating the abbreviations for years and time references as small caps with periods. Although some recent resources omit the periods and small caps, this book holds fast to the traditional styling approach, using small capitalization and periods.

The traditional approach is outlined in the following examples. Note all are set in small capitals with periods.

Time Abbreviation	Meaning
A.M.	ante meridiem
P.M.	post meridiem

Date Abbreviation	Meaning
A.D.	*anno Domini*
A.H.	*anno Hegirae*
B.C.	before Christ
B.C.E.	before the Christian Era *or* before the Common Era
C.E.	Common Era

A.D. (*anno Domini*): The translated meaning is "in the year of the Lord." This abbreviation is used to show that a time falls within the Christian Era. The Christian Era is the period of time that comes after the birth of Christ.

A.H. (*anno Hegirae*): The translated meaning is "in the year of the Hegira." This abbreviation is used to indicate a time division that falls within the Islamic Era. The Islamic Era is the era used in Muslim countries for numbering the Islamic calendar years ever since the Hegira, which was Muhammad's flight from Mecca in A.D. 622.

B.C.: This abbreviation means "before Christ." This means a reference to the years prior to the birth of Christ.

B.C.E.: This abbreviation means "before the Christian Era" or "before the Common Era."

C.E.: This abbreviation makes reference to the "Common Era."

All these abbreviations follow the year citation except for A.D. and A.H., both of which precede the year.

> In A.D. 330, Constantinople became the capital of the Roman Empire.
>
> It wasn't until third century B.C. that sugar arrived in the Middle East from India.

Other Everyday Abbreviations

Abbreviation	Meaning
abbr.	abbreviation
adj.	adjective
ad lib.	*ad libitum*
a.k.a.	also known as
anon.	anonymous
bib.	biblical, bibliography
chap.	chapter
col.	column
conj.	conjunction
cont.	continued
def.	definition
dept.	department
dict.	dictionary
div.	division
ea.	each
ed.	edition, editor
e.g.	*exempli gratia* (for example)
encyc.	encyclopedia
Eng.	English
eng.	engineer
esp.	especially
et al.	*et alia* (and others)
etc.	*et cetera* (and so forth)
ex.	example
fem.	female, feminine
fig.	figure
HQ	headquarters
ibid.	ibidem (in the same place)
ID	identification
i.e.	*id est* (that is)
infin.	infinitive
interj.	interjection
intro.	introduction

continues

continued

Abbreviation	Meaning
lang.	language
lit.	literature
masc.	masculine
misc.	miscellaneous
n.b.	*nota bene* (take careful note)
neg.	negative
no.	number
non seq.	*non sequitur* (it does not follow)
obs.	obsolete
op. cit.	*opere citato* (in the work cited)
p., pg.	page
para.	paragraph
part.	participle
pl.	plural
P.P.S.	*post postscriptum* (later postscript)
prep.	preposition
pron.	pronoun
pro tem.	*pro tempore* (for the time being)
P.S.	*postscriptum* (postscript)
pt.	part
RIP	*requiescat in pace* (may s/he rest in peace)
RSVP	*respondez s'il vous plaît*
sec.	section
sing.	singular
Span.	Spanish
subj.	subject
syn.	synonym
trans.	translator, translated by
univ.	university
vol.	volume
v., versus	versus
yr.	year
web, www	World Wide Web

Biblical Abbreviations

The Bible has its own set of abbreviations, including the versions and the books of the Bible.

BIBLE VERSIONS

Abbreviation	Meaning
KJV	King James Version
NLT	New Living Translation
NIV	New International Version
TNIV	Today's New International Version
JB	Jerusalem Bible
NEB	New English Bible
Apoc.	Apocrypha

THE BOOKS OF THE OLD TESTAMENT (OT)

Abbreviation(s)	Meaning
Gen.	Genesis
Ex./Exod.	Exodus
Lev.	Leviticus
Num.	Numbers
Deut.	Deuteronomy
Josh.	Joshua
Judg.	Judges
Ruth	Ruth
I and II Sam.	I and II Samuel
I and II Kings	I and II Kings
I and II Chron.	I and II Chronicles
Ezra	Ezra
Neh.	Nehemiah
Esther	Esther
Job	Job
Ps.	Psalms
Prov.	Proverbs
Eccles.	Ecclesiastes
Song	Song of Solomon

continues

continued

Abbreviation(s)	Meaning
Isa.	Isaiah
Jer.	Jeremiah
Lam.	Lamentations
Ezek.	Ezekiel
Dan.	Daniel
Hos.	Hosea
Joel	Joel
Amos	Amos
Obad.	Obadiah
Jon.	Jonah
Mic.	Micah
Nah.	Nahum
Hab.	Habakkuk
Zeph.	Zephaniah
Hag.	Haggai
Zech.	Zechariah
Mal.	Malachi

THE BOOKS OF THE NEW TESTAMENT (NT)

Abbreviation(s)	Meaning
Matt.	Matthew
Mark	Mark
Luke	Luke
John	John
Acts	Acts
Rom.	Romans
I and II Cor.	I and II Corinthians
Gal.	Galatians
Eph.	Ephesians
Phil.	Philippians
Col.	Colossians
I and II Thess.	I and II Thessalonians
I and II Tim.	I and II Timothy
Titus	Titus

Abbreviation(s)	Meaning
Philem.	Philemon
Heb.	Hebrews
James	James
I and II Pet.	I and II Peter
Jude	Jude
Rev.	Revelation

Geographical Abbreviations

The current trend is to use two-letter postal codes, sans periods. I've provided this current treatment abbreviations list. I tend to follow more traditional approaches in most areas of writing, but in this instance my preference is actually for the newer style of abbreviation. But I've also included the older, but still correct, treatment of abbreviations.

THE UNITED STATES AND TERRITORIES

Abbreviation(s)	Meaning
AK, A.K.	Alaska
AL, Ala.	Alabama
AR, Ark.	Arkansas
AS	American Samoa
AZ, Ariz.	Arizona
BC, B.C.	British Columbia
CA, Calif.	California
CO, Colo.	Colorado
CT, Conn.	Connecticut
DC, D.C.	District of Columbia
DE, Del.	Delaware
FL, Fla.	Florida
GA, Ga.	Georgia
GU	Guam
HI, H.I.	Hawaii
IA, Ia.	Iowa
ID, Ida.	Idaho
IL, Ill.	Illinois
IN, Ind.	Indiana
KS, Kans.	Kansas

continues

10.3

continued

Abbreviation(s)	Meaning
KY, Ky.	Kentucky
LA, La.	Louisiana
MA, Mass.	Massachusetts
MD, Md.	Maryland
ME, Me.	Maine
MI, Mich.	Michigan
MN, Minn.	Minnesota
MO, Mo.	Missouri
MS, Miss.	Mississippi
MT, Mont.	Montana
NC, N.C.	North Carolina
ND, N.Dak.	North Dakota
NE, Neb. or Nebr.	Nebraska
NH, N.H.	New Hampshire
NJ, N.J.	New Jersey
NM, N.Mex.	New Mexico
NV, Nev.	Nevada
NY, N.Y.	New York
OH, O.H.	Ohio
OK, Okla.	Oklahoma
OR, Ore. or Oreg.	Oregon
PA, Pa.	Pennsylvania
PR, P.R.	Puerto Rico
RI, R.I.	Rhode Island
SC, S.C.	South Carolina
SD, S.D.	South Dakota
TN, Tenn.	Tennessee
TX, Tex.	Texas
UT, U.T.	Utah
VA, Va.	Virginia
VI, V.I.	Virgin Islands
VT, Vt.	Vermont
WA, Wash.	Washington
WI, Wis.	Wisconsin
WV, W.Va.	West Virginia
WY, Wy.	Wyoming

The proper nouns of places, which are spelled out when they are used as nouns, can be presented in their abbreviated form only when they are used as adjectives (*UN*, *United Nations*; *U.K.*, *United Kingdom*; *U.S.*, *United States*).

Noun: The United Nations examined the issue.

Adjective: The UN activity caused massive gridlock.

WORLDWIDE ABBREVIATIONS

Abbreviation(s)	Meaning
AB	Alberta
Fr.	France
Ger.	Germany
Grk.	Greek
Isr.	Israel
It.	Italy
Neth.	Netherlands
NS	Nova Scotia
NT	Northwest Territories
ON	Ontario
Russ.	Russia
UAE	United Arab Emirates
U.K.	United Kingdom
U.S.	United States

The following table lists some common abbreviations used in referencing addresses.

ADDRESSING ABBREVIATIONS

Abbreviation(s)	Meaning
Ave.	Avenue
Bldg.	Building
Blvd.	Boulevard
Ct.	Court
Dr.	Drive
Expy.	Expressway
Fl.	Floor
Hwy.	Highway

continues

continued

Abbreviation(s)	Meaning
La.	Lane
Pkwy.	Parkway
Pl.	Place
PO Box (or POB)	Post Office Box
R.R.	Rural Route
Rd.	Road
Rm.	Room
Rt.	Route
Sq.	Square
St.	Street
Ste.	Suite

Here is a list of common directional, compass-oriented abbreviations.

DIRECTION ABBREVIATIONS

Abbreviation(s)	Meaning
N, NE, NW, NNE	north, northeast, northwest, north northeast
E	east
S	south
W	west

Acronyms

Acronyms are abbreviations created by using the first letter(s) of each word of a compound word or word phrase. The abbreviation is usually created by initial letters only, but in some instances, the acronym becomes so well known that it takes on such meaning without needing further definition. *Radar* and *laser* are two such examples.

Acronym	Meaning
AWOL	absent without leave
CIA	Central Intelligence Agency
CSI	Crime Scene Investigation
FBI	Federal Bureau of Investigation

Acronym	Meaning
FYI	For Your Information
laser	light amplification by stimulated emission of radiation
NATO	North Atlantic Treaty Organization
radar	radio detecting and ranging
snafu	situation normal all fouled up
USA	United States of America
VIP	Very Important Person
www	World Wide Web
ZIP	zone improvement plan

Shortened Forms

Shortened forms of words or names are just that: shortened forms of words or names. They are not all caps, and they do not take any periods.

Shortened Form	Meaning
ad	advertisement
gym	gymnasium
auto	automobile
phone	telephone
exam	examination
lab	laboratory

In this chapter, I've discussed all aspects of spelling: the parts of words, contractions, and word choices. I've addressed spelling challenges, offering options for dealing with them. In keeping with the discussion about spelling challenges, I've identified abbreviation issues and provided multiple listings to give guidance with how to abbreviate titles and degrees, times and dates, biblical and geographical terms, as well as providing discussion on acronyms.

11

NUMBERS, SIGNS, AND SYMBOLS

11.1 Numbers

11.2 Signs and Symbols

11.1 NUMBERS

Numbers Starting Sentences

Whole Numbers

Round Numbers

When Numerals Are Preferred

Times and Dates

Names and Titles

Knowing when to use numerals (*1*, *2*, *3*) and when to spell out a number (*one*, *two*, *three*) can sometimes make even the most experienced grammarian's head spin. When can you use numerals? When do you have to spell out a number?

Numerals might be the preferred choice when making lists or with mathematics equations, but that's not always the case within running text. Within running text, you must follow many rules when determining whether the number should be spelled out. Whether a number is written as a numeral or spelled out depends on a few basic considerations:

- Is the number large or small? Is it 101 or larger?
- Is the number a round number?
- If the number is a round number, is it surrounded by other numbers greater than one hundred that are not round numbers?
- What is the context in which the number is used?

The following rules are meant for use with general writing projects. These rules, although generally accepted, might not mesh seamlessly with specific rules for certain technical writing assignments. If you're doing technical writing, follow the guidelines provided by your instructor, or ask whenever there's a difference of opinion.

Numbers Starting Sentences

Always spell out numbers at the start of a sentence. If spelling out the numbers results in an awkward setup, rewrite the sentence so the troublesome number is no longer the first word.

Incorrect: 1 is the loneliest number.

Correct: One is the loneliest number.

Recast: The loneliest number is 1.

Whole Numbers

If the number is a whole number (not a fraction or with a decimal) between one and one hundred, it should be spelled out.

She has two or three children under the age of ten.

He lived to the ripe old age of ninety–three.

Whenever the number is 101 or greater and not a round number (*two thousand, four hundred,* etc.), it should be presented in numeral form.

His SAT results were disappointing, especially the 499 in mathematics and the 485 in world history.

Whenever multiple numbers are in close proximity or in the same discussion, and some are whole numbers one hundred or less and other numbers are greater than one hundred, write all the numbers as numerals for consistency.

Winfield had a population of 100 in the 1800s, in 1976 it jumped to 550, and as recently as 2005 the township was closing in on the big 600 with a revised population count of 596.

Round Numbers

If the number is larger than 101 but is a round number, then it would also be spelled out. A round number is a number ending with one or more zeros.

There were an estimated seven hundred fifty million people watching as Diana married Prince Charles.

There are already more than two thousand bookies taking bets on who will win the next Kentucky Derby.

When Numerals Are Preferred

As outlined in the preceding sections, sometimes numbers should be spelled out. But sometimes numerals should be used instead. Use numerals for days and years.

July 4, 1776

A.D. 13

321 B.C.

Numerals are also used when writing out addresses.

1 East Vanderbilt Street
2903 Grand Avenue
New York, New York 10009

Use numerals when writing out rural routes, highways, and thoroughfares. This applies to their abbreviated versions as well.

Rural Route 603	RR 603
Highway 79	Hwy. 79
Interstate 70	I–70
U.S. 40–61	

Like a digital watch, use numerals when writing about exact times of day.

9:33 A.M.
5:05 P.M.
7:20

Note: Certain groups in the world of grammar and usage have put forth faddish notions in recent editions of their texts. One of those notions is that "A.M./P.M." do not need to be small caps or that when they are small caps that they do not have to include the periods because they are not necessary. There are a lot of rules in this world that are not absolutely 101 percent necessary, however, I still plan on wearing my seatbelt whenever I get behind the wheel—and I also plan to stop at all stoplights. There's nothing innovative about changing the rules for referencing ante meridiem (A.M.) or post meridiem (P.M.), so I'm not sure what the logic was for their assertion of these new approaches. Until and unless the sense of something new proves compelling and convincing, my methodology will continue to support and promote traditional approaches to grammar and style.

When writing about money in exact amounts, with decimals and money symbols, use numerals. When providing references to money in written dialogue or in round numbers, spell out the dollar amounts.

75¢	$4.23
$2.6 million (*also* $2,600,000)	$7,549.00

Numerals are the preferred treatment for fractions, percentages, and decimals when being referenced in charts, graphs, etc.

$2\frac{1}{2}$, $5\frac{3}{4}$, $\frac{3}{16}$

33% (*also* 33 percent)

3.333

Within running text, decimals would continue to be presented as numerals. However, other references of fractions and percentages used in running text would be spelled out or at least partially spelled out.

They were two–thirds of the way home.

He picked up his half before heading back.

The investment provided a 12 percent profit the first year.

Scores and measurements of all manner are often listed in numerals when placed in charts or lists or provided as comparisons. Within running text, such numbers are usually spelled out except when to do so would cause the read to be more difficult or when part of multiple examples.

6 to 1	30–15
a ratio of 5 to 2 (*also* 5:2)	1 cup

Times and Dates

Numerals are usually used to note time, days, and years. However, if the month and day are noted without the year, it's okay to spell out the day in terms of *ordinal numbers*, as opposed to *cardinal numbers*.

WORDS TO GO . . .WORDS TO GO . . .WORDS TO GO

Ordinal numbers are numbers representing an ordered-sequence placement: *first, 1st,* etc.

Cardinal numbers are used in basic counting: *one, 1, forty-three, 43.*

When in running text, times of day are usually spelled out. If attached to *o'clock*, the hour is always spelled out.

That six thirty alarm clock rings earlier each day.

She was expected to stay until quarter to five, but she left early, around four fifteen, for a doctor's appointment.

I left at eleven o'clock, but Peter stayed until midnight.

Numerals should be used, however, if a specific time is being mentioned or emphasized.

> Her flight was landing at 5:47.
>
> He arrived with ring in pocket at 3:43 and sweated out the next two hours.

When writing military time—the twenty–four–hour time method used by the military and much of Europe—the time is always represented by four digits without a colon between the hours and minutes.

1200 (noon)	2400 *or* 0000 (midnight)
0003 (12:03 A.M.)	1333 (1:33 P.M.)

> The sergeant had us in a forced, full–pack march up to Dead Man's Bluff until 2400.

Cardinal numbers are used to express specific dates.

> After 2001, September 11 will never be just another day.
>
> (*Also*: 9/11, September 11th)

When years are mentioned on their own, they tend to be in numeral form. If a year starts a sentence, spell it out or recast the sentence so the year doesn't lead off.

> *Incorrect:* 2008 will be the next leap year.
>
> *Correct:* The next leap year will be 2008.

The opposite is true when the day is mentioned but no mention is made of the month or year. In this case, spell out the date.

> I'm going to have to leave on the twenty–third to make it home in time for Christmas.
>
> I'll be back by the first.

Dates with the month, date, and year included generally use numerals for the day and year, and spell out only the month.

> Her fiftieth birthday was November 17, 2006.
>
> As President Franklin D. Roosevelt said, that Sunday, December 7, 1941, was truly a day that will "live in infamy."

When abbreviating a year, use an apostrophe in place of the first two digits in the year.

> Life will be heaven in '07!
>
> The banner read: WELCOME WINFIELD WARRIORS CLASS OF '84!

Decades can go either way. If they're spelled out, set them lowercase and be sure it's clear to the reader what century you're referring to. Decades can also be written out in numerals.

I barely made it out of the <u>sixties</u>.
The music of the <u>seventies</u> gets a bad rap.
She came into her own in the <u>'90s</u>.
He was in outer space for most of the <u>1990s</u>.

When referring to a specific century, spell it out. No capitalization is required.

Welcome to the <u>twenty–first century</u>.

References to eras can be treated in many ways. My preference is for the old standards of A.D. and B.C. (which stand for *anno Domini*, "in the year of the Lord" and "before Christ," respectively), with small capitals and periods.

Recently, some other style books decided to make treatments of era references open to interpretation but they never gave a good reason for the reversal from the rule, so I tend to feel they got tired of fighting the good fight and caved to the dumbing down of America. There will be no such capitulation from this writer. Note that A.D. precedes the date, whereas B.C. follows.

A.D. 13
465 B.C.

Names and Titles

Personal names and titles for members of the monarchy and papacy with the same name as others are identified by the use of numerals, usually roman numerals.

Henry VIII
Elizabeth I (*also* Queen Elizabeth I)
Adlai E. Stevenson III
James J. Walker II
Pope John II

When referencing titles of sequels, the determination of how to reference the number of the title depends upon what the originator and rights holder decided.

Jaws II
The Godfather, Part II
Friday the 13th, Part 2
Merriam–Webster's Collegiate Dictionary, 11th edition

The following examples identify how to treat governmental, political, and judicial names that are presented with numbers.

109th Congress, 2nd Session
Fourth Ward
Seventieth Precinct
Twelfth Dynasty (*also* Dynasty XII)

And when numbers are included in reference to military terms, these following examples provide the appropriate treatments.

Fourth Infantry Division
173rd Airborne Brigade
Eighty–second Airborne Division

In this section we covered the treatment of numbers. We looked at how to approach numbers that fall at the beginning of a sentence. Additionally, whole and round numbers were discussed. I also touched on the times when numerals are preferred over the spelled–out version. And I wrapped up discussing how to treat numbers that are part of times, dates, names, and titles.

11.2 SIGNS AND SYMBOLS

Mathematics

Punctuation

Accents

Copyediting and Proofreading Marks

This section provides multiple listings of signs and symbols that may be confusing as you encounter them. These include signs and symbols for mathematics. I also revisit punctuation and accent markings. And I wrap up this chapter with an extensive charting of copyediting and proofreading marks.

Mathematics

@	"at" sign	<	less–than sign
$	dollar sign	>	more–than sign
¢	cents sign	≤	less–than–or–equal–to sign
%	percent symbol	≥	greater–than–or–equal–to sign
#	number sign	=	equal sign
+	plus sign	≈	almost–equal–to sign
–	minus sign/hyphen	≠	not–equal–to sign
±	plus–minus sign	∞	infinity
×	multiplication sign	∫	integral
÷	division sign	£	pound sign
/	division slash	¤	currency sign
√	square root	¥	yen sign

Punctuation

.	period	'	apostrophe or single quotation mark
...	ellipses	( )	parentheses (left and right)
,	comma	[ ]	brackets (left and right)
;	semicolon	{ }	curly brackets (left and right)
:	colon	/	slash (solidus)
!	exclamation mark	\	back slash (reverse solidus)
?	question mark	–	hyphen
"	double quotation mark		

continues

continued

Punctuation			
–	en dash	°	degree sign
—	em dash	©	copyright symbol
&	ampersand	®	registered trademark
*	asterisk	™	trademark
¡	inverted exclamation mark	℠	service mark
¿	inverted question mark	¶	paragraph symbol

Accents	
ˆ	circumflex accent
´	acute accent
`	grave accent
˜	tilde
¨	dieresis or umlaut (depends on where it is placed)
˘	macron
¸	cedilla

Copyediting and Proofreading Marks

If you've ever reviewed someone else's work—or deciphered the scribbles and lines a proofreader made on one of your letters or papers, you know that copyeditors and proofreaders have their own set of symbols and marks. You might not know, however, what they all mean.

The copyediting and proofreading symbols that follow will be of invaluable assistance for any class, work, or personal experience that involves any sort of writing or review of written materials. The proofreading symbols and abbreviations presented here are broad in scope and should be universally useful. I've provided both the marks and information on when, where, and how to apply them. Not only has the meaning for each mark been provided, but the meaning has been further defined along with a usage demonstration.

COPYEDITING AND PROOFREADING MARKS

Symbol	Meaning	Defining Example
Punctuation Marks		
	insert a comma	There should be a comma inserted etc. before we move on.
	insert a period	Insert a period That's all I have to say on the subject
	insert a question mark	Who me Why confuse things by forgetting a question mark
	insert an exclamation mark	Stop Help This is in need of a couple more exclamation marks!
	insert a semicolon	It's easy just insert the semicolon and move on.
	insert a colon	I have just six words for you You should have inserted a colon.
or	insert an apostrophe or single quote marks	"Shes saying no to the addition of an apostrophe and a single quotation mark?" I asked with incredulity.
/	insert quote marks	I wanted to know what frizzbeck meant but couldn't find a definition.
	insert a hyphen	To my worn out, light headed friends: Inserting a hyphen won't hurt at all.
	insert an en dash	When the connected words are uneven, an en dash style mark is called for. (The term "Post Cold War" is another example of proper en dash use.)
		NOTE THE DASH
	insert an em dash	To show a break or interruption in flow too many times would be annoying place an em dash.
or	Insert 2-em or 3-em dash	Mrs. X *or* Shakespeare, William. *Hamlet.* ~~Shakespeare, William.~~ *Macbeth.*
/	insert parentheses	To show comment, you can insert parentheses such as this.
/	insert brackets	To comment outside of quoted material, brackets can be used.
Operational Marks		
/	separating slash	Use slash to indicate the end of the symbol or with a word~~(s)~~ insertion. Place slashes to the right of each mark. note slash
	delete, remove	Take it ~~out~~ out.
	close up	Remove ex tra sp ace.
	delete and close up	Takke it out and close up ~~up~~.
( )	close up vertically	Once upon a time, there was a clown named Beulah Belle who made children laugh with each honk of her horn and tinkle of her bell.

11.2

COPYEDITING AND PROOFREADING MARKS

Symbol	Meaning	Defining Example
^	insert	Caret shows something is coming
#	add a space	Tootight.Seriouslytootight.
hair # / hr #	add a small space	"She asked me, "What?"
eq #	equalize spacing	Uneven is odd spacing weirdness....Help clarify.
STET	let it stand	Ignore marks and leave original text.
sp	spell out	Use this when 1 or more words should be spelled out.
tr / ∾	transpose	Change the order the of words. Does that sense make?
¶	new paragraph	A new paragraph should begin. No one misunderstands.
□	indent type	Indent type the amount of space that is equivalent to one em dash This can be used to indent from either the left or the right. You decide.
]	move to the right	Move the type to the right.
[	move to the left	Move the type to the left.
] [	move to the center	Center the type on a line or lines.
⊓	move up	Move the type up.
⊔	move down	Move the type down.
fl. lft.	flush left	Move the type flush left.
fl. rt.	flush right	Move the type flush right.
=	align type horizontally	Fix type on line to be horizontally aligned.
‖	align type vertically	Align the type vertically to follow design or logical flow.
⊚	reverse	Reverse the direction of the character or symbol.
ok?	okay to do this?	Is this okay?

Typographical Marks

Symbol	Meaning	Defining Example
ital	set in italics	The underlined or circled word(s) should be set in italicized type.
rom	set roman	The underlined or circled word(s) should be set in roman type.
lc	set lowercase	Letter(s) or Word(s) that have a SLASH thru them should be lowercased.
cap	set in capitals	the letter(s) or word(s) that are circled should be capitalized. the same goes for the letter(s) or word(s) with three lines underneath them.
sc / sm cap	set in small capitals	This should read: two lines underneath MEANS SET IN SMALL CAPITALS.
wf	wrong font	Wrong font needs to be reset in the correct type.
X	type is broken	Check the original setting material for the problem; fix the broken type.
cln	clean a blemish	Check the original setting material for the problem (often a printer issue).

12

TRADEMARKS, COPYRIGHTS, PERMISSIONS, AND FAIR USE

12.1 Trademarks

12.2 Copyright Information

12.3 Permissions

12.1 TRADEMARKS

Identifying Trademarks
Use of Trademarks

A trademark is a word, phrase, symbol, or design—or a combination of words, phrases, symbols, or designs—that identifies the "source of the goods of one party from those of others," according to the U.S. Patent and Trademark Office. For instance, the word *Kleenex* is a trademarked term, whereas *facial tissue* is not.

A *service mark* is basically the same as a trademark, but it identifies the source and owner of a service instead of a product.

Options Analysis for Reengineering℠
Personal Analysis for Reengineering℠
Product Line Technical Probe℠

Two degrees of trademarks exist. There are trademarks, often denoted on product packaging or within advertisements for the products by the addition of the ™ symbol. You'll also see registered trademarks, which could be identified on the product package or advertisement with a ® symbol.

Identifying Trademarks

To know whether a word or phrase related to a product or service is trademarked, the trademark holder has probably noted its ownership by placing either the ™ or the ® beside the word or words that are either trademarks or registered trademarks.

Beyond looking on the product itself, you can look to many resources to find out whether or not a word or a phrase is trademarked. First, check out a dictionary. A good dictionary, such as *Merriam-Webster's Collegiate Dictionary*, 11th Edition, is a great resource for much more than how to spell words, including helping identify trademarked terms.

Interestingly, within the title *Merriam-Webster's Collegiate Dictionary*, "Merriam-Webster" is a trademarked term, while "Collegiate" is a registered trademark. Both of these trademarked terms are owned by Merriam-Webster, Incorporated. It was very simple for me to find that information by looking on the copyright page of that dictionary. The **copyright page** of a book, magazine, or journal is the most overlooked resource even though it generally provides a good deal of information, including all pertinent trademark information concerning that publication.

A copyright notice generally includes the word *copyright* and the copyright symbol ©, the year the book was published, and the copyright owner's name. (Note: A published work is not required to include a copyright notice due to the protection of the Copyright Act of 1989.)

WORDS TO GO . . . WORDS TO GO . . . WORDS TO GO

A **copyright page** is almost always the reverse side of the title page, or the second page in a book. The copyright page includes standardized information, including, of course, the copyright information:

Copyright © 2007 by Lara M. Robbins.

Of course you could always look online to find trademark information. Using a search engine such as Google or Yahoo!, type in the word or phrase in question to see a variety of resources. It's imperative to verify that the site and information you use are reliable and accurate. And unless you come across the trademark owner's website and obtain your confirmation that way, it's a good idea to do a quick bit of double- and triple-checking to make certain the info you have is correct.

One of the sites with which I often begin my trademark hunts is www.inta.org. This site has yet to steer me wrong, but I still double-check to confirm the exact trademarked terms—perhaps by visiting the trademark owner's website for added confirmation. You know the old saying, "Measure twice, cut once"? In this context, I'd adjust it just a bit: "Look it up two or three times, write it down once."

You can also do a free search with the United States Patent and Trademark Office, which can be accessed via www.uspto.gov/index.html. There are currently about four million registered, pending, and "dead" trademarks accounted for.

It would be impossible to provide an exhaustive list of all trademarked terms that exist today. If there were enough pages in this book to accommodate such a listing, as of tomorrow it would be outdated! Instead, the following is a handy list of common, everyday terms for quick reference at your fingertips.

Trademarks

A.1.
Academy Awards
Air Jordan
Amazon.com
American Express (AmEx)
American Idol
AT&T
Band-Aid

continues

continued

Trademarks

Ben & Jerry's

Blow Pop

BOTOX

Bubble Wrap

Bugs Bunny

Campbell's

C-SPAN

Cap'n Crunch

Chap Stick

Cheez-It

Choc full o'Nuts

Cinn-A-Burst

Coca-Cola

Coke

Day-Glo

Day-Timer

Diet Coke

Dippity-do

Doc Martens

Dom Pérignon

Dr Pepper

Dunkin' Donuts

Dumpster

eBay

Edy's

Elmer's

Etch A Sketch

Ex-Lax

Expedia.com

E-ZPass

Fabergé

Federal Express (FedEx)

Frisbee

Fudgsicle

Game Boy

G.I. Joe

Gore-Tex

Got Milk?

Hacky Sack

Häagen-Dazs

Hard Rock Café

Harley-Davidson

Harry Potter

Hershey's Kisses

Iams

I Can't Believe It's Not Butter

IMAX

iTunes

J.Crew

Jack Daniel's

JCPenney

Jell-O

Jeopardy!

Jet Ski

Just Do It.

Kleenex

Kool-Aid

Laundromat

La-Z-Boy

L.L. Bean

M&M's

Major League Baseball

Martha Stewart Living

MasterCard

Moon Pie

MTV

O, The Oprah Magazine

o.b.

Ping-Pong

Porta Potti

Porta-John

Post-it

Q-tips

ReaLemon

Realtor

Rolls-Royce

Smith & Wesson

Sno-Kone

Spider-Man

StairMaster

Star-Kist

Styrofoam

Tastee-Freez

Tater Tots

Thermos

ThighMaster

TiVo

Toys "R" Us

TV Guide

U-Haul

United Parcel Service (UPS)

USA Today

V8

Wal-Mart

WD-40

Windbreaker

Wite-Out

World Series

Xbox

Xerox

Yahoo!

Yoo-hoo

An interesting note on trademarked terms: As identified within the preceding trademarks list, *Styrofoam* is a trademarked term owned by The Dow Chemical Company. According to www.dow.com/styrofoam/what.htm, Styrofoam was invented by that company more than fifty years ago and all products made with this material have a distinct blue color.

A common trademark infringement error that a lot of writers make is to reference disposable, hot-beverage cups as "Styrofoam cups." Dow has always insisted—continues to assert, check out the website noted above—that such a reference is not only incorrect but a misuse of their trademarked term. According to the website, the material that composes such disposable items tends to be "white in color and are made of expanded polystyrene beads." Dow suggests using the generic term of "foam" for referencing such non-Styrofoam materials.

Use of Trademarks

When citing a trademarked term, it's important to cite the exact trademarked term. Any lowercasing, hyphens, or other punctuation marks that are shown as part of the trademarked term(s) should be retained. That said, when using trademarks within running text, there's no need to use either the ™ or the ® symbols to indicate the trademark. Simply capitalizing the trademarked terms will suffice.

Throughout my years in publishing, I've seen a few books in which the authors apparently insisted on including the ® and ™ symbols within running text. Despite all attempts to persuade them that the excess of trademark symbols is unnecessary, for whatever reason, a few authors are always determined to have the symbols placed with every mention in their text. To seasoned vets, the placement of such symbols within running text is a sure sign of a novice writer. Not to mention that the resulting reading experience is clunky and frustrating.

12.2 COPYRIGHT INFORMATION

What Is a Copyright?

Ineligible for Copyright Protection

Registering Copyrights

Copyrighting Benefits

Copyright Duration

In this subchapter, I present a basic explanation of the copyright process and laws. It's important if you have specific concerns regarding copyright uses and laws that you seek professional assistance through a copyright attorney or the United States Copyright Office.

What Is a Copyright?

A copyright, according to the United States Copyright Office, "is a form of protection provided by the laws of the United States to the authors of 'original works of authorship.'" A copyright protects original works, including artistic, dramatic, literary, musical, and some other works—whether published or unpublished.

Works that are copyrightable include, but are not limited to, the following:

- Architectural works
- Audiovisual works
- Choreographic works
- Dramatic works
- Graphic works
- Literary works
- Motion picture works
- Musical works
- Pantomime
- Pictorial works
- Sculpture works
- Sound recording works

These categories should be considered broadly; they are somewhat open to interpretation. For instance, certain computer programs could be accepted as "literary works."

Section 106 of the 1976 Copyright Act generally gives the owner of copyright the exclusive right to do and to authorize others to:

- duplicate the work;
- create subsequent works derived from the original;
- distribute copies of the work by sale, renting, leasing, lending, or some other temporary or permanent ownership transfer;
- display, present, or perform the work publicly.

What a Copyright Does and Does Not Do

Holding a copyright does not protect ideas, concepts, systems, or methods of doing something. Ideas can be expressed via writings or drawings and the copyright claims can be placed in the description, but a copyright does not protect ideas.

The power of copyright protects the form of expression, not the subject matter of, say, the writing. For example, a written description of a machine could be copyrighted, but that would prevent others only from copying the description; it would not prevent others from writing a description of their own or from making and using the machine. The machine itself could possibly be patented or trademarked, but probably not copyrighted.

It's also important to note that simply having possession or ownership of a work such as a book, manuscript, painting, photograph, etc., does not automatically provide the owner with the copyright.

Who Owns a Copyright?

Copyright protections begin as soon as the created work is finished. The copyright is owned by the originator (the original author/creator) of the creation of the work. Only the author, or someone the author endows, can claim the copyright. That said, if something is created as a "work for hire," the employer owns the copyright.

A "work for hire" is defined in section 101 of the Copyright Law of the United States of America as:

1. a work prepared by an employee within the scope of his or her employment; or

2. a work specially ordered or commissioned for use as:
    - a contribution to a collective work
    - a part of a motion picture or other audiovisual work
    - a translation
    - a supplementary work
    - a compilation
    - an instructional text
    - a test
    - answer material for a test
    - an atlas

If more than one person authors a work, each person shares in the ownership of the work's copyright—unless some other arrangement is made and is agreed to by all parties involved. If multiple contributions are made to a collective work of some sort, it is important to note that each individual contributor holds the copyright for his or her specific portion of the work. There is also a copyright for the whole of the work. Ownership of the copyright for the whole of the work would be agreed to by all contributors.

To make sure that you understand fully your individual, collaborative, or work-for-hire rights and responsibilities regarding copyrights, a visit to the United States Copyright Office via its website at www.copyright.gov is a good idea. If your concerns aren't easily resolved, consider seeking the advice of an attorney who specializes in the field of copyright law.

Ineligible for Copyright Protection

Some materials or categories of materials are not usually viable for copyright protection under the federal copyright laws. Some things that aren't covered by the protection of federal copyright law include the following:

- Works that are not yet finalized to an appreciable degree or manner
- Titles and names
- Brief phrases and slogans
- Common and customary symbols or designs
- Modifications of typographic ornamentation, lettering, or coloring
- Basic listings of ingredients or contents

- Ideas, procedures, methods, processes, concepts, principles, discoveries, or devices
- Works made up completely of common property information that has no original authorship (lists or tables taken from public documents or other common sources, calendars, etc.)

—United States Copyright Office

Registering Copyrights

Copyrights are registered through the Copyright Office of the Library of Congress. There's a fee to register for copyrights; as of this writing, it's $45. However, the cost can vary, so please confirm this with the Copyright Office. Other fees might also be involved, depending on what exactly you want to register. You can access all fees-related information at www.copyright.gov/docs/fees.html.

Copyrighting Benefits

There is no requirement to register with the United States Copyright Office to make a claim of copyright. Copyright ownership is automatic whenever a "work" is created. And the "creation" of a work is whenever there is at least one copy of it—meaning after it's first completed. If a work is not created all at once, but rather over time, the portion of the work that is basically final at a given time equals the work as of that point in time.

Registration can be made anytime throughout the life of the copyright. Still, there are benefits to registration—and the earlier the registration, the greater the benefits. Here are some of the benefits:

- To establish a public record (in case there should be a dispute in the future).
- Registration is needed for works of origin in the United States before any suits claiming rights infringement can be filed with a court. The registration needs to be made within five years of the publication dates. When registration is made before an infringement of the work occurs—and within three months of publication—then the copyright owner can get awarded not only actual damages and profits, but also additional damages and attorney's fees that are granted within a court judgment.
- Registration also enables the copyright owner to record their rights with the U.S. Customs Services in order to gain protection against the importing of bogus copies of what they own.

For more information, check out the U.S. Customs and Border Protection website at www.cbp.gov/xp/cgov/import.

Copyright Duration

Works Created January 1, 1978, or Later Works that were first created (or at least first fixed in tangible form) on or after January 1, 1978, are protected from the time of their creation. The term of protection is usually the length of the author's life plus an added seventy years after the author's death. If more than one author created the work in question, then the copyright protection continues until seventy years after the death of the last author. If a work was a "work for hire" or was written under a pseudonym or anonymously, the copyright protection is to be either ninety-five years from the publication date or 120 years from the creation date, whichever date is shorter.

Works Created Before January 1, 1978 (Published or Registered Before January 1, 1978) The copyright protection laws get a bit more complex for works that were created and published or registered before January 1, 1978. The Copyright Act of 1976 changed the renewal term to seventy-five years for copyrights that were in existence as of January 1, 1978. Then on October 27, 1998, the 105th Congress enacted Public Law 105-298, which added more time to the protection term of copyrights that were in effect on January 1, 1978, for a total of ninety-five years of protection.

Works Created Before January 1, 1978 (Unpublished or Unregistered) Works that were created before January 1, 1978, but were left unpublished or unregistered were automatically brought under the newest statute and provided with federal copyright protection. The length of copyright protection for these works is just like the works created on January 1, 1978, or after: usually the length of the author's life plus an added seventy years after the author's death. If more than one author created the work in question, then the copyright protection continues until seventy years after the death of the last of the authors. If a work was a "work for hire" or was written under a pseudonym or anonymously, then the copyright protection is to be either ninety-five years from the publication date or 120 years from the creation date, whichever date is shorter.

For more information on copyrights and copyright registration, please visit the United States Copyright Office at www.copyright.gov.

12.3 PERMISSIONS

Permissions Letter

Fair Use

When parts of previously published or copyrighted works are included in a new work—even if it's been altered—it's important to include an acknowledgment in the new work. If space is available, the acknowledgment should be placed on the copyright page of the new work.

> An excerpt from *TITLE* by AUTHOR NAME copyright © DATE by is used by permission. All rights reserved.

When space is limited on the copyright page, a simple notification line redirecting the reader to a permissions page can be added to the copyright page. Then a permissions page (or pages) can be placed at the very end of the book. It's important to include copyright information for the previously published work if that work falls under the protection of copyright law.

> A complete listing of permissions is provided on page XXX.

It's also a common practice to note short credit information directly beside uses of others' photos, art, maps, and quoted text, assuming it fits in with the chosen book style. If the permission and credit information appear to interrupt the general flow and style of the book, it's a better option to collect it all in one place, either on the copyright page or on the permission page(s) at the end of the book.

Permissions Letter

If you plan to use someone else's copyright-protected work, it's your responsibility, as creator of the new work, to get the copyright owner's permission. This can often be done by writing a request for permission letter to the copyright holder.

You/Your Company
Street Address
City, State, Zip Code
E-mail
Phone Number
Fax Number

Date

Copyright Owner's Name/Company
Street Address
City, State, Zip Code
Reference Information

Dear *Copyright Owner's Name,*

This letter is being sent to request your permission to reproduce the following selections taken from your publication:

Author Name:
Title:
Date of Publication:
Page Numbers in the Copyright Owner's Publication:
Any Additional Identification Information:

The selection(s) will be used, as they were published in your title (above), in the following title, which is currently in production for publication:

You/Your Company Name:
Proposed Title of Your Work:
Estimated Publication Date:
Specify the rights you are seeking as well as all of the editions and languages where the material will be used.

Explicitly restate your request for permission to reprint their material and ask for their crediting information. Provide a space for them to acknowledge that they are giving their permission and a space for the signing date and credits information.

If the plan is to use someone else's copyright protected work, then it is the responsibility of the creator of the new work to get the copyright owner's permission.

Fair Use

Simply providing a credit or an acknowledgment of the source does not equal getting permission in writing. The only exception is when the portion being used is considered to be "fair use."

The 1961 *Report of the Register of Copyrights on the General Revision of the U.S. Copyright Law* cites examples of activities that courts have regarded as fair use:

> "... quotation of excerpts in a review or criticism for purposes of illustration or comment; quotation of short passages in a scholarly or technical work, for illustration or clarification of the author's observations; use in a parody of some of the content of the work parodied; summary of an address or article, with brief quotations, in a news report; reproduction by a library of a portion of a work to replace part of a damaged copy; reproduction by a teacher or student of a small part of a work to illustrate a lesson; reproduction of a work in legislative or judicial proceedings or reports; incidental and fortuitous reproduction, in a newsreel or broadcast, of a work located in the scene of an event being reported."

Copyright protects the particular way an author has expressed himself; it does not extend to any ideas, systems, or factual information conveyed in the work.

There is no legal specification of the exact number of words, musical notes, or portion of a work that can be used without explicitly granted permission. Determining what is allowable must be done on a case-by-case basis. Consider these four factors when deciding whether a specific use is fair:

- What is "the purpose and character of the use"? Factor in whether the work borrowed from will be utilized for a commercial or for a nonprofit or educational use.
- What is the nature of the work under copyright protection?
- What portion of the copyrighted work is being used?
- What is the impact of the use with regard to the value and market of the original copyrighted work?

Public Domain

If the original work falls into the realm of "public domain," there's no restriction of use. Public domain means either the works never held copyright status or the works have aged out of the restrictions of the copyright laws.

Songs, Books, Articles

When borrowing lyrics from songs or poems that are usually small in words and lines already, two lines or less than 10 percent (whichever is the more conservative option) tends to be the maximum covered under the fair-use maxim.

Images

Permission to reproduce art that is separate from text, such as illustrations and photographs, must also be gained prior to actual use—unless, again, the image in question satisfies the requirements of "fair use," as outlined previously.

In some instances, permission can be given by the publisher of the previous work. Even if their contract does not grant that option, the publisher might redirect your efforts to the true owner of the rights to the artwork. A fee will be incurred when permission is granted. The fee is the responsibility of the author, not the publisher, in most instances—to negotiate and to pay.

All art that is used must be acknowledged with a crediting line either beside the artwork itself or in a listing on the copyright page, if space allows it. If space on the copyright page is limited, then a single-line notation on the copyright directing the reader to a page dedicated for credits will suffice.

Up/Downloads

Uploaded and downloaded materials that are protected by copyright also require the permission of the copyright owner before they can be used for reproduction and/or distribution. If the rights of the copyright owner are willfully ignored, the penalties can be huge ($30,000 to $150,000) for each work concerned. For far more information on this matter or law, please check out the U.S. Copyright Office website at www.copyright.gov/docs/regstat090903.html.

Reproductions

Many photocopying and photography stores are reluctant to make reproductions of old photographs and other such materials because they're concerned about potential copyright violations that could lead to them being sued. For photographs, it can be challenging to figure out who is the actual owner of the copyright. The person who has actual, physical possession of a copy of a photography is not necessarily the same as the owner of the work. The photographer, or, in some situations, the person who hired the photographer to take the pictures, is usually the owner of the work. The only way to transfer the ownership of these works is also in writing. Notably, the subject of a photo (the person in the picture) has no rights of copyright ownership.

13

CITATION

13.1 Source Citation

13.1 SOURCE CITATION

Direct Quotes
Online Sources
Shortened Citations
Initial Articles
Source Citation Chart
Poetry and Prose Extract Citations

Copyright laws dictate that writers cite all sources of quoted material and, whenever possible, identify all facts or opinions that are not original to the author. Whenever you quote information from another source in your writing, it's imperative that you clearly and correctly give credit to the source of the quotation. In keeping with these guidelines, in addition to referencing the sources quoted, you will also want to include background or supplemental information readers may need to fully understand and locate the original form of the quoted text. There are several ways to document quoted sources, including footnotes, endnotes, and bibliographies.

If the citation information you are provide isn't clear, you could be plagiarizing someone else's work. How you go about citing your sources can vary, as you'll see in this subchapter.

Direct Quotes

Look around on book covers, magazines, billboards, etc., and you'll see review quotes touting the virtues of specific books, movies, art showings, phone services, and just about everything else under the sun. These sorts of quotes show up on books, on billboards, and just about everywhere else possible—even on the sides of buses. Generally, in such instances, the quote's source follows directly after the quote.

"★★★★.
A mind-blowing comedy classic ....
It will make you laugh till it hurts and you'll still beg for more. ...
You won't know what outrageous fun is until you see [this movie]."
—Peter Travers, *Rolling Stone*

If a direct quote is included within running text, it needs to be clearly attributed to its source as well. The attribution either can be included in the introduction to the quote or can follow the quote.

> In a review of the book *The Ladies of Grace Adieu*, the reviewer notes that within the book "humans do make friends within the faerie world . . ." (*People*), but there are clearly deeper meanings throughout.

Online Sources

When citing from a well-known and recognizable online source such as an online magazine (or "webzine"), that does not use ".com" as part of its name, then italicize the online magazine title and leave off the *.com* at the end. This is also the case for quotes taken from the website for a corresponding print publication.

> *Salon* (not Salon.com)

When citing from a website that is not well known or is strictly a website, and does include ".com" as part of its name, then set the website in roman type and do include the *.com*, *.net*, or *.whatever* at the end.

> AllReaders.com
> AllSciFi.com

In both of these situations, there is no reason whatsoever to include the http:// or www. preceding the website name.

Shortened Citations

After a title is provided in full in running text, a list of references, or a notes or bibliography section, subsequent references to it can be referenced in a shortened fashion.

> The best dictionary for daily reference would be *Merriam-Webster's Collegiate Dictionary*, 11th edition. Everyone at my office references *Web11* these days.

Use the keyword(s) of the full title for the short version. In the preceding example, if instead of saying "*Web11*" I had said "dictionary," then what I was referencing wouldn't be clear at all.

Initial Articles

Initial articles in titles such as *A*, *An*, or *The* might not always jibe with the flow of the text. In such instances, those initial articles can be dropped. You could also recast the sentence so it makes sense with the initial articles.

Awkward: Though no one knows the author's name, everyone knows "The Man on the Flying Trapeze."

Recast: Though no one knows George Leybourne's name, everyone knows his lyrics for "The Man on the Flying Trapeze."

Treatment of *The* differs depending on whether the use is the citation of a source set apart from the quoted material or whether the citation is being used within running text. When citing a source separate from running text, include the initial *The* with the initial cap and italicization whenever it appears in the title of the source. However, when the title is referenced within running text, the initial *the* should be set roman and lowercase.

Separate: "Big, expensive parties and intimate little lunches: the beast must be fed." —*The New York Times*

In running text: His performance was panned by the *New York Times*.

The entire title should be used in citation of sources. You have many resources for verifying exact titles, including *The Literary Marketplace* (LMP) and various online sites. You could also use search engines such as Google, Yahoo!, etc.

The New York Times *The New York Observer*

Certain titles are so nonspecific that the city and/or state must be provided to avoid confusion. When a newspaper is not well known, the city name must be added to the full title for the source citation.

San Francisco Chronicle *San Antonio Express-News*
San Francisco Examiner

If the city name is used but the city name is not well known, then the state must be added, too. The state, using postal code abbreviations within parentheses, is added directly after the city's name.

The Columbia (SC) State *The Macon (GA) Telegraph*

If the source being cited is from another country, the name of the city where the source originates is added in parentheses. In this instance, the city name in parentheses is added and follows the title. In this instance, the city name is not italicized.

The Observer (London) *North Shore News* (Vancouver)

Source Citation Chart

The following table provides an extensive listing of the proper citation of many various sources.

SOURCE CITATION CHART (MAGAZINES, NEWSPAPERS, ONLINE SOURCES)

Masthead/Title	Location/Format	Cite As
Advocate, The	(Baton Rouge, Louisiana)	*The Baton Rouge Advocate*
Advocate, The	(magazine)	*The Advocate*
Affaire de Coeur	(magazine)	*Affaire de Coeur*
Albany Herald, The	(Georgia)	*The Albany (GA) Herald*
AllSciFi.com	(website)	AllSciFi.com
Arizona Republic, The	(Phoenix, Arizona)	*The Arizona Republic*
Arkansas Democratic Gazette	(Little Rock, Arkansas)	*Arkansas Democratic Gazette*
Armed Forces Journal	(magazine)	*Armed Forces Journal*
Associated Press, The	(news service)	The Associated Press
Atlanta Journal-Constitution, The	(Georgia)	*The Atlanta Journal-Constitution*
Atlantic Monthly, The	(magazine)	*The Atlantic Monthly*
Booklist	(Chicago, Illinois)	*Booklist*
BookLovers.co.uk	(U.K.; website)	BookLovers.co.uk
BookNook.com	(website)	BookNook.com
Book-of-the-Month Club (BOMC)	(book club)	Book-of-the-Month Club
BookPage	(webzine)	*BookPage*
Bookwatch, The	(newsletter of the *Midwest Book Review*)	*The Bookwatch*
Books 'n' Bytes	(webzine)	*Books 'n' Bytes*
Boston Globe, The	(Massachusetts)	*The Boston Globe*
BusinessWeek	(magazine & website)	*BusinessWeek*
Charlotte Observer, The	(North Carolina)	*The Charlotte Observer*
Christian Science Monitor, The	(Boston, Massachusetts)	*The Christian Science Monitor*
Commercial Appeal, The	(Memphis, Tennessee)	*The Commercial Appeal*
Copley News Service	(news service)	Copley News Service
Courier-Journal, The	(Louisville, Kentucky)	*The Courier-Journal*

continues

continued

Masthead/Title	Location/Format	Cite As
Daily Mail	(London, U.K.)	*Daily Mail* (London)
Dallas Morning News, The	(Texas)	*The Dallas Morning News*
Daytona Beach News-Journal	(Florida)	*Daytona Beach News-Journal*
Decatur Daily, The	(Alabama)	*The Decatur (AL) Daily*
Des Moines Register, The	(Iowa)	*The Des Moines Register*
Detroit News and Free Press, The	(Michigan)	*The Detroit News and Free Press*
Doubleday Book Club	(book club)	Doubleday Book Club
Entertainment Weekly	(magazine)	*Entertainment Weekly*
Evening Standard, The	(London, England)	*The Evening Standard* (London)
Fargo Forum, The	(Fargo, North Dakota)	*The Fargo Forum*
Fresno Bee, The	(Fresno, California)	*The Fresno Bee*
Gazette, The	(Colorado Springs, Colorado)	*The Colorado Springs Gazette*
Gazette, The	(Gaithersburg, Maryland)	*The Gaithersburg Gazette*
Gazette, The	(Ottawa, Canada)	*The Gazette* (Ottawa)
Guardian, The	(U.K.)	*The Guardian* (U.K.)
Harper's Bazaar	(magazine)	*Harper's Bazaar*
Hello!	(London, England; magazine)	*Hello!* (London)
Hollywood Reporter, The	(California)	*The Hollywood Reporter*
Independent, The	(London, England)	*The Independent* (London)
Kansas City Star, The	(Kansas City, Missouri)	*The Kansas City Star*
Kirkus Reviews	(magazine)	*Kirkus Reviews*
Knoxville News-Sentinel, The	(Knoxville, Tennessee)	*The Knoxville News-Sentinel*
Library Journal	(magazine)	*Library Journal*
Literary Guild, The	(book club)	The Literary Guild
Literary Times, The	(magazine)	*The Literary Times*
Locus	(magazine)	*Locus*
Los Angeles Times	(Los Angeles, California)	*Los Angeles Times*

Masthead/Title	Location/Format	Cite As
Metro Newspaper Service	(New York, New York)	Metro Newspaper Service
Midwest Book Review	(Oregon, Wisconsin)	*Midwest Book Review*
Milwaukee Journal Sentinel	(Milwaukee, Wisconsin)	*Milwaukee Journal Sentinel*
Mirabella	(magazine)	*Mirabella*
Mystery Guild	(book club)	Mystery Guild
Mystery Scene	(New York, New York; magazine)	*Mystery Scene*
NAPRA Review	(industry publication)	*NAPRA Review*
New Republic, The	(Washington, D.C.; magazine)	*The New Republic*
News & Record	(Greensboro, North Carolina)	*Greensboro (NC) News & Record*
New Yorker, The	(New York, New York; magazine)	*The New Yorker*
New York Observer, The	(New York, New York)	*The New York Observer*
New York Times, The	(New York, New York)	*The New York Times*
New York Times Book Review, The	(New York, New York)	*The New York Times Book Review*
New York Times Magazine, The	(New York, New York)	*The New York Times Magazine*
Observer, The	(London, U.K.)	*The Observer* (London)
Orlando Sentinel	(Orlando, Florida)	*Orlando Sentinel*
Paris News, The	(Paris, Texas)	*The Paris (TX) News*
People	(New York, New York; magazine)	*People*
Philadelphia Inquirer, The	(Philadelphia, Pennsylvania)	*The Philadelphia Inquirer*
Publishers Weekly	(New York, New York; magazine)	*Publishers Weekly*
Rocky Mountain News	(Denver, Colorado)	*Rocky Mountain News*
Sacramento Bee, The	(California)	*The Sacramento Bee*

continues

continued

Masthead/Title	Location/Format	Cite As
Salon	(webzine)	*Salon*
San Diego Union-Tribune, The	(San Diego, California)	*The San Diego Union-Tribune*
San Francisco Chronicle	(San Francisco, California)	*San Francisco Chronicle*
San Francisco Examiner	(San Francisco, California)	*San Francisco Examiner*
Seattle Post-Intelligencer	(Seattle, Washington)	*Seattle Post-Intelligencer*
Seattle Times, The	(Seattle, Washington)	*The Seattle Times*
SFRevu	(webzine)	*SFRevu*
St. Louis Post-Dispatch	(St. Louis, Missouri)	*St. Louis Post-Dispatch*
State, The	(Columbia, South Carolina)	*The Columbia (SC) State*
Stuart News, The	(Stuart, Florida)	*The Stuart News*
Sun, The	(Baltimore, Maryland)	*The Baltimore Sun*
Sunday Times, The	(London, U.K.)	*The Sunday Times* (London)
Telegraph, The	(Macon, Georgia)	*The Macon (GA) Telegraph*
Time	(magazine)	*Time*
Time Out	(magazine)	*Time Out*
Times, The	(Trenton, New Jersey)	*The Trenton Times*
Times-Picayune, The	(New Orleans, Louisiana)	*The Times-Picayune*
Tulsa World	(Tulsa, Oklahoma)	*Tulsa World*
United Press International (UPI)	(news service)	UPI
USA Today	(McLean, Virginia)	*USA Today*
U.S. News & World Report	(magazine)	*U.S. News & World Report*
Us Weekly	(magazine)	*Us Weekly*
Village Voice, The	(New York, New York; newspaper)	*The Village Voice*
Wall Street Journal, The	(New York, New York)	*The Wall Street Journal*
Washington Post, The	(Arlington, Virginia)	*The Washington Post*
Washington Post Book World, The	(Arlington, Virginia)	*The Washington Post Book World*
Women's Wear Daily (WWD)	(New York, New York)	*WWD*

Poetry and Prose Extract Citations

Citations that follow block quotations of poetry or prose follow the quoted material directly. There are at least two heads about where to place the citation.

You can place the citation in parentheses following the last bit of punctuation from the quote. With this method, no concluding punctuation for the citation beyond the surrounding parentheses is necessary. This way, there's no confusing the citation as part of the quotation itself.

> "For God so loved the world that he gave his one and only Son, that whoever believes in him shall not perish but have eternal life. For God did not send his Son into the world to condemn the world, but to save the world through him. Whoever believes in him is not condemned, but whoever does not believe stands condemned already because he has not believed in the name of God's one and only Son." (John 3:16–18, NIV)

The second approach finds that there is more potential confusion by placing the citation of the block quote's source outside the concluding punctuation. And outside of the first approach there are a couple of other options.

> Then quotation was taken from the New International Edition of the Bible:
>
> > "Love is patient, love is kind. It does not envy, it does not boast, it is not proud. It is not rude, it is not self-seeking, it is not easily angered, it keeps no record of wrongs. Love does not delight in evil but rejoices with the truth. It always protects, always trusts, always hopes, always perseveres. Love never fails" (1 Corinthians 13:4–8).
>
> It was clear by the placement of the quote over the door to see that they were a Bible believing family.

Here's another example:

> "Love is patient, love is kind. It does not envy, it does not boast, it is not proud. It is not rude, it is not self-seeking, it is not easily angered, it keeps no record of wrongs. Love does not delight in evil but rejoices with the truth. It always protects, always trusts, always hopes, always perseveres. Love never fails."
>
> —1 Corinthians 13: 4–8

When a poem is quoted, the citation is placed to follow the poem as separate from the poem. The placement of the source citation could be preceded by an em dash and centered. It also can be set flush left or right, or the em dash can be used as a center point. Be sure whichever treatment you use is applied consistently throughout your work. The design is really usually up to the designer of the paper, book, or magazine. And making certain the design elements are set consistently is the responsibility of the proofreader and editor.

I'm Nobody! Who are you?
Are you—Nobody—too?
Then there's a pair of us!
Don't tell! They'd advertise—you know!

How dreary—to be—Somebody!
How public—like a Frog—
To tell one's name—the livelong June—
To an admiring Bog!

—Emily Dickinson, No. 288 (c. 1861)

In this chapter, we've gone in depth with our discussion of the citation of sources. We've looked at how to cite direct quotes and online sources and how to present citations in more condensed fashion. The treatment of the citation of titles with initial articles has been examined and explained. And finally, this section wrapped up with discussion about how to provide citations for poetry extracts.

14

DOCUMENTATION AND REFERENCE

14.1 Footnotes

14.2 Endnotes

14.3 Glossaries

14.4 Bibliographies

14.5 Indexes

14.1 FOOTNOTES

Definition and Use
Footnote Numbering
Footnote Symbols
Footnote Citation Style
Footnote Pros and Cons

Have you ever read a Shakespearean play? Chances are, you have—and, chances are, it was heavily annotated with footnotes that explained what all those Elizabethan words meant. Footnotes act as an easy reference tool to help the reader understand the text.

Definition and Use

A footnote is a note that comes at the foot of a page (not to be confused with an endnote, which is a note that comes at the end. But more on that later).

Footnotes are brief notations used throughout a text to clarify, cite, or comment and help the reader understand the text. Set at the bottom of the page within a chapter or article, footnotes correspond to numbers or symbols within the text and usually appear on the same page as the related material.

Footnotes offer additional information to the reader; they define or explain a term or phrase, cite an outside text or cross-reference other parts of the work, or comment on or acknowledge something relevant to the text but not integral to the overall work. Commonly used in nonfiction and scholarly works, footnotes are an accessible way for the reader to better understand the work.

Footnote Numbering

Generally, footnotes are numbered consecutively throughout a chapter or article, with each new chapter or section starting over and beginning with footnote 1. This is helpful if you have a long work with many footnotes that are numbered consecutively from start to finish. By starting each new chapter or section with 1, you reduce the risk of throwing off the numbering of the entire piece by adding or deleting a footnote. Always break up a long work into smaller chunks and begin numbering the footnotes in each section with 1.

When you use footnotes, set the numbers within the text in superscript (small type set above the line). At the bottom of the page, the same number is used to identify the footnote with the number in the text.

Here's what a footnote number looks like in the text:

> Shakespeare wrote that true nobility is exempt from fear[1].
> Try thalassotherapy[6] for relaxation.

Here's what you'd see at the bottom of the page:

> [1]From *Henry VI*, Part Two, 4.1.129.
> [6]*Thalasso* means "sea" in Greek.

Alternatively, the number identifying the footnote can be placed as regular text at the bottom of the page and set off by a period. Either way, remember that consistency is key.

Examples in the text:

> Shakespeare wrote that true nobility is exempt from fear[1].
> Try thalassotherapy[6] for health and relaxation.

At the bottom of the page:

> 1. From *Henry VI*, Part Two, 4.1.129.
> 6. *Thalasso* means "sea" in Greek.

Keep your footnotes short, as shown in these examples, with no more than two or three on a page. The first line of a footnote must appear on the same page as its reference in the text, but then it may run on to the next page, if necessary. Longer notes and/or more frequent use may be better suited to endnotes.

SEE ALSO 14.2, "Endnotes"

Footnote Symbols

If your footnotes are few and far between, or if you are using both footnotes and endnotes—or if you just don't like numbers—you can identify footnotes using a symbol system. Generally, these symbols are used in tables with numerals, where numeric footnotes may add confusion.

If using symbols, begin with an asterisk (*) to mark the reference in the text, and another at the bottom to identify the footnote. If more than one footnote appears on a page, use different symbols to avoid confusion. The following is the most common order of acceptable symbols to use in a text.

*	asterisk	§	section mark
†	dagger	| |	parallels
‡	double dagger	¶	paragraph mark

Here's how footnotes with symbols would look in the text:

Shakespeare writes, "Come, Let's have one other gaudy* night."‡
Endomeso therapy combines both mesotherapy* and endermologie‡.

And at the bottom of the page:

*Here *gaudy* is used to mean "joyful."
‡From *Antony and Cleopatra*, 3.8.182.
*Mesotherapy uses injections to fight cellulite.
‡Endermologie uses a machine for deep-muscle massage.

Footnote Citation Style

Footnote citation style depends largely on whether there is also a bibliography and/or endnotes. Footnote citations should be shortened whenever possible, but only if the full citation can be included somewhere else.

Short Citation Style

Use the short citation style for footnotes when a complete citation is included elsewhere (such as the endnotes or bibliography) and when space prevents you from providing more information. This condensed citation generally includes nothing but the author's last name, the title of the work (abbreviated, if necessary), and the page numbers, when applicable.

[1]Geier, *Cafe Flora Cookbook*, 25–40.
[3]Robbins, *Grammar and Style*, 12–24.

Long Citation Style

The long citation style appears in full with all of its publication information in the footnote, just as it would in a bibliography. There is no need to be redundant; if the complete citation is in the endnotes or bibliography, use only the short citation in the footnotes. And if you aren't including a notes or bibliography section, you can get by with the long citation footnotes alone.

[1]Geier, Catherine, with Carol Brown. *Cafe Flora Cookbook*. (New York: HPBooks, 2005), 25–40.

[3]Robbins, Lara M. *Grammar and Style at Your Fingertips* (Indianapolis: Alpha Books, 2007), 12–24.

SEE ALSO 14.4, "Bibliographies"

Footnote Pros and Cons

As previously stated, footnotes are best used for brief notations that you want the reader to consider while reading the main text. Footnotes can enhance meaning, cite other sources, or add color commentary to a text, and because they are located within the main text, they are easy to find. But they need to be concise. If you have too many footnotes on one page or if they are too long or complicated, your readers are likely to be overwhelmed. The page will be cluttered and difficult to read, and the footnotes will distract the reader from the main text.

Longer, more detailed passages are better presented in a separate endnotes section. And extensive citations are usually better placed in the endnotes or in a bibliography.

Consider how your reader will use this additional information. If the information is short and helpful to the text, use a footnote. If the information is long and primarily for research or reference purposes, move it to the endnotes.

14.2 ENDNOTES

Endnote Numbering

Endnote Citation Style

Ibid.

Endnote Pros and Cons

An endnote is a note that comes at the end of a section of text (compare to a footnote, which is a note that comes at the foot of a page). Endnotes offer additional information about the text. Similar to footnotes, they clarify, cite, and comment on the text; however, they allow more options and greater flexibility. Endnotes can expand on the text with long and complex explanations, and they can include tables and graphs, as well as unabridged resource identification.

SEE ALSO 14.1, "Footnotes"

This information is compiled at the end of a text, in a section generally called "Notes." In most cases, this is one section at the back of a book, but in multi-author works, the endnotes may fall at the end of an individual article, chapter, or section.

Often coupled with bibliographies, endnotes tend to be more user-friendly and more concise than bibliographies. If a bibliography is not included in the work, then all the necessary publication details for directly quoted material should be listed in the endnotes.

SEE ALSO 14.4, "Bibliographies"

Endnote Numbering

Endnotes are numbered consecutively throughout a chapter or article, with each new chapter or section starting over with endnote 1. The notes section at the back is then broken down by chapter or section, with the corresponding endnote numbers listed underneath. If you have a long work with many endnotes, avoid numbering them from start to finish. Adding or deleting even one endnote can throw off all the other numbers. Always break up a long work into smaller chunks and begin numbering the endnotes in each at 1.

Place endnote numbers within the text in superscript type (small type set above the line). In the notes section, use the same number to identify the endnote with the number in the text.

This is what you would list in the text:

> Shakespeare writes, “Come, Let’s have one other gaudy night.”[2]
>
> A recent study[7] shows that three out of five women agree that environmental concerns affect their children.

Here’s what you’d compile in the endnotes:

> **Chapter 4**
>
> 2. Quoted from *Antony and Cleopatra*, 3.8.182. Note the unusual usage of the word *gaudy*, which in this case means “joyful.” This word refers to nighttime celebrations at Oxford University from the school song “Gaudeamus igitur.”
>
> **Chapter 9**
>
> 7. According to a 2003 study by General Testing Associates, 609 out of 1,016 women agreed that environmental concerns, including air and water pollution as well as global warming, directly affect their children and their health.

When using both endnotes and footnotes, endnotes are always distinguished by numbers and footnotes by symbols, to avoid confusion.

SEE ALSO 14.1, “Footnotes”

Endnote Citation Style

If your work includes a bibliography, you can use short citations in the endnotes. This condensed citation generally includes the author’s last name, title of the work (abbreviated, if necessary), and page numbers, when applicable.

> 4. Geier, *Cafe Flora Cookbook*, 25–40.
>
> 10. Robbins, *Grammar and Style*, 12–24.

If your text does not contain a bibliography, though, use a full citation with all the publishing details in the endnotes.

> 4. Geier, Catherine, with Carol Brown. *Cafe Flora Cookbook*. (New York: HPBooks, 2005), 25–40.
>
> 10. Robbins, Lara M. *Grammar and Style at Your Fingertips*. (Indianapolis: Alpha Books, 2007).

Either of these examples may be followed by commentary or annotations to further explain the citation or to elaborate on something related to the text. Start the commentary just after the citation or on the next line using indented paragraph style.

4. Geier, *Cafe Flora Cookbook*, 25–40. Several delicious recipes stand out from this Seattle restaurant …

4. Geier, Catherine, with Carol Brown. *Cafe Flora Cookbook.* (New York: HPBooks, 2005), 25–40.

Several delicious recipes stand out from this Seattle restaurant …

Ibid.

For the sake of expediency and to avoid redundancy, the abbreviation *ibid.* is sometimes used to show that the endnote refers exactly to the citation immediately preceding it. *Ibid.* means literally "in the same place" and replaces the author's name, the title, and as many other publication details as are identical; page numbers for the original source may be added to differentiate between sources. Do not use *ibid.* if the preceding endnote mentions more than one source, unless all sources are again used in the following endnote.

2. Munro, *Runaway*, 87–125.
3. Ibid.
4. Ibid., 236–269.

Endnote Pros and Cons

Endnotes are not restricted by length the way footnotes tend to be. Basically, anything that helps the reader understand the text can be put in an endnote; excerpts of poetry, artwork, or anything that requires special typography or placement can be set in endnotes without disrupting the main text.

The only drawback to using endnotes is that the reader must flip back and forth between the text reference and the notes section. Therefore, endnotes may paraphrase or otherwise recall what was mentioned in the text to facilitate the reader's use. Conversely, footnotes should be as concise as possible and should avoid repetition.

Endnotes may be used in conjunction with footnotes and/or bibliographies, or they may stand alone.

Endnotes, and pretty much all types of documentation, help to keep everyone honest. By documenting the sources used throughout the text, authors are able to highlight their own work and ideas, while also giving proper acknowledgment to the others they have cited.

14.3 GLOSSARIES

When in doubt, look it up! A glossary—a list of commonly used words and unusual and foreign terms used in a text, explaining or defining the terms—provides the readers with all the tools they'll need to read the text, in a handy list at the back of a book. Think of it as a very abridged dictionary specific to what you're reading.

Glossaries are helpful for readers who may not be familiar with the subject matter of the text. Glossaries are especially helpful when some ambiguity exists among terms, or even to define made-up words used within the text.

There are several ways to stylize a glossary, although the basic structure is always the same: The words are arranged alphabetically, and each new term begins on a separate line, followed by its definition. The terms should begin with a lowercase letter, unless they appear capitalized within the text. Likewise, terms should be set in regular roman type, unless they appear italicized in the text. A period or colon should follow the term before the definition. Terms may be bolded if space and design constraints allow.

glossary. A collection of special terms with their meanings.
glossary: A collection of special terms with their meanings.
glossary. A collection of special terms with their meanings.

The term may be set in small or full capital letters or without punctuation following the term, but only if there's no chance of causing a misread.

GLOSSARY: A collection of special terms with their meanings.
GLOSSAR Y. A collection of special terms with their meanings.
glossary A collection of special terms with their meanings.

SEE ALSO Appendix A, "Words to Go Glossary"

Glossaries are not intended to be all-inclusive; they are meant only to provide an easy reference tool for frequently used terms. Defining terms in a glossary can help the author avoid bogging down the running text with clunky definitions while still providing the reader with the essential information he or she needs.

Terms and definitions do not ordinarily need to be documented by their sources, as long as they are written in the author's own words. Glossary entries are not included in the index.

SEE ALSO 14.5, "Indexes"

14.4 BIBLIOGRAPHIES

Bibliography Basics
Print Publications
Electronic Publications
Unpublished and Informally Published Works

Often used in conjunction with notes (either footnotes or endnotes), bibliographies direct readers to outside information and cite information that is directly quoted or that is not new or unique to the document at hand.

Bibliography Basics

Also called a ***reference list***, the bibliography compiles all the publication details for the sources cited or consulted by the author in the process of writing the text.

Not all works require bibliographies. If the work does not rely heavily on outside resources, or if the citations are included in the notes, a bibliography may be unnecessary or redundant.

You can follow the bibliographical recommendations in this book in most all circumstances, as long as the overall style of the bibliography is consistent. However, if your work requires a special style for the bibliography, please refer to specific guidebooks in your field, such as *The MLA Handbook*, *The Chicago Manual of Style*, *The AMA Style Guide*, *The Associated Press Stylebook*, etc. The systems of citing bibliographical information are quite similar, but each has distinct requirements related to its individual field of study, publication, or audience. Depending on your needs, you can use styles from various sourcebooks; the trick, as always, is to combine those styles and then use them consistently throughout your bibliography.

Basic Setup

When citing sources, include only the key elements:

- Author or authors
- Title of the work, including subtitle, if there is one
- Editor or translator
- Volume and series, if applicable

- Page numbers, when relevant
- Place of publication
- Date of publication
- Publisher

Not all works require bibliographies. If the work does not rely heavily on outside resources, or if the citations are included in the notes, then a bibliography may be unnecessary or redundant.

For simplicity's sake, only the most commonly used citation styles are included here, as well as the two most common types of bibliographies.

Full Bibliography

A full bibliography includes all works cited in the text and notes, and any sources cited while researching, even if not directly quoted. Most often the heading is "Bibliography" or "Works Cited."

All works, printed and electronic, should be included in alphabetical order by author's last name, following a consistent style. Full bibliographies may be annotated, although this is not necessary if footnotes or endnotes are elsewhere in the text. These annotations would follow the bibliographical information.

Select Bibliography

A select bibliography includes only the most pertinent sources referenced in the text. By convention, this is more often used in literary and historical works; legal and scientific works generally use a full bibliography. The heading can be "Select Bibliography" or "Suggested Readings," if the list is quite short. Included is usually a headnote explaining the delineation of sources listed.

Print Publications

Slight variations are made between types of publications, but for the most part, titles of works are italicized or set in quotation marks, and everything else is set in regular text. Placement of punctuation should be consistent throughout the bibliography.

Books

Author's names are usually inverted (last name first) and should follow the same style that appears on the book's title page. Authors such as J. K. Rowling, who are known by their initials, should be listed as such. The title, publisher, and place of publication information can be cited from the title page; publication date and most other information can be retrieved from the book's copyright page.

Geier, Catherine, with Carol Brown. *Cafe Flora Cookbook*. New York: HPBooks, 2005.

Robbins, Lara M. *Grammar and Style at Your Fingertips*. Indianapolis: Alpha Books, 2007.

Entries such as translations and revised editions contain additional information and are cited as shown. Note the annotation explaining which edition is used within the main text.

Gavalda, Anna. *I Wish Someone Were Waiting for Me Somewhere*. Translated by Karen L. Marker. New York: Riverhead Books, 1999.

Strunk, William, Jr., and E. B. White. 1959. *The Elements of Style*. 4th ed. Boston: Allyn and Bacon, 2000. Page references are to the 2000 edition.

Journals, Newspapers, and Magazines

Periodicals follow a similar style; however, names of articles are set within quotation marks and names of periodicals are set in italics. Also, volume and page numbers or other locators are included as appropriate.

Gorman, Christine. "What Ails the CDC." *Time* 168, no. 22 (November 27, 2006): 21.

Winne, Mark. "A New Idea Grows in Alabama." *The Nation* 283, no. 18 (November 27, 2006): 18.

In these magazine citation examples, the volume number comes after the title of the publication, followed by the issue number, its publication date within parentheses, and the page number.

The following examples illustrate newspaper citations. Newspaper references tend to be made in the footnotes or endnotes rather than in the bibliography.

Barrett, Joe. "On Brooklyn Streets, Shopping Carts Roll in a Renegade Derby." *The Wall Street Journal*, February 2, 2006, national edition, sec. 1.

Pollack, Andrew. "In Trials for New Cancer Drugs, Family Pets Are Benefiting, Too." *The New York Times*, November 24, 2006, national edition, sec. 1.

Plays

When citing plays, the documentation follows other print materials. However, when it's necessary to identify an exact quotation or passage, the act, scene, and line (or book, canto, and stanza) should also be provided. These are generally set in numerals, separated by periods.

Hansberry, Lorraine. *A Raisin in the Sun*, scene 1. New York: Random House, 1994.

Shakespeare, William. *Henry VI*, Part Two, 4.1.129. Ed. Sylvan Barnet. New York: Signet Classics, 2005.

Electronic Publications

Electronic media are constantly changing, and the vast wealth of information available on the Internet demands that authors cite as many details as possible about material taken from the web. The URL is not generally sufficient on its own, but it should be included along with other vital facts about the work. Note that electronic media usually do not include page numbers, so that element is omitted, contrary to print publication style.

Online Books

For works that are published online and that are available to all users, follow the same guidelines as for printed books. Include the title, author, place and date of publication, and the URL. If the material is especially time sensitive, you should include the date the URL was accessed. This is not necessary for non-time-sensitive information.

Griffin, Gerald. *The Collegians*, 1829. Ed. Michael Sundermeier. Omaha, NB: Creighton Electronic Editions, 2000. http://mockingbird.creighton.edu/english/micsun/.

IrishResources/collegians/collcont.htm (accessed October 20, 2006).

Online Journals and Magazines

Treat online journal and magazine articles exactly as you'd treat their print counterparts, but add the URL and the accessed date, if necessary.

Curtis, Bryan. "For Your Eyes Only: The Secret Life of James Bond." *Slate*, November 16, 2006. http://www.slate.com/id/2153937/.

Miller, Laura. "The Fall of the House of Pynchon." Review of *Against the Day*, by Thomas Pynchon. *Salon*, November 21, 2006. http://www.salon.com/books/review/2006/11/21/pynchon/.

Online News Sites and Services

Style any online news sites and services in the bibliography as you would online magazines. Common news services include the Associated Press (AP), Reuters, and United Press International (UPI). Regularly cited news websites include Yahoo! News, Google News, CNN.com, NYTimes.com, etc.

Associated Press. "Court OKs Broad Web Libel Immunity." *CNN.com*, November 20, 2006. http://www.cnn.com/2006/LAW/11/20/internet.libel .ap/index.html.

Reuters. "Study Finds Australia Nuclear Power Option Viable." *Google News*, Nov. 21, 2006. http://www.alertnet.org/thenews/newsdesk/SYD228117.htm.

Note that if a URL needs to be broken at the end of a line, it should break after a slash or before a period. To avoid a very loose line, words may be broken at the syllable. Never introduce a hyphen into a URL because it could cause a misread.

Unpublished and Informally Published Works

When citing material that hasn't been formally published, try to gather as many details as you can. Whether it's a letter or a website or a speech, provide as much information in the bibliography as you can, following the same style for other publications as closely as you can.

Websites and E-Mail

These days, virtually everything that is posted on the Internet can be considered published, albeit informally. Authorship may be unknown and publication details scant. Try to collect as much information as possible about the site—if there is no author, the name or owner of the site can stand in; if there is no title, a brief description will work.

Fifth Avenue Committee. "Mission Statement," http://www.fifthave.org/.

U2's official website, "News," http://www.u2.com/news/ (accessed November 1, 2006).

If you have permission to use e-mail or other electronic communications, the following is an appropriate citation method:

John Smythe, e-mail message to author, July 1, 2007.

John Young, memo to all first-year associates, June 3, 2006.

For e-mails or other electronic communications, do not include personal e-mail addresses without the owner's permission.

Print and Other Forms

Essays, theses, speeches, and other works that have not been formally published should be cited with as much information as possible.

Murphy, Dan. "The Great Northern Plains, 1880–1920." Ph.D. diss. Georgetown University, 2003.

Restoration in the 1950s. Papers. Derry Township Historical Society, Hershey, Penn.

SEE ALSO Chapter 13, "Citation"

14.5 INDEXES

Index Basics

Index Setup

Index Alphabetizing

Indexing is a true art form—one that's best left to the professionals. However, if you're crafting your own index or even hiring someone else to create one for you, there's a lot you should know. Your work may be chockfull of information, but without a high-quality index, your readers will have a hard time finding and using that information.

Index Basics

An index provides a road map for your text. It breaks down your text into its key terms, ideas, and names, and organizes them into an easily accessible list at the back of the book with page or section numbers corresponding to the text. Depending on the content of the work and the needs of its readers, the index may be extremely detailed, cross-referencing and grouping like terms and specifying every virtually nuance. Or the index may need to capture only the major ideas and how they relate to one other.

I've worked with indexes in excess of sixty book pages for a six-hundred-page reference book, and those with as few as two pages for a how-to book that was mostly illustrations. Consider how your readers will use the index and what information your readers will need to find what they're looking for. A dense work, especially one used for reference, legal, scientific, or medical purposes, requires a sophisticated index, with the key terms extensively cross-referenced. This may require capturing some hundreds of terms, and an implicit understanding of how these terms relate to one another is essential.

All pages of the main body of text should be read and indexed, along with all footnotes and endnotes. The preface, foreword, introduction, and appendixes may be indexed if they provide information that supplements the text; however, glossaries and bibliographies are not usually included in the index. Tables, charts, graphs, photographs, and other nontext elements should be included in the index as well.

Indexes use numbers as locators to explain where the index entries are found in the main text. Most often the locators are page numbers, but they may also be paragraph or section numbers, as well as figure or table numbers. In any case, the number locator in the index must direct the reader to the reference in the main text. Use a numbering system that best suits the stylistic and organizational needs of your work.

Indexes must be created from the final version of the text and after the page proofs have been typeset and proofread. Avoid editing the text after the index has been created because any movement of the text will cause a shift in the number locators in the index. If edits are necessary after indexing and the main text reflows, the page numbers in the index will have to be rekeyed.

Index Setup

Indexes are arranged alphabetically by their main entries. The main entries are broken down into subentries and occasionally subsubentries. The main entries are the key terms, ideas, and names that the reader will look up; the subentries describe different elements as they relate to the main entry. The main entries need to be as logical as possible, covering a broad topic that is then made more specific by the subentries.

Use a flush-and-hang style of index for printed texts. This means that the main entry is set flush left (not indented) and all subsequent information is indented below it. The subentries can be set in one of two ways.

Indented Style

With the indented style, each main entry and its subentries are set on their own lines, with the subentries indented after the main entry.

apple pie, 12–28

apples
  Gala, 13, 15, 28
  Granny Smith, 13, 14, 25
  McIntosh, 12, 16, 26–27
  Red Delicious, 12, 15, 27

Run-In Style

Sometimes space constraints do not allow for the indented style. The run-in style saves room but may also be more difficult to read. The subentries are not set on individual lines, but instead follow one after another and are separated by a semicolon.

apple pie, 12–28

apples
    Gala, 13, 15, 28; Granny
    Smith, 13, 14, 25; McIntosh,
    12, 16, 26–27; Red Delicious,
    12, 15, 27

Index Punctuation

In the preceding examples, you'll notice a comma placed after the term and before the page numbers. This is the preferred style for most indexes. An alternative style does not use the comma after the term. This style can be useful when the entries themselves often contain commas, but it can present problems if the entries contain numerals.

apple pie 12–28

apples
    Gala 13, 15, 28
    Granny Smith 13, 14, 25
    McIntosh 12, 16, 26–27
    Red Delicious 12, 15, 27

Number locators are always separated by commas, and an en dash is always used to show a range of numbers.

46, 82, 99–105

3.4, 5.5–5.9, 6.8

SEE ALSO 6.9, "Hyphens, Dashes, and Slashes"

Index Capitalization and Type Treatment

Generally, the first letter of a main entry is lowercase unless it appears capitalized in the text, such as a proper noun. Occasionally, all main entries can be capitalized regardless of their use in the text, but this is best only if there are many subentries and an initial capital entry would be easier to read. Subentries always begin with a lowercase letter, unless the words are capitalized in the text.

Likewise, any special type treatment that appears in the text should be carried over into the index. So if a title is italicized or appears in quotation marks in the text, it should also be italicized or in quotation marks in the index. The index should follow the overall style set out in the main text, so all secondary spellings used in the text should also be used in the index.

Definitions, Photos, Tables, Etc.

Special elements such as definitions, photographs and illustrations, and tables and charts may be denoted differently within the index. The most common way to do this is to set the number locator in italics or boldface, or to assign a letter or abbreviation after the number to make it distinct from a reference in the text.

For example, you might want to identify tables with italics and definitions with boldface. Or you could distinguish such elements by adding a letter after the number, such as *t* for tables and *d* for definitions.

tax brackets, 171–204, **172**, *181*, *200*
tax brackets, 171–204, 172d, 181t, 200t

In either case, a headnote should be placed at the beginning of the index to explain what the different typeface or letters mean. This headnote is set in italics after the index heading and before the first index entry.

Page numbers in italics refer to tables; those in bold refer to definitions.

The letters t *and* d *following the page numbers refer to tables and definitions, respectively.*

Similarly, if for any reason you want to call out certain entries in the index, you can set the words in boldface or capital letters. For example, in a guidebook for colleges, the author might want to highlight the Ivy League schools in bold to separate them from the other schools and make them stand out. The rationale for such treatment should also be explained in a headnote.

College names in boldface represent Ivy League schools.

Amherst College, 70–76
Columbia University, 109–115
Cornell University, 116–121
Dartmouth College, 122–129
Duke University, 130–136

See and *See Also*

An essential cross-referencing technique is to use the words *see* and *see also* to connect related entries in the index. *See* is used after a main entry when the information is listed elsewhere but the reader might not think to look there first. A period follows the main entry, and *See* is capitalized and italicized.

gorillas. <u>See</u> primates

Great War. <u>See</u> World War I

Gulf of Mexico. <u>See</u> Mexico, Gulf of

guns. <u>See</u> weapons

If, however, a *see* reference is made to a subentry, it's set lowercase and usually within parentheses.

surveys, 42–59; polling,
53–54; reporting, 55–56;
results (<u>see</u> tabulation)

Use *see also* to direct the reader to more information. This reference comes after the number locators, the last of which ends with a period. If there is more than one reference, separate them with a semicolon.

moon, 17–24. <u>See also</u> astronomy; planets

music, 33–51, 59. <u>See also</u> individual styles

mustard, 69–78
    brown, 70
    dry, 77. <u>See also</u> seeds, mustard
    spicy, 72

Be warned that too many *see* and *see also* references may actually make the index less user-friendly, as the reader will have to flip too often. For ease of use, some information may be listed under both entries rather than using *see* or *see also* references.

NASA, 227

National Aeronautics and Space Administration (NASA), 227

Other cross-referencing tools are *see under* and *see also under*, to be used when the referenced directive may not be immediately clear. For example, use *see under* instead of *see* when directing the reader to a subentry under the cross-referenced main entry.

Granny Smith. <u>See under</u> apples, types

Gulf of Mexico. <u>See under</u> water, bodies of

Watch out for *see* or *see also* references that direct the reader to another *see* or *see also* reference. These are called a "blind" cross-references and should *always* be avoided.

Bad Breaks and Continued Line

When the index is typeset, it usually appears in two or three columns per page. When reviewing the index before publication, look for any awkward placement, such as a main heading falling at the end of a column with its subentries beginning the next column. This is considered a *bad break* in the flow of the index, and the main entry should be moved to the top of the next column.

Similarly, if a listing of subentries carries over from a right-hand page (recto) to a left-hand page (verso), a *continued* line should be added for clarity. This line restates the main entry followed by the word *continued* within parentheses; the remaining subentries then continue below it. The continued line is not needed on right-hand pages because it's easy enough to see that the entries are carried over from the facing page. It's necessary only on left-hand pages because otherwise the reader would have to turn the page to find the main entry.

apples, types (*continued*)
  McIntosh 12, 16, 26–27
  Red Delicious 12, 15, 2

Index Alphabetizing

Yes, we all know that *B* comes after *A*, and *C* comes after *B*, but there are actually two ways to alphabetize an index: letter by letter or word by word.

Alphabetizing Letter by Letter

In the letter-by-letter method, words are alphabetized letter by letter until the first comma or parenthesis, and all spaces and other punctuation marks are disregarded. This is my preference.

cat
cat, bat, and rat
cat-a-mountain
cat and mouse
catch
catch-up
catch up
catch-22
cat got your tongue

catgut
cat (kitten)
Cather, Willa
cats
cats and dogs
cats, dogs, and frogs
CAT scan
cat's cradle
catsup
cat rig
cattails

Alphabetizing Word by Word

An alternate method is to alphabetize word by word. Words are alphabetized by the first word and then by any following words. The order after the first word is determined by parentheses, then commas, then spaces. Other punctuation, such as hyphens and apostrophes, is ignored.

cat
cat (kitten)
cat, bat, and rat
cat and mouse
cat got your tongue
cat rig
CAT scan
cat-a-mountain
catch
catch up
catch-22
catch-up
catgut
Cather, Willa
cats
cats, dogs, and frogs
cats and dogs
cat's cradle
catsup
cattails

If a title or term begins with an article (*the*, *an*, or *a*), it's alphabetized according to the first letter of the next word, and the article is moved to the end.

Armies of the Night, The, 360, 399
Light Bearer, The, 234
Separate Peace, A, 23–25

However you choose to organize your citation and documentation materials, the greatest requirement is for consistency, consistency, consistency.

A

WORDS TO GO GLOSSARY

abbreviation The shortened form of a word or a word phrase. It can be used instead of the word itself.

absolute phrase A phrase that includes a noun (or pronoun) and a participle, and is not linked to the rest of the sentence by a connecting word.

abstract noun Word that identifies an intangible idea or quality.

acronym Abbreviation created by joining the first letter(s) of each word that makes up the parts (major parts only in certain instances) of a compound word or word phrase.

active voice When the subjects are the ones in action.

adjective A word used to modify a word or group of words that serve as nouns and pronouns.

adjective pronoun (or **pronominal pronoun**) Pronoun that serves as the modifier of a noun. Most pronouns can be used as adjectives.

adverb A word that modifies—describes, restricts, or otherwise qualifies—verbs, adjectives, or other adverbs. Adverbs can also modify clauses, phrases, and entire sentences.

agreement The consistency in form between subject and verb.

alliteration A stylistic device that repeats the consonant sound at the beginning of two or more words used consecutively or in close proximity.

allusion A stylistic device that intentionally references an idea, person, or happening that exists outside the current context.

antecedent The word, phrase, or clause to which a subsequent pronoun refers.

apostrophe Single punctuation mark used to form the possessive for nouns and pronouns; to identify omissions within contractions; and to create plural versions of letters, numbers, and words as words.

appositive A word or a group of words that renames or explains the word or group of words that follow it. Generally, appositives are nouns renaming nouns and are often set between commas.

article (or **determiner**) Word that indicates that a noun follows (such as *a*, *an*, *the*).

assonance A stylistic device that provides for a similar sound within multiple syllables or words. These similar sounds—usually repeating vowel sounds without the repeating of consonants—tend to be close to each other at the beginning of the words (alliteration) or within the word, but do not tend to be placed at the end of the words.

attributive adjective Adjective placed beside the noun it modifies.

attributive noun A noun that modifies another noun and usually acts as an adjective.

auxiliary verb A verb that goes along with other verbs to express tense, person, number, and mood tense.

bibliography A compilation of all the publication details for the sources cited or consulted by the author in the process of writing the text.

boldface Type that is heavier and darker than regular type.

capitalize To write with a capital letter or letters. When referenced within the context of the spelling of a word, phrase, or sentence, only the first letter of the first word is intended to be written with a capital letter.

cardinal number The number form used in basic counting (*one*, *1*, *forty-three*, *43*).

case The form a noun or pronoun takes to indicate its relationship with the other words in a given sentence.

cliché Any figure of speech that has become so trite and commonplace, it no longer carries much meaning.

collective noun Word that identifies a group.

colloquialism A local or regional word or expression.

colon Punctuation used to introduce explanations; formal or long, extracted quotations; summaries; statements introduced by the words *the following* or *as follows*; concluding appositives; and series listings.

comma Punctuation used as a separator within sentences, in addition to its other technical uses, including mathematical and bibliographical uses. Commas provide an opportunity for a short pause, the smallest break value within a sentence's structure. Commas also provide separation for a string of related words.

comma splice A run-on sentence that has two main clauses set apart by a comma but no coordinating conjunction to link them. Comma splices can often be corrected simply by changing the comma to a period or a semicolon.

command (or **imperative sentence**) Sentence that consists of predicates that are infinitive verbs but have no explicit subjects. The subject *you* is implied.

common noun Word that references general classes of people, places, things, or ideas.

comparative form The form of adjectives and adverbs that compares what is modified with some other thing.

complement A word or group of words that provides a wholeness to the understanding of the meaning of a subject, an object, or a verb.

complete predicate The simple predicate plus any additional modifiers, objects, and/or complements.

complete sentence Sentence that consists of an independent clause and at least one dependent clause.

compound noun Noun made by combining two other words to form a new word.

compound sentence Sentence comprised of two or more independent clauses (or simple sentences) joined by a conjunction (such as *and*, *but*, *or*, *nor*, *so*, *yet*, and *for*) or a semicolon.

compound verb Verb that is complete only when combined with one of the various forms of auxiliary words such as *be*, *can*, *have*, *do*, or *will*.

compound word A new single-unit word comprised of at least two previously independent words that are now combined as either an open, solid, or hyphenated compound.

compound-complex sentence Sentence that consists of two complex sentences or one simple sentence with one complex sentence, joined by a conjunction or a semicolon.

concrete noun Word that identifies things that have form and are tangible.

conjugation A change in inflection.

conjunction Word that links words, or word groupings, that have equal grammatical status within the sentence.

consonance A stylistic device that repeats the consonant sound in a series of words. Consonance differs from alliteration in that the repeated sound can be found anywhere within the word, although it is most often located at the end.

contraction Reduced, succinct version of combined-word expressions with an apostrophe in place of the letters that have been removed.

correlative conjunction (or **correlative**) Tag-team pair of conjunctions used together to link either similar or differing elements.

count noun Word that identifies things that can be counted.

dangling modifier A word or phrase that is set to modify another word that does not link up well with it or with another word that has been left out.

declarative sentence The most usual sort of simple sentence, used to communicate information. Its organization tends to be simple: subject + verb + object (in that order).

demonstrative pronoun Pronoun used to identify, set apart, point out, or specify.

descriptive adjective Adjective that more definitively and fully identifies a characteristic of a noun.

determiner Word that indicates that a noun will follow (such as *a*, *an*, *the*, *my*, and *your*).

diction Vocabulary, but also the choice of specific words over others and the emotions associated with them.

direct object A word, phrase, or clause identifying the ultimate goal or desired outcome of the verb's action.

ellipsis Punctuation mark used to show a pause or an omission of a word or multiple words.

endnote A note that comes at the end of a section of text.

euphemism A word, phrase, or expression that has been softened so it is not offensive or disagreeable and is used in place of one that could cause offense or indicate some form of unpleasantness.

exclamation An expression of great excitement or some other burst of emotion.

exclamation mark Punctuation used to demonstrate that the preceding words were meant as an emphatic statement, an interjection, or a command.

figure of speech A word or phrase used to express something other than its literal meaning.

footnote A note that comes at the foot of a page.

fragment Incomplete sentence.

future tense Tense achieved simply by adding *will* to precede the verb's basic dictionary spelling. Within the first person, *shall* can be substituted instead of *will*. This addition shows that the action is anticipated.

gender Denotes nouns and pronouns as having one of three classifications—feminine, masculine, or neuter.

genitive case The possessive form used in constructions where the *of* is omitted. *See also* **possessive case.**

gerund Present participle used as a noun and ending with *-ing*. Gerunds can function as the subject of a verb, the object of a verb, a predicate nominative or complement, or the object of a preposition.

glossary An explained or defined list of commonly used words and unusual and foreign terms culled from a section of text.

helping verb (or **auxiliary verb**) Verb that relates subjects with their predicates to identify tense and also voice, person, number, or mood.

hyperbole A figure of speech that uses deliberate exaggeration for heightened effect and is not intended for literal interpretation.

hyphenated compound Two or more words connected by one or more hyphens.

hyphen Punctuation used to divide compound words, various elements of words, or numbers.

idiom A figure of speech in which the words together form a unique meaning that is understood only because of its specific manner of use.

imperative The verb stem being used to issue a command, make a request, or utter an exclamation.

imperative mood Gives voice to commands or provides direction.

indefinite pronoun Pronoun that typically indicates an unspecified, even generic, person or thing.

index A breakdown of the text into key terms, ideas, and names, organized into an easily accessible list at the back of the book with page or section numbers corresponding to the text.

indicative mood Reports facts and opinions, or asks questions.

indirect object An object that is the secondary consideration or goal of the verb's action.

indirect question A question that repeats a question someone else has asked but has not been presented as a direct quotation. For these sorts of questions, a period is used instead of a question mark at the conclusion of the sentence.

infinitive form (or **plain form**) The main-entry or dictionary form of the verb. This is the form used to show that the verb action takes place in the present.

When using the infinitive form, the subject of the sentence is either a plural noun or one of these pronouns: *I*, *we*, *you*, or *they*.

inflection A change in the form of a word to indicate distinctions such as case, gender, number, tense, person, mood, or voice.

intensive pronoun A pronoun used to give added emphasis to a preceding personal pronoun.

interjection Expression of emotion, unique in that it is always independent of the overall sentence. Often interjections are single words or short phrases set off by commas within the sentence, or on their own with an exclamation point. The stronger the emotion, the more likely it is to use an exclamation point.

interrogative pronoun Pronoun that asks questions.

intransitive verb Verb that doesn't—and can't—take on a direct object. The intransitive verbs clearly and completely communicate without a direct object.

irregular verb Verb that does not follow the system for regular verbs.

italic A slanted type akin to cursive script.

kinship name Word that identifies relatives according to their genealogical relationships.

language Communication of ideas or feelings using written marks with accepted meanings (a.k.a. words), sounds, or gestures.

lexical meaning The essence of the root of a word.

limiting adjective Adjective that narrows the scope of a noun to some degree.

limiting modifier Word that modifies the expression that falls directly after it in a sentence.

linking verb Verb that connects the subject to another word in the sentence, either a predicate noun, a pronoun, or an adjective.

lowercase Written without capital letters.

main verb The infinitive, present participle, or past participle in all verb phrases that carries the main meaning.

mass noun Word that identifies things that are not usually able to be counted.

masthead A publication's name, which is generally presented at the top of the first page (as in a newspaper) or on the cover (as in a magazine). It can also be a list of those involved with putting the publication together.

mild command A sentence that directs authoritatively or gives an order.

misplaced modifier A modifier placed too far from the word or words it's supposed to modify.

modifier A word or group of words that describes or qualifies the meaning of another word or word group. Included in the modifier family are lone-word adjectives and adverbs, as well as word groups, phrases, and clauses acting as adjectives and adverbs.

mood The verb form that indicates the feeling or attitude of the writer toward what's written.

nominative case (or **subjective case**) The case used when the pronoun is the subject of a sentence or clause, the complement of a subject, or an appositive identifying a subject.

nonrestrictive element An element that simply provides supplemental information about the word or words it references, but is not a limiting component. These elements can easily be deleted from a sentence without changing its basic meaning.

noun A word that identifies a person, place, thing, or idea.

number The form of a noun or pronoun (verbs and demonstrative adjectives also) that indicates whether the word is singular (one) or plural (more than one).

object A noun, pronoun, or word group serving as a noun, which is received or is influenced by the action of a verb or a preposition.

object of the preposition The noun or pronoun connected by a preposition.

objective case The pronoun case showing its use as the object of a verb or a preposition.

onomatopoeia A figure of speech that identifies the kinds of words we use to name or imitate sounds (*boing*, *ding-dong*, etc.).

open compound Word used as a single unit of meaning but still written separately as two words.

ordinal number Number representation in terms of the ordered-sequence placement it holds (*first*, *1st*, etc.).

oxymoron A figure of speech that couples opposite or incongruous terms to create a new meaning.

parallelism Sentence construction that has repeated syntactical similarities.

parentheses Punctuation marks used to isolate elements within sentences that are not exactly necessary but add to the reader's understanding. These parenthetical expressions include examples, explanations, facts, and digressions.

parenthetical expressions Words that serve as explanations or transitions.

participle The verb form that can take either the verb form or the adjective form.

participle adjective A participle used to modify a noun.

passive voice Identifies the object or receiver of the action. The verb takes an object; the subject of passive sentences does not instigate or execute the action specified by the verb.

past indicative The form that adds *-ed* to the end of the verb stem for all regular verbs.

past participle Shows that the work of the verb has been completed. Generally, the past participle ends in *-ed*.

past tense Shows that the verb's action took place in the past. The past-tense verb generally is formed by simply adding *-d* or *-ed* to the infinitive form.

perfect tense Shows that a verb's action was or will be completed before some other time or action takes place. The helping verb *have* is added to a verb's past participle to form the perfect tense.

period Punctuation mark that indicates the conclusion of a sentence.

person The characteristic that indicates whether the person referenced is doing the speaking (first person), being spoken to (second person), or being talked about (third person). Only personal pronouns and verbs change their forms to show a variance in person.

personal names The names of people.

personal pronoun Pronouns used to refer to a specific person or group.

personification A figure of speech that attributes human characteristics or qualities to animals, inanimate objects, or abstract ideas.

plural More than one.

positive form The basic dictionary version of a descriptive modifier.

possessive case (or **genitive case**) Indicates ownership or a relationship.

possessive compound Compound word or sentence used in the possessive form.

predicate A part of each sentence that is neither the subject nor its modifiers. The predicate must contain a verb and may include objects and modifiers of the verb.

predicate adjective Adjective joined to the noun it modifies by a verb that links the two (noun + adjective).

prefix Letters added to the front of a word that change the meaning of the word.

preposition A word or phrase that functions as a connector.

prepositional phrase The preposition plus its object and any modifiers.

present indicative The verb stem for singular and plural persons in the present tense.

present participle Shows that the verb is currently in action or at least not yet completed. Generally, the present participle is formed by adding *-ing* to the infinitive form of the verb.

present subjunctive Uses a past-tense verb to express or imply some sort of doubt or impracticability.

present tense The infinitive verb stem, which is also referenced as the present indicative form. For the third-person singular in the present tense, add *-s* at the end of the word.

pronoun Substitution word used in place of the noun or noun phrase it represents.

proper adjective Adjective derived from proper nouns. These are almost always capitalized.

proper noun Word that references specific people, places, or things.

pun A figure of speech, also known as a "play on words," that intentionally confuses similar words or phrases for rhetorical effect. These clever and usually humorous expressions most often employ homonyms, metaphors, or words with several different meanings.

punctuation The universally accepted, standardized marks that help clarify the meaning of a sentence or structural portions of writing.

question mark The concluding punctuation for a direct question.

question (or **interrogative sentence**) Sentence whose function is to inquire or ask.

quotation marks (or **quote marks**) Punctuation used to envelop direct quotations, whether from spoken or written word. Quotation marks must always be used in pairs, regardless of whether they are doubles or singles.

reciprocal pronoun A pronoun used when those referenced are expected to bear an equal relationship with one another.

reflexive pronoun Pronoun that refers to the subject of the sentence, clause, or phrase in which it's located.

regular verb A verb able to take on its past-tense and past participle forms simply by adding *-d* or *-ed* to its infinitive state.

relative pronoun A connecting word that introduces a subordinate clause and provides a link from one clause to another.

repetition A stylistic device that repeats individual words for greater effect.

restrictive element Word that limits the meaning of the word or words to which the restrictive elements apply.

root word The most basic form of a word, where the word's lexical meaning originates.

run-on sentence (or **fused sentence**) Sentence that has two or more independent clauses joined in one sentence that lacks punctuation or conjunctions. These sentences fuse clauses that could ordinarily stand on their own.

***-s* form** The verb form used when the action of the verb is happening in the present time. This form ends in *-s* or *-es*.

semicolon Punctuation used to separate main clauses that are not linked with a coordinating conjunction.

serial commas (or **series commas**) Commas used to separate three or more items in a list; the last two items are joined by a conjunction. The use of serial commas helps avoid confusion and ambiguity.

sibilance Sibilant sounds—those created by *s* and *sh*, which are pronounced *s*, *z*, *sh*, *zh*, *ch* (*tsh*), or *j* (*dzh*)—that create these very noticeable types of consonance.

simile A figure of speech that compares two unlike concepts and joins them by the words *like*, *as*, or *than*.

simple predicate A verb and any auxiliaries (helping verbs).

simple sentence Sentence that contains only one clause and may be as short as one word. These sentences have a subject and a predicate, and they may include modifiers.

simple tense Used to show that a verb's action or "state of being" is in either present tense, past tense, or future tense.

slang Terms that are informal, nonstandard words, phrases, or expressions, the use of which indicates everything from colloquialism to illiteracy and may include words changed arbitrarily as well as many variations on figures of speech.

small capital Capital letter set smaller than an ordinary capital letter.

solid compound Compound word that is closed up—no space, no hyphen.

statement The reporting of facts or opinions, a declaration, a remark, or an assertion.

stylistic device The method a writer chooses to convey information by manipulating language in various techniques to achieve differing results.

subject The word (or words functioning as a unit) that's the focus of the action or state of the predicate within a sentence or clause.

subjunctive mood States a necessity, a desire, a suggestion. The subjunctive mood can also name a condition that appears contrary to the current facts.

subordinating conjunction (or **subordinate conjunction**) Conjunction that joins clauses that are not equal in grammatical weight.

subscript Small type set below the regular text line.

substantive A word or group of words that functions as a noun.

subtitle The second part of a title, often to explain the main title or to give more information about it.

suffix Letters joined to the end of a word that change the meaning of the word.

superlative form The form of adjectives and adverbs that compares what's modified with two or more other things.

superscript Small type set above the regular text line.

symbol A stylistic device that represents something other than itself, especially a visible sign representing something invisible.

tense The characteristic of a verb that identifies the time of the action of the verb with the time when the writer writes about the action.

terminal preposition Preposition that ends a sentence.

trademark A word, phrase, symbol, design, or combination therein that identifies the source of the goods of one party from those of others.

transitive verb A verb that conveys action and requires an object.

verb A word or a group of words used to indicate an act or an action, an occurrence, or a state of being.

whole number Integer that is not negative.

B

REFERENCE AND RESOURCE BIBLIOGRAPHY

Books

Ayers, Elizabeth. *Writing the Wave: Inspired Rides for Aspiring Writers*. New York: Perigee, 1997.

Bartlett, John. *Bartlett's Familiar Quotations: A Collection of Passages, Phrases, and Proverbs Traced to Their Sources in Ancient and Modern Literature*. 16th ed. Justin Kaplan, general editor. Boston: Little, Brown and Company, Inc., 1992.

Bawer, Bruce. *The Contemporary Stylist*. New York: Harcourt Brace Jovanovich, Inc., 1987.

Bernays, Anne, and Pamela Painter. *What If?: Writing Exercises for Fiction Writers*. 2nd ed. New York: Longman, 2003.

Bolander, Donald O. *The New Webster's Desk Reference*. New York: Berkley, 1991.

Elliott, Rebecca, Ph.D. *Painless Grammar*. Hauppauge, NY: Barron's, 1997.

Fowler, H. Ramsey. *The Little, Brown Handbook*. 3rd ed. Boston: Little, Brown and Company, Inc., 1986.

Gibaldi, Joseph, and Walter S. Achtert. *MLA Handbook for Writers of Research Papers*. 3rd ed. New York: The Modern Language Association of America, 1988.

Goldberg, Natalie. *Writing Down the Bones: Freeing the Writer Within*. Boston: Shambhala, 1986.

Hart, Thomas B., Carolyn Keefe, and Bob R. Derryberry. *The Complete Book of Speechwriting for Students and Professionals*. 2nd ed. Edina, MN: Burgess International Group, Inc., 1988.

Henry, Laurie. *The Fiction Dictionary*. Toronto: Story Press Books, 1995.

Johnson, Edward D. *The Handbook of Good English: A Comprehensive, Easy-to-Use Guide to Modern Grammar, Punctuation, Usage, and Style*. New York: Washington Square Press, 1991.

Lederer, Richard. *Anguished English: An Anthology of Accidental Assaults Upon Our Language*. Charleston, SC: Wyrick & Company, 1987.

Mead, Hayden, Ph.D., and Jay Stevenson, Ph.D. *The Essentials of Grammar*. New York: Berkley, 1996.

Merriam-Webster. *Merriam-Webster's Collegiate Dictionary*. 11th ed. Springfield, MA: Merriam-Webster, Inc., 2003.

———. *Merriam-Webster's Encyclopedia of Literature*. Springfield, MA: Merriam-Webster, Inc., 1995.

Miner, Margaret, and Hugh Rawson, ed. 1992. *A Dictionary of Quotations from Shakespeare*. 2nd ed. New York: Meridian, 1996.

Murphy, Bruce, ed. *Benét's Reader's Encyclopedia*. 4th ed. New York: HarperCollins, 1996.

O'Conner, Patricia T. *Woe Is I: The Grammarphobe's Guide to Better English in Plain English*. Rev. ed. New York: Riverhead Books, 2003.

Peck, Richard. *Invitations to the World: Teaching and Writing for the Young*. New York: Dial Books, 2002.

Perrine, Laurence. *Literature: Structure, Sound, and Sense*. 4th ed. New York: Harcourt Brace Jovanovich, Inc., 1983.

Prentice Hall. *Words into Type*. 3rd ed. Englewood Cliffs, NJ: Prentice Hall, 1974.

Semmelmeyer, Madeline, M.A., and Donald O. Bolander, M.A., Litt. D. *The New Webster's Grammar Guide: A Complete Handbook on English Grammar, Correct Usage and Punctuation*. New York: Berkley, 1991.

Shaw, Harry. *Dictionary of Problem Words and Expressions*. Rev. ed. New York: McGraw-Hill Book Company, 1987.

Strunk, William, Jr., and E. B. White. *The Elements of Style*. 4th ed. New York: Longman, 2000.

University of Chicago Press. *The Chicago Manual of Style*. 15th ed. Chicago: University of Chicago Press, 2003.

Urdang, Laurence. *The Basic Book of Synonyms and Antonyms*. 2nd ed. New York: Signet, 1985.

Walker, Janice R., and Todd Taylor. *The Columbia Guide to Online Style*. New York: Columbia University Press, 1998.

Webster's New World Thesaurus. New rev. ed. New York: Simon & Schuster, Inc., 1985.

Wilson, Lee. *Fair Use, Free Use and Use by Permission: How to Handle Copyrights in All Media*. New York: Allworth Press, 2005.

Websites

Bartleby.com

www.bartleby.com

This free service website provides verification of famous—and infamous—quotations and their originators as well as links to other such sites.

Chicago Manual of Style Online

www.chicagomanualofstyle.org/home.html

This is the online, searchable version of the fifteenth edition of *The Chicago Manual of Style*. There is a free trial option, but this is a fee-based annual subscription service.

Daily Grammar

www.dailygrammar.com

Daily grammar lessons Monday through Friday—free of charge—with a quiz each Saturday.

Encyclopædia Britannica Online

www.britannica.com

Encyclopædia Britannica online offers a free trial option, but this is a fee-based annual subscription service. The yearly fee provides current and archived articles as well as online access to the dictionary, thesaurus, and updated world atlas with thousands of images and videos.

Famous Poets and Poems

www.famouspoetsandpoems.com

This website provides reference to current and historical poets and their poetry.

Figures of Speech Served Fresh

www.figarospeech.com

This writer's blog contains helpful information and examples of various figures of speech.

Grammarphobia.com

www.grammarphobia.com

The website of the authors of *Woe Is I: The Grammarphobe's Guide to Better English in Plain English*, *Words Fail Me: What Everyone Who Writes Should Know About Writing*, and *You Send Me: Getting It Right When You Write Online*, Patricia T. O'Conner and Stewart Kellerman. This site provides not only information about the authors and their books but also writing tips as well as debunking writing myths.

IdiomSite

www.idiomsite.com

This blog explains the background and origins of dozens of common idioms.

International Trademark Association

www.inta.org

This is a not-for-profit association comprised of thousands of trademark owners and others from nearly two hundred countries. The purpose of this association is to support the advancement of trademarks. This site also provides an extensive listing of trademarks.

Internet Public Library (IPL)
www.ipl.org
The IPL is a free online reference resource that provides both information as well as interactive features, such as the IPL TeenSpace Poetry Wiki. Also included are links to a variety of other reference websites.

Merriam-Webster Collegiate.com
www.merriam-webstercollegiate.com
This is the comprehensive online equivalent of *Merriam-Webster's Collegiate Dictionary*, 11th edition. This is a fee-based reference source.

National Geographic
www.nationalgeographic.com
This active and interactive website provides researchers with current and historical facts.

Online English Grammar (OEG)
www.edufind.com/english/grammar/TOC.CFM
A free online reference source for the elements of grammar studies.

Online Grammar Handbook
www.onlinegrammar.org
This is a useful Internet tool for those looking for help with researching, writing, speechmaking, and even reading. Through the Online Grammar Handbook, the researcher has access to the websites of multiple colleges, universities, etc.

Owl Online Writing Lab
owl.english.purdue.edu/handouts/grammar
This website is provided by the Purdue University Online Writing Lab and offers helpful information regarding grammar, punctuation, and spelling, including handouts and excercises.

Poets.org
www.poets.org
This website of the Academy of American Poets holds nearly two thousand poems and more than five hundred poets' biographies—and much more.

Pun of the Day
www.punoftheday.com
This site has list after list of puns, which are broken down into various categories. Here you can also sign up for a "Pun of the Day," a free delivery service.

Refdesk.com
www.refdesk.com
This site provides a comprehensive assortment of links leading researchers to all manner of information regarding almanacs and maps; calendars and time(s); dictionaries, thesauruses, and encyclopedias; people and places; grammar and style; quotations; libraries; travel and weather; etc. This is a great start toward finding facts fast.

Schoolhouse Rock Site
school-house-rock.com
This is the unofficial site of the *Schoolhouse Rock* series of fun, educational songs and videos dealing with grammar, history, math, and science. It's a wonderful, nostalgic experience for parents and an enjoyable way for children to learn!

SlangSite.com
www.slangsite.com
This is a dictionary of slang, webspeak, made-up words, and colloquialisms.

United States Census Bureau: Geographic Areas Reference Manual
www.census.gov/geo/www/garm.html
The website for the U.S. Census Bureau's *Geographic Areas Reference Manual*, which provides detailed information about geographic areas.

United States Copyright Office
copyright.gov
This is the official website of the U.S. Copyright Office, a division of the Library of Congress. This site provides thorough information about copyrights: the rules of registering, the restrictions of use, how to register for a copyright, etc.

United States Patent and Trademark Office
uspto.gov
This is the official website of this agency of the U.S. Department of Commerce. This site provides all information necessary to applying and registering for a patent or trademark as well as helping identify trademarks and patents and their holders.

Wikipedia
www.wikipedia.org
The slogan says it all: "The free encyclopedia." This site is written and maintained by people from all around the world, and each contributor volunteers their time and information.

Wikiquote
www.wikiquote.org
This is a free source of notable quotations and their sources (whenever possible).

INDEX

A

a/an, 181
abbreviations, 186
  Biblical, 191–192
  commas and, 104
  common, 189–190
  degrees, 186
  geographical, 193–196
  plurals, 122–123
  small capitals, 160
  time/date, 187–188
  titles, 186
absolute phrases, commas, 99
academic titles, capitalization, 137
accept/except, 181
acronyms, 196–197
active voice, 40
adjectival articles, 48
adjective pronouns, 15
adjectives, 46
  adjectival articles, 48
  attribute, 49
  descriptive, 47
  limiting, 47
  participle, 48
  predicate, 49
  pronominal adjectives, 15
  proper, 49
adverbs, 50–51
affect/effect, 182
aircraft names, 154
alliteration, 88
allusion, 90
antecedents, pronouns, 12–14
antonyms, 172–179
apostrophes
  compound words and, 111
  joint possession and, 111
  omission and, 112
  possessive, 111
  sole possession and, 111
appositives, 4
  possessives, 130
articles
  adjectival, 48
  copyright, 224
article titles, italics, 150
assonance, 89
attribute adjectives, 49
attribute nouns, possessives, 131
auxiliary verbs, 23
avoiding wordiness, 185
awhile/a while, 182

B

Biblical abbreviations, 191–192
bibliography
  books, 247
  electronic publications, 249–250
  full bibliography, 247
  informally published works, 250
  journals, 248
  magazines, 248
  newspapers, 248
  online books, 249
  online journals, 249
  online magazines, 249
  online news sites, 249

overview, 246
plays, 248
print publications, 247–249
select bibliography, 247
unpublished works, 250
websites, 250
block quotes, 235
boldface
display, 159
for emphasis, 159
books
bibliography, 247
copyright, 224
italics, 148
building names, capitalization, 144

C

capitalization
academic titles, 137
building names, 144
civil titles, 137
days, 142
geographical terms, 144
governmental agencies/terms, 145
historical happenings/items, 143
holidays, 142
indexes, 254
kinship names, 136–137
languages, 141
medical terms, 145
military titles, 137
nationalities, 141
nouns, 3
peoples, 141
personal names, 134–136
personal titles, 136
political agencies/terms, 145
prepositions, 57
proper nouns, 3
religious terms, 145
religious titles, 137
royal titles, 137
time zones, 143
cardinal numbers, dates, 204
case
plain, 17–18
possessive, 17–18
channel titles, 153
citation
block quotes, 235
chart, 231–234
direct quotes, 228
endnotes, 243
footnote style, 240
initial articles, 229–230
online sources, 229
poetry, 235
shortened, 229
civil titles, capitalization, 137
clauses, commas, 99–100
clichés, 86
closed compounds, plurals, 124
collective nouns, subject/verb agreement, 44
colloquialisms, 85
colons, 107
column titles, italics, 150
commands, 76
commas
with abbreviations, 104
absolute phrases, 99
with clauses, 99–100
comma splices, 99
with dates, 103
with locations, 103
with nonrestrictive appositives, 101
with nonrestrictive elements, 100
with numbers, 103
with parenthetical expressions, 101–103
with phrases, 99
with quotations, 104
with restrictive elements, 100
serial commas, 98
with transition expressions, 101–103
comma splices, 79, 99
commonly misspelled words, 180
common nouns, 2
versus proper nouns, 3–4

comparative form, modifiers, 52
complements, verbs, 25
complex sentences, 73
compound-complex sentences, 74
compound nouns, 8–9
compound sentences, 72–73
  coordinating conjunctions and, 62–63
  possessives, 129
compound words, 8
  apostrophe and, 111
  hyphenated, 9
  hyphens, 113
  open compounds, 10
  plurals, 124–125
  possessives, 130
  solid compounds, 9
conjugation of verbs, 34–37
conjunctions, 61
  coordinating, 61–63
  correlative, 63–64
  subordinating, 64–66
consonance, 89
contractions, 172
coordinating conjunctions, 61
  compound sentences and, 62–63
  starting sentence with, 62
copyright
  articles, 224
  benefits, 219
  books, 224
  duration, 220
  fair use, 223
  images, 224
  overview, 216–217
  ownership, 217–218
  protection eligibility, 218
  public domain, 224
  registering, 219
  reproductions, 224
  songs, 224
  uploads/downloads, 224
correlative conjunctions, 63–64, 81
count nouns, 5
cross-references, indexes, 256

D

dangling modifiers, 53
dates, commas and, 103
days, capitalization, 142
declarative sentences, 74
degrees, abbreviations, 186
demonstrative pronouns, 14
descriptive adjectives, 47
diction, 91
direct quotes, 228
display, small capitals, 161
double quotation marks, 109
downloads, copyright, 224

E

electronic publications, bibliography, 249–250
ellipses, 106
em dashes, 115
  multiple, 115
  other punctuation and, 115
  sudden breaks and, 115
emphasis
  boldface, 159
  italics, 154
en dashes, 114
endnotes, 242
  citation style, 243
  ibid., 244
  numbering, 242–243
  pros/cons, 244
ensure/insure, 183
essays, italics, 148
euphemisms, 84
exclamation marks, 105
exclamations, 75

F

fair use, 223
fewer/less, 183

figures of speech, 82
  clichés, 86
  colloquialisms, 85
  euphemisms, 84
  hyperbole, 86
  idioms, 83
  metaphors, 82
  onomatopoeia, 87
  oxymorons, 87
  personification, 87
  puns, 86
  similes, 83
  slang, 85
film titles, 152
footnotes
  citation style, 240
  definition, 238
  numbering, 238–239
  pros/cons, 241
  symbols, 239–240
  use, 238
foreign words/phrases, italics, 155
fragments, 77–78
full bibliography, 247
future tense, 38

G

gender, 19
geographical abbreviations, 193–196
geographical terms, capitalization, 144
gerunds, possessives, 129
glossary
  overview, 245
  style, 245
governmental agencies/terms, capitalization, 145
governmental texts, italics, 148

H

headnotes, indexes, 255
helping verbs, 23
holidays
  capitalization, 142
  possessives, 131
hyperbole, 86
hyphenated compounds, plurals, 125
hyphenated words, compound, 9
hyphenation, solid compounds, 9
hyphens, 113
  compound words and, 113
  letter-to-letter separation and, 114
  number separation and, 114
  syllabic division and, 113

I

ibid., 244
idioms, 83
images, copyright, 224
imperative mood, 40
imperatives, 76
imperative verb form, 37
imply/infer, 183
indefinite pronouns, 15
  subject/verb agreement, 43
indented style indexes, 253
indexes
  bad breaks, 257
  capitalization, 254
  continued line, 257
  cross-references, 256
  definitions, 255
  headnotes, 255
  indented style, 253
  italics, 254
  letter-by-letter alphabetization, 257
  overview, 252
  photos, 255
  punctuation, 254
  run-in style, 253
  see/see also, 256
  tables, 255
  word-by-word alphabetization, 258
indicative mood, 39
indict/indite, 184
infinitives, 31, 39
informally published works, bibliography, 250
initial articles in citations, 229–230

initials, punctuation, 97
intensive pronouns, 15
interjections, 76–77
Internet articles, italics, 151
interrogative pronouns, 14
interrogative sentences, 74–75
intransitive verbs, 29
irregular plurals, 121
irregular verbs, 26, 29
italicized words
  plurals, 125
  possessives, 131
italics
  emphasis, 154
  foreign words/phrases, 155
  indexes, 254
  letters as letters, 157
  letters as shape, 158
  plurals and, 156
  possessives and, 156
  punctuation and, 158
  quotations, 156
  sounds, 155
  thoughts, 155
  titles, 148–154
  within italics, 158
  words as words, 157
its, 128

J–K

journals
  bibliography, 248
  titles, italics, 150

kinship names, capitalization, 136–137

L

languages, capitalization, 141
lay/lie, 184
letters
  plurals, 122–123
  possessives, 127
letters as letters, italics, 157
letters as shapes, italics, 158
lexical meaning of word, 166
limiting adjectives, 47
limiting modifiers, misplaced modifiers, 54
linked subjects, subject/verb agreement, 43
linking verbs, 23–25
lists, 80
locations, commas and, 103

M

magazines, bibliography, 248
main verb, 24
mass nouns, 6–8
medical terms, capitalization, 145
metaphors, 82
military titles, capitalization, 137
misplaced modifiers
  limiting modifiers, 54
  prepositional phrases, 53
  subordinate clauses, 54
modifiers
  comparative form, 52
  dangling modifiers, 53
  limiting modifiers, 54
  misplaced, 53–54
  positive form, 52
  superlative form, 52
mood, 39
  imperative, 40
  indicative, 39
  subjunctive, 40

N

names
  aircraft, 154
  buildings, capitalization, 144
  kinship, capitalization, 136–137
  numbers, 205–206

personal, capitalization, 134–136
punctuation, 97
ships, 154
nationalities, capitalization, 141
network titles, 153
newspapers, bibliography, 248
nominative case, 18
nonrestrictive appositives, commas and, 101
nonrestrictive elements, commas and, 100
nouns
attribute, possessives, 131
capitalization, 3
common, 2
compound nouns, 8–9
count nouns, 5
definition, 2
gender, 19
mass nouns, 6–8
number, 19
person, 19
proper, 3
proper nouns, plurals, 123–124
proper nouns, possessives, 127
numbers, 81
commas and, 103
endnotes, 242–243
footnotes, 238–239
names, 205–206
nouns, 19
numerals preferred, 201–203
plurals, 123
possessives, 127
round numbers, 201
separation with hyphen, 114
starting sentences, 200
time and date, 203–205
titles, 205–206
verbs, 41
whole numbers, 201

O

objective case, 18
omission, apostrophes and, 112
online books, bibliography, 249
online journals, bibliography, 249
online magazines, bibliography, 249
online news sites, bibliography, 249
online sources, 229
onomatopoeia, 87
open compounds, 10
plurals, 124
oxymorons, 87

P

parallelisms, 80
correlative conjunctions, 81
lists, 80
numbers, 81
parentheses, 117
parenthetical expressions, commas and, 101, 103
participle adjectives, 48
parts of book, italics, 149
passive voice, 40
past indicative verb form, 36
past participles, 31, 37
past subjunctive verb form, 37
past tense, 38
past-tense verbs, 31
peoples, capitalization, 141
perfect tense, 39
periodicals, titles, italics, 150
periods
with abbreviations, 96
with acronyms, 97
with initials, 97
with names, 97
with sentences, 95–96
with shortened words, 97

permissions, 221
articles, 224
books, 224
fair use, 223
images, 224
letter, 221–223
public domain, 224
songs, 224
person
nouns, 19
verbs, 41
personal names, capitalization, 134–136
personal pronouns, 14
personal titles, capitalization, 136
personification, 87
phrases
absolute, 99
commas, 99
plain case, 17–18
plays
bibliography, 248
italics, 148
plural nouns, subject/verb agreement, 44
plurals, 120
abbreviations, 122–123
compound words, 124–125
exceptions, 121
irregular, 121
italicized words, 125
italics and, 156
letters, 122–123
nouns, proper, 123–124
numbers, 123
poetry, quoting, 235
political agencies/terms, capitalization, 145
positive form, modifiers, 52
possessive apostrophe
compound words and, 111
joint possession and, 111
omission and, 112
sole possession and, 111
possessive case, 17–18
possessives, 126
appositives, 130
attributive nouns, 131
compound sentences, 129
compound words, 130
gerunds, 129
holidays, 131
italicized words, 131
italics and, 156
its, 128
letters, 127
nouns, proper nouns, 127
numbers, 127
pronouns, 127
whose, 128
predicate adjectives, 49
predicates, 68–70
types, 69
prefixes, 167–169
prepositional phrases
misplaced modifiers, 53
punctuation, 59–60
prepositions, 56
capitalization, 57
terminal, 57
present indicative form of verbs, 35
present participles, 32, 35
present subjunctive verb form, 36
present tense, 38
print publications, bibliography, 247–249
pronominal adjectives, 15
pronouns, 11
adjective, 15
antecedents, 12–14
demonstrative, 14
gender, 19
indefinite, 15
intensive, 15
interrogative, 14
nominative case, 18
objective case, 18
personal, 14
possessive case, 18

possessives, 127
reciprocal, 16
reflexive, 15
relative, 15
proper adjectives, 49
proper nouns, 3
plural, 123–124
possessives, 127
versus common nouns, 3–4
public domain, 224
punctuation, 94
apostrophes, 111–112
brackets, 117
colons, 107
commas, 98–104
ellipses, 106
em dashes, 115
en dashes, 114
exclamation marks, 105
hyphens, 113–114
indexes, 254
italics and, 158
parentheses, 117
periods, 95–97
prepositional phrases, 59–60
quotation marks, 105, 109
semicolons, 107
slashes, 115
puns, 86

Q

question marks, 105
questions, 74–75
quotation marks
double, 109
single, 109
titles and, 109
quotations
commas and, 104
italics, 156
quotes
block quotes, 235
chart, 231–234
direct quotes, 228
initial articles, 229–230
online sources, 229
poetry, 235
shortened citations, 229

R

radio show titles, 152
reciprocal pronouns, 16
reference list, 246
reflexive pronouns, 15
regular verbs, 25
relative pronouns, 15
religious terms, capitalization, 145
religious texts, italics, 148
religious titles, capitalization, 137
repetition, 90
reproductions, copyright, 224
restrictive elements, commas and, 100
resume/résumé, 184
root words, 166
round numbers, 201
royal titles, capitalization, 137
run-in style indexes, 253
run-on sentences, 78

S

sans serif type, 162–163
section titles, italics, 150
select bibliography, 247
semicolons, 107
sentences, numbers starting, 200
sentence structure
commands, 76
comma splices, 79
complex sentences, 73
compound-complex sentences, 74
compound sentences, 72–73
declarative sentences, 74
exclamations, 75
fragments, 77–78
imperative sentences, 76
interjections, 76–77

interrogative sentences, 74–75
parallelisms, 80–81
periods, 95–96
predicates, 68–70
questions, 74–75
run-on, 78
simple sentences, 71
subjects, 68–70
serial commas, 98
series names (book), italics, 149
serif type, 162–163
service marks, 212
ship names, 154
shortened citations, 229
shortened forms of words, 197
signs, 207
similes, 83
simple sentences, 71
single quotation marks, 109
slang, 85
slashes, 115
small capitals, 160
abbreviations, 160
display, 161
signs, 160
time and date, 160
solid compounds, 9
songs, 224
sounds, italics, 155
spelling
commonly misspelled words, 180
preferred spellings, 179
stylistic devices, 88
alliteration, 88
allusion, 90
assonance, 89
consonance, 89
diction, 91
repetition, 90
symbols, 90
subject/verb agreement
collective nouns, 44
indefinite pronouns, 43
linked subjects, 43
plural nouns, 44
separated subjects and verbs, 42
third-person subject, 42
titles of works, 44
subjects, 68–70
identifying, 70
types, 69
subjunctive mood, 40
subordinate clauses, misplaced modifiers, 54
subordinating conjunctions, 64–66
suffixes, 169–172
superlative form, modifiers, 52
symbols, 90, 207
footnotes, 239–240
synonyms, 172–179

T

television show titles, 152
tense
future, 38
infinitives, 39
past, 38
perfect, 39
present, 38
terminal prepositions, 57
third-person subject agreement, 42
thoughts, italics, 155
time and date
abbreviations, 187–188
numbers, 203–205
small capitals, 160
time zones, capitalization, 143
titles
abbreviations, 186
academic, capitalization, 137
civil, capitalization, 137
italics, 148–154
military, capitalization, 137
numbers, 205–206
personal, capitalization, 136
quotation marks and, 109
religious, capitalization, 137
royal, capitalization, 137
subject/verb agreement, 44

trademarks, 212
identifying, 212–215
using, 215
transition expressions, commas and, 101–103
transitive verbs, 29

U

underlined text, 164
unpublished works, bibliography, 250
uploads, copyright, 224

V

verbs, 22
auxiliary verbs, 23
complements, 25
conjugation, 34–37
future tense, 38
helping verbs, 23
imperatives, 37
infinitive form, 31
infinitives, 39
intransitive verbs, 29
irregular verbs, 26, 29
linking verbs, 23–25
main verb, 24
mood, 39–40
number, 41
past indicative form, 36
past participles, 31
past participle verb form, 37
past subjunctive, 37
past tense, 31, 38
perfect tense, 39
person, 41
present indicative form, 35
present participles, 32, 35
present subjunctive form, 36
present tense, 38
regular verbs, 25
-s form, 33
subject/verb agreement, 43–44
transitive verbs, 29
voice, 40
verb stem, 35
voice
active, 40
passive, 40

W–X–Y–Z

websites
bibliography, 250
italic titles, 151
whole numbers, 201
whose, 128
who/whom, 184
word choices
a/an, 181
accept/except, 181
affect/effect, 182
awhile/a while, 182
ensure/insure, 183
farther/further, 183
fewer/less, 183
imply/infer, 183
indict/indite, 184
lay/lie, 184
resume/résumé, 184
-ward/-word, -wards/-words, 184
who/whom, 184
wordiness, avoiding, 185
word parts
prefixes, 167–169
root words, 166
suffixes, 169–172
words as words, italics, 157
works of art, titles, 153
works of music, titles, 153

...ne is the ...mmodity of al

...ts readers pinpoint the exact informa- ...nrelated material. Each book covers ...omplete bites that are easy to find and easy to understand. ... that time is the scarcest commodity of all, *At Your Fingertips* offers readers the shortest path to the answers they need.

978-1-59257-657-9

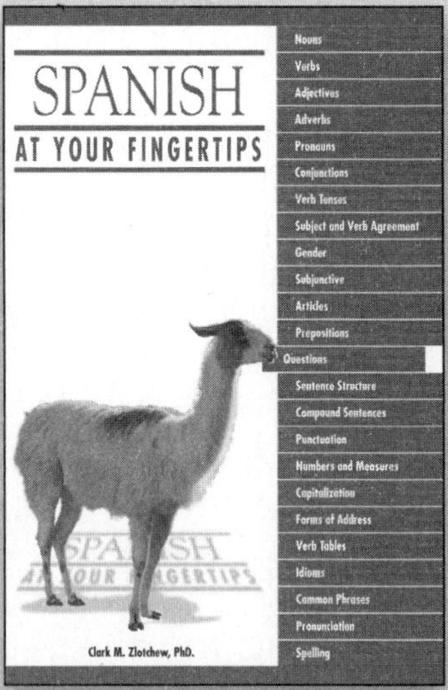

978-1-59257-638-8

978-1-59257-644-9

978-1-59257-649-4

ALPHA
Penguin.com